D1472974

IRAN 1977/8

Editorial Contributors: DEREK FRENCH, ROBIN HOWE,
                            NINA NELSON, PETER SHELDON,
                            MICHAEL VON HAAG

Drawings: D. NORMAND, W. RONDAS,
                            BERYL SANDERS

Photographs: DOUGLAS DICKINS,
              IRAN INFORMATION AND TOURIST CENTER,
                            ADELAIDE McCRIRICK

Production: EILEEN ROLPH

FODOR'S

IRAN 1977/8

*Illustrated edition with map, city and
archeological plans*

**EUGENE FODOR
ROBERT C. FISHER**
Editors

RICHARD MOORE
Executive Editor

PETER SHELDON
Area Editor

DAVID McKAY COMPANY INC. — NEW YORK

© 1977 FODOR'S MODERN GUIDES INC.

ISBN 0 679 00200 6 *David McKay, New York*
0 340 21413 9 *Hodder & Stoughton, London*

The following travel books edited by Eugene Fodor are current in 1977:

AREA GUIDES:

CARIBBEAN, BAHAMAS
AND BERMUDA
EUROPE
INDIA
JAPAN AND KOREA

MEXICO
SCANDINAVIA
SOUTH AMERICA
SOUTH-EAST ASIA
SOVIET UNION

USA

COUNTRY GUIDES:

AUSTRIA
BELGIUM AND
LUXEMBOURG
CZECHOSLOVAKIA
FRANCE
GERMANY
GREAT BRITAIN
GREECE
HOLLAND
HUNGARY*

IRELAND
ISRAEL
ITALY
MOROCCO
PORTUGAL
SPAIN
SWITZERLAND
TUNISIA*
TURKEY
YUGOSLAVIA

U.S.A. REGIONAL GUIDES:

NEW ENGLAND*
NEW YORK AND
NEW JERSEY*
MID-ATLANTIC*
THE SOUTH*
INDIAN AMERICA

THE MID-WEST*
THE SOUTH-WEST*
ROCKIES AND PLAINS*
THE FAR WEST*
HAWAII
THE OLD WEST

CITY GUIDES:

LONDON – PARIS – PEKING – VENICE* – VIENNA

LANGUAGE GUIDE:

EUROPE TALKING*

AND THE LATEST:

CRUISES EVERYWHERE
RAILWAYS OF THE WORLD

CANADA
IRAN

* *Not available in Hodder & Stoughton edition*

Printed in Great Britain by The Anchor Press Ltd
and bound by Wm Brendon & Son Ltd, both of Tiptree, Essex

FOREWORD

Iran is a land of contrasts, often of violent contrasts. Even the two names by which it is most commonly known evoke different facets of its nature. "Persia" suggests dreams of wine and roses, of fabulous carpets, langorous dancers and recumbent poets. "Iran" calls forth the dynamic present, oil-wells and tractors, schemes for the betterment of the backward regions, programs of hospital-building and irrigation. This thread of dichotomy will run through your visit to the country, too. There is a strong element of time-travel about a trip to Iran. One can swing through two thousand years in an hour, from an air-conditioned hotel to a ruined place where "the lion and the lizard keep the courts where Jamshid gloried and drank deep".

We cannot pretend that Iran is a country to go for a cheap holiday, unless you are prepared to rough it, really to rough it. It *is* a country to visit for active tourism, for traveling around, drinking in the thousand-and-one forms that beauty and history can take. Iran is the kind of place, and there are not many left around the globe, where the visitor with a certain amount of travel experience under his belt has a great advantage over the tenderfoot. You will have to be ready to ignore the minor irritations of less-than-perfect hotel service, and immerse yourself in the joys of an ancient land (one of the most ancient of all lands), incredibly rich in history and art.

It is a huge country, about the size of Continental Europe, and somewhere around half of it is totally dead land. Only recently, with the access of oil-wealth, have schemes for improving the lot of the vast proportion of the population been possible. The broken rocky nature of the countryside has not been helped by the fact that an earthquake zone runs clear across the middle. It is this combination of wilderness and oasis that gives the particular quality of contrast to the Iranian scene.

We advise that you spend a short time in Tehran, seeing the glories that it has to offer, and then leave its bustle and prices behind for the endlessly magic carpet of the rest of the country. The intense colors of the landscape, the satisfying shapes of mosque and minaret, the glorious textures of rugs and metalwork, of flowers and rock will all enchant you. As will the kindness and attractiveness of the Iranian people. From the turbulence of Tehran to the dreaming

5

gardens of Shiraz, from the ruined glories of Persepolis to the modern boom-town of Abadan, Iran has mystery and wonders in abundance.

*　　　*　　　*

We would like to thank the following people for their generous help in the production of this book: Mr. Nouredin Sharif, Director of Iran Information and Tourism Center in New York; the Director and his staff at the Iran Information and Tourist Center in London, who have been unfailingly courteous and informative; Mrs. Nina Nelson, for her advice and editorial assistance; Mr. and Mrs. H. C. Seherr-Thoss, for their helpful comments; and especially Mr. Peter Sheldon whose field-work and historical knowledge have helped us enormously.

*　　　*　　　*

Errors are bound to creep into any guide—when a hotel closes or a chef produces an inferior meal, when the management of a hotel changes or a landslide carries away a minor road. We are always interested to have letters from our readers, giving us their experiences. They help us to pinpoint trouble spots, and correct any errors we may have overlooked.

Our two addresses are:

in the USA: Fodor's Modern Guides, 750 Third Ave., New York, NY 10017;

in Great Britain: 27B, Old Gloucester St., London WC1N 3AF.

TABLE OF CONTENTS

7

TABLE OF CONTENTS

SUPPLEMENTS

MAPS

FACTS AT YOUR FINGERTIPS

FACTS AT YOUR FINGERTIPS

Contents

FACTS AT YOUR FINGERTIPS

PLANNING YOUR TRIP

WHEN TO GO. The travel season begins towards the end of March when it is still cold on the plateau. The whole of Iran is more agreeable to visit from the 15th of May to the end of October. True, these are the hottest months, but once an altitude of 1,500 m (5,000 feet) has been reached the sun's rays are quite bearable. It rains in spring and autumn, but the showers are short and often very welcome.

The Khuzistan plain, the Baluchistan and the Persian Gulf coasts enjoy moderate temperatures in December and January; this would be the ideal time to explore them, although there is the risk of having the roads cut off due to inundations.

In winter, the rest of the Iranian plateau is covered with snow and ice, but the sky is usually clear. Communications become difficult. It would be wise to be well equipped if one decides to travel during this season and to avoid visiting the furthermost parts of the Elburz, Zagros and Azerbaijan regions.

SPECIAL EVENTS. *Norouz*, the Iranian New Year, falls on March 21st; the Shah receives the diplomatic corps, people visit their families in the provinces, the hotels in Tehran are packed. Thirteen days after, the *sizdah* occurs; on this day all city-dwellers go picnicking in the country. The Moslem religion has two great festivals: *Ramadan*, when there is fasting between the rising and setting of the sun; and *Muharram*, which involves processions and dramatic presentations. These feasts do not have a fixed date, and advance 11 days each year, with respect to the Gregorian calendar. In 1977 Ramadan will last a month, from mid-August, and Muharram will fall in mid-December. Most of the national feast days are religious holidays and are based on the lunar calendar. There are at least 25 of them each year. The *Shiraz-Persepolis Festival* takes place annually in the first fortnight of September.

WHAT TO SEE. It would take months to visit Iran thoroughly, since it is a vast and varied country where each province has its own peculiarities. In Azerbaijan there is the *Armenian Monastery of St. Thaddeus*, the capital of the province, *Tabriz* and its Blue Mosque. The Mongol and Seljuk tombs of *Maragheh* are worth the detour, if you are interested in ancient faience monuments, as well as the Shah Safi mausoleum at *Ardabil*. Then there is the mortuary mosque of Sultan Ojljaitu Khodabendeh at *Soltanieh*. *Tehran* is exciting only because of its museums.

Isfahan and its region are much more interesting: in the Safavid capital you can see the royal palace, the principal mausoleums, and the minarets and bridges which abound in the city.

In *Shiraz*, capital of the Fars province, there are beautiful remains of the Zand period (18th century) but it is especially in its surrounding area that you will find the highlights of ancient Persia: *Persepolis, Pasargadae, Naqsh-e Rustam*, the Achaemenid residences and tombs, *Bishahpur* with its bas-reliefs and its sculptured grotto of the Sassanid period.

On the road which extends along the desert, there are other beautiful Islamic monuments at *Qom, Kashan, Natanz, Kerman* and *Bam*. In the Khuzistan, *Susa* is perhaps not spectacular but the ziggurat of *Choga Zanbil* is the most beautiful in the Middle East. In the vicinity of *Kermanshah* there are the most interesting examples of Sassanid sculpture at *Taq-i-Bostan* and Achaemenid bas-reliefs at *Bisutun*. On the northern route which runs from the Caspian Sea to the Khorasan region, you should see the mausoleum at *Gonbad-e-Qabus*. At *Meshed*, you can only admire the monuments within the holy enclosure, but the historical museum and the mausoleum of Nadir Shah are well worth a visit.

 ITINERARIES. The general topography does not easily lend itself to an itinerary which would cover the whole country. It would take approximately four weeks to visit Iran thoroughly, but by airplane it's possible in *one week* to see Tehran and the three main sites: Isfahan, Shiraz and Persepolis, with a side-trip by car to spend a day at the Caspian Sea. With an additional day you can include Kermanshah, Taq-i-Bostan and Hamadan.

If you have *2 weeks* at your disposal, you would have enough time to visit the whole of the country by airplane. To the preceding itinerary, add the towns of Meshed, Tabriz and Ahwaz, as well as the sites of Susiana, Kashan and Yazd plus the Minab excursion.

By car, you should choose one of the two following plans as they will enable you to see the most picturesque aspects of the country. The first will show you the desert towns and the style of life imposed upon its inhabitants; the second will take you through the Zagros, then Khuzistan and the oil towns.

Itinerary No. 1. Turkish frontier, Monastery of St. Thaddeus, Tabriz, excursion to Maragheh, return to Tabriz, Ardabil by the Ahar road, Astara, Rasht, Chalus, Tehran (one day); Isfahan (2 days); Shiraz and Persepolis (one day); Yazd, Kerman; return to Yazd, Kashan, Qom, Tehran, Zinjan, Soltanieh and Tabriz. With two additional days, you can return to Tabriz from Tehran by way of Hamadan, Kermanshah and the site of Taq-i-Bostan, Sanandaj, Maragheh (to which you would not have made an excursion upon arrival).

Itinerary No. 2. The second plan, identical to the first until Shiraz (except for the excursion to Maragheh and St. Thaddeus), returns via Bishahpur, Behbehan, Abadan, Ahwaz, Susa and Choga Zanbil, Dizful, Khurramabad, Kermanshah and Taq-i-Bostan, Sanandaj, Maragheh and Tabriz.

With *3 weeks*, you can accomplish itinerary no. 1 (including Kermanshah and Sanandaj) to which you can add excursions to Minab and Bam from Kerman. You can also combine itineraries 1 and 2 in the following manner: Turkish frontier, Tabriz, Maragheh, Sanandaj, Kermanshah, Kurramabad, Dizful, Susa and Choga Zanbil, Ahwaz, Abadan, Behbehan, Bishahpur, Shiraz and Persepolis, Yazd, Isfahan via Naïn, Natanz, Kashan, Qom, Tehran, Chalus, Rasht, Astara, Ardabil and Tabriz via Ahar. *Four weeks* are required for this plan if you include excursions to Kerman, Minab and Bam.

These last two itineraries give a rather complete picture of the country, although the holy city of Meshed and its surroundings are missing. Another week is required to go there and return, strolling around Pahlavi Dej (Turkoman market on Thursdays) and Gonbad-e-Qabus.

Finally, in *6 weeks*, you can make the grand tour by using the preceding itineraries: Tabriz, Tehran via the Caspian, then the desert road, Kashan, Yazd, Kerman, excursion to Minab, Bam, Zahedan, excursion to Zabol, Birjan, Meshed, return to Tehran via Gonbad-e-Qabus. Then finish by touring the western part of the country via Isfahan, Shiraz and the Fars, Ahwaz and Khuzistan, Dizful, Khurramabad, Kermanshah, Sanandaj and Tabriz via Maragheh. The road which joins Naïn to Gonbad enters both deserts and passes through Tabas, but it does not really have any particular interest, except for the achievement of doing it, which is not superhuman. In order to follow these itineraries within the time allotted here, a strongly-built, reliable and relatively fast car is required.

WHAT IT WILL COST. You have fixed the date and general itinerary for your trip. It is time to consult a travel agent (see next section). Even an experienced traveler finds it a good idea to consult an expert, if only to learn about changes in a country where everything is rapidly evolving. But even so, some knowledge of the costs will be helpful.

Outside Tehran, where the cost of living can sometimes be higher than in most Western capitals, it is possible to stay for a quite reasonable sum in Iran. Naturally, European-style comfort and conveniences are relatively expensive. Hotel prices are theoretically controlled by the Ministry of Tourism but are sometimes arbitrary. A good provincial hotel costs between 500 and 1,000 rials for a single room with air-conditioning and private bath. In the one-star category you can get hot water and a ventilator or gas heater, depending on the climate, for 150 to 300 Rs per person. It is in this category of establishment (very numerous) that the price fluctuates greatly between one customer and the next.

Food is not expensive. A regular meal in a big hotel in Tehran costs 400 Rs, drinks not included. Local beer sells for 30 to 60 Rs a bottle. In the stores you will pay approximately 200 Rs for a bottle of Iranian vodka, 75 Rs for a Shiraz wine, 1,000 Rs for a bottle of Scotch.

A chauffeured car will cost 150 Rs for the first hour and 85 Rs for those following, plus 6 Rs per kilometer outside the city limits. The collective taxis are cheap (around 6 Rs a run). However, the cars parked in front of the luxury hotels ask up to 150 Rs to take you anywhere in the city. Trains and buses are cheaper than domestic Iranian airlines which are expensive (Tehran–Tabriz, about 1,000 km (620 miles) from 260 Rs by train, 250 Rs by bus, 1,800 Rs by plane).

Traveling by car is reasonable since gasoline (petrol) is only about 40 Rs a gallon. But driving your own car involves problems of vast distances, language, booked-out hotels, which justify the higher cost of organized excursions, especially to out-of-the-way places.

It is difficult to estimate an average daily budget, for this depends on whether you want to travel in relative comfort or on a lower scale—meals can cost 350 Rs or 100 Rs, tea 10 Rs or 2 Rs, cigarettes 50 Rs or 10 Rs, etc. An organized excursion in the Fars, from Shiraz to Bishahpur for example, costs over 3,000 Rs with a guide, and 450 Rs by bus.

DAILY BUDGET IN A THREE-STAR TEHRAN HOTEL

Room	900	Rs
Breakfast	120	,,
Two meals (no alcohol)	800	,,
Transportation	80	,,
Beverages	200	,,
Cigarettes (foreign)	50	,,
Museums, miscellaneous	100	,,
	2,250	**Rs**

If you wish to use the services of a guide-interpreter and spend an evening in a nightclub, these expenses must be added on to the budget.

DAILY BUDGET, STUDENT-STYLE

Room	150	Rs
Breakfast	40	,,
Two meals (local style)	220	,,
Transportation	60	,,
Teas, one beer	60	,,
Local cigarettes	10	,,
Museums, miscellaneous	50	,,
	590	**Rs**

 HOW TO GO. When you have decided where you want to go, your next step is to consult a good travel agent. If you haven't one, the *American Society of Travel Agents*, 360 Lexington Ave, New York, or the *Association of British Travel Agents*, 53 Newman St., London W1P 4AH, will advise you. Whether you select *Maupintour Associates*, *Cooks*, *American Express*, or a smaller organization is a matter of preference. They all have branch offices or correspondents in the larger cities.

Travel abroad today, although it is steadily becoming easier and more comfortable, is also growing more complex in its details. As the choice of things to do, places to visit, ways of getting there, increases, so does the problem of *knowing* about all these questions. A reputable, experienced travel agent is a specialist in details, and because of his importance to the success of your trip, you should inquire in your community to find out which organization has the finest reputation.

If you wish your agent to book you on a package tour, reserve your transportations and even your first overnight hotel accommodation, his services should cost you nothing.

If, on the other hand, you wish him to plan for you an individual itinerary and make all arrangements down to hotel reservations and transfers to and from rail and air terminals, he will make a service charge on the total cost of your planned itinerary.

There are many tour operators with programs that cover Iran, and, indeed, for the inexperienced traveler it is the best possible way of visiting the country. *Pennworld* have a 28-day tour, $791 plus airfare, which travels by motorcoach and involves a bit of roughing it. *Maupintour* run a 15-day tour from $998, plus airfare, that uses only first class facilities.

From Britian W. F. & R. K. Swan have tours in the fall and spring, with highly qualified guest lecturers. These tours are called *Art Treasures of Persia*, and run from £625, all included, 15-days.

 WHAT TO TAKE. The less you take, the better you will feel and the less you will have to carry. Those who travel by air are limited from the start to the traditional 20 kilos, and, leaving a few kilos leeway at the beginning, means you will be able to return with souvenirs without being obliged to pay extra freight charges. By car you probably would be tempted to take along more. However, you must remember that, although the hotel where you spend the night can ensure your car's safekeeping, you may have to park in the street from time to time, and in this case it is preferable to empty the car. The risks of being robbed are no higher than in some European countries or in the U.S., but it is better not to tempt the devil.

For summer, extremely light clothing is necessary (dresses and suits of cotton, linen, silk). Do not forget that you will be in an Islamic land where discreet dress, especially for women, is required everywhere. Madame's shorts are to be rigorously excluded! Trousers are preferable to the mini-skirt and, accompanied by a tunic, they are the perfect solution. For visits to the mosques and other religious edifices it is useful to carry a scarf. The severity of the winter climate requires a complete wardrobe of warm coats, hats and fur-lined boots. Do not forget your mountain or ski shoes and boots as these may be difficult to find on the spot.

Ready-made clothes, underwear and shoes may be found in Iran, but the prices are rather high. On the other hand, certain materials, such as Yazd silk and satin, are very good buys.

Iranian pharmacies are well-stocked with foreign medicines made in Iran under license; however, if you have a special treatment to follow, it is wiser to take along your own supply of medicine—in particular for stomach trouble. Cosmetics of all makes are easily found in Tehran, less easily in the provinces.

NEW YORK-TEHRAN ROUND TRIP

		Availability
First class	$2,144	All year
Economy high season	$1,544	1 June–31 August
Economy low season	$1,400	1 September–31 May
14–21 day excursion, stopovers permitted	$1,141	1 June–31 August
,, ,,	$1,059	1 September–31 May
14–21 day excursion, no stopovers	$ 900	1 June–31 August
,, ,,	$ 812	April–May & September–October
,, ,,	$ 747	1 November–31 March
14–21 day excursion, 1 stop Europe and 1 stop Middle East	$ 951	1 June–31 August
,, ,,	$ 864	April–May & September–October
,, ,,	$ 806	1 November–31 March

LONDON-TEHRAN RETURN

		Availability
First class	£611.00	All year
Economy	£423.00	All year
10–30 day excursion	£271.00	All year

 PASSPORTS, VISAS, VACCINATIONS. Whatever your means of transport, you must have a valid passport. British passport holders do not require a visa for visits of up to 3 months; U.S. and Canadian passport holders do require visas, but these are issued gratis. Other nationalities should inquire about visa fees. Visas can be obtained at the appropriate Embassy or Consulate in your own country.

Tourists who arrive by air from countries where there is no Iranian Consulate can obtain a 15-day visa at the Abadan or Tehran airport. A 3-month visa can be renewed for an equal amount of time at *Service for Foreign Residents*, Farah Jonoubi Ave., in Tehran.

A *smallpox* vaccination is required for entry into Iran while travelers arriving overland are advised to obtain cholera vaccinations. In case of an epidemic in these countries, a health barrier can detain travelers for 48 hours at the Iranian border (at Tayebat, coming from Afghanistan and at Mirjaveh, coming from Pakistan). Vaccinations must be entered on the yellow international vaccination certificate and officially stamped.

Automobile drivers should consult our motoring section for if you go through some of the Eastern European countries (including Hungary, Yugoslavia, Bulgaria), you will need transit visas which you can get either in the Consulates of the countries concerned or at the frontier. (Some of the formalities have been eased recently and this was still the case at press time: ask for the latest information.) A *carnet de passage*, issued by the AA or RAC, is compulsory for any car staying in Iran for longer than one month.

GETTING TO IRAN

BY AIR. Aircraft arriving from Europe land at Tehran-Mehrabad. The national airline, *Iran Air*, provides regular connecting flights to London, Paris, Frankfurt, Geneva, Istanbul, Rome, Moscow, Kabul, etc. and to the emirates (principalities) of the Persian Gulf, etc., and operates both a one-stop (London) 707 flight from New York to Tehran five days a week, and a non-stop Jumbo 747SP flight from New York to Tehran twice a week. Tehran is also served by most of the major airlines, *Air France*, *British Airways*, *PanAm* etc.

Abadan also has an international airport.

BY SEA. Not a practical solution for this large continental country. Khorramshahr on the Persian Gulf is the largest port and some of the freighters which stop there take passengers. *P&O* (*Cargo Division*) do occasional trips from Britain, via Suez and Kuwait. *Hellenic Lines Ltd.* sail from the States on a round-the-world cargo voyage, dropping in at Iran occasionally. In both cases, check with the line.

BY TRAIN. As the exotic days of the *Orient Express* are no more, the best way to get to Iran by rail is to go to Istanbul by express from either London or Paris. Once there cross by rail to Hydarpasa. There are trains on Wednesdays, Thursdays, Fridays and Saturdays onward to Tehran. You should be warned, however, that there can be up to 12 hours' delay in outward connections. This is now a trip for those with patience, time and a sense of adventure. This part of the trip is on the *Vangölü Express*.

An even more adventurous route is to go to Istanbul, then catch the *Taurus Express* to Bagdad via Ankara and Aleppo in Syria (80 hrs. Istanbul–Bagdad). From Bagdad to Iran (if the two countries are speaking to each other at the time), take a bus (slow and dusty) or the once-weekly airplane (*Pakistan International Airlines*).

BY BUS. Though buses are air-conditioned, the distance and unpaved roads in Turkey make for a strenuous journey. Still, you get a good idea of the country before arriving at your destination. There is a regular service which takes you from Munich to Tehran in 8 days. For more information, write to *Touring Bureau*, Starnberger Bahnhof, Munich, West Germany; the price is about $90 (£55), without meals or lodging.

You may also write to *Generalcar*, 10 Rue de la Montagne, 1000-Brussels, Belgium (*Orientbus* line) which works in conjunction with the Iranian company *TBT* in Tehran.

BY CAR. From the Continent you must count on an average of 5 stopovers, or 4 stops with a fast car, to cover the 3,000 km (1,850 miles) to Istanbul. From Le Havre, the easiest itinerary goes through Rouen, around Paris, Châlons-sur-Marne, Metz and Saarbrücken where you join the German autobahn system; Mannheim, Karlsruhe, branch off towards Stuttgart and Munich, Salzburg, Vienna, Hegyeshalom (the Hungarian frontier, transit visa at the frontier, car insurance obligatory: 15 minutes if all goes well); Budapest, Szeged (Yugoslavian frontier), Subotica, Belgrade, Nis, Dimitrovgrad (Bulgarian frontier, visa at the frontier and also compulsory car insurance of 72 hrs), Sofia, Plovdiv, Haskovo, Svilengrad, Turkish frontier, Edirne, Istanbul.

Travelers coming from Ostend will go around Brussels, then via Liège, Cologne, Frankfurt. Take the autobahn via Nuremberg, which is less crowded, and then join the above-mentioned highway at Munich.

From Salzburg, you can also go down towards Graz and the Yugoslavian frontier. The Maribor–Zagreb road is not bad but it is winding and narrow. At Zagreb you rejoin a two-lane highway with a speed limit which leads to Belgrade. The road is straight, slightly deteriorated and crowded with trucks, especially at night.

The three main variations which can be used to reach Istanbul are matched by an equal number to continue to Iran. The shortest but least attractive route is the E5 to Ankara, then the E23 via Yozgat, Sivas, Erzincan to Erzerum, theoretically paved all the way since 1975 but in actual fact with long stretches which are exceedingly dusty or muddy (according to season) where widening or straightening is in process. Scenically greatly superior is the 200 km (125 miles) detour from Ankara via Samsun, then along the Black Sea coast to Trabzon, turning inland over two passes of more than 2,000 m (6,500 feet) in altitude, which are difficult in winter so that snow chains are needed from November 15th to May 1st.

Four days are required to cross Turkey to Erzerum. E23 continues paved to Horasan, where it deteriorates into a dusty washboard for 102 km (65 miles) while after Ağri potholes abound to the Iranian border at Bazargan. A third choice is Route 60 from Ankara via Kayseri, Malatya, Bingöl to Mus, then over some very bad stretches west of Lake Van to Ağri. But keep in mind that in the East the shortest in miles is often the longest in time, so better take the road round Lake Van, paved except for the last 80 km (50 miles) to Ağri.

From Ankara, you can avoid the mountain passes by going via Aleppo (Syria) and Bagdad (Iraq) and entering Iran at Kermanshah. This itinerary includes a bad stretch of 400 km (248 miles) the length of the Euphrates and requires two supplementary visas that can be obtained at Ankara.

In Iran. Bazargan, Tabriz, Tehran, well-kept and busy Route 4, but insufficient filling stations from the border to Tabriz. Then the northern route: Sari, Shahpasand, Meshed, Youssoufabad (Afghan frontier)—paved all the way to Herat in Afghanistan, but with a pass more than 6,500 feet high in the Elburz (same advice as for the mountain passes).

A Note of Warning About Road Travel. A survey by the Consumers Association in Britain (1972) showed that 1 out of 5 responding to the questionnaire on driving their own cars to the Middle East (including Iran) stated they had either been physically assaulted or cheated on the road. Frontier guards were little better than highwaymen in some cases, and pretty girls needed constant protection.

Road maps. Most of the official tourist services, Hungarian, Yugoslavian, Bulgarian, etc., give or sell abridged maps which suffice to cross the country.

FACTS AT YOUR FINGERTIPS

For an overall look at the Paris, Brussels or Geneva–Istanbul run there is a "Balkans" map put out by Kümmerley and Frey; a quick glance shows all the possible routes from Germany to Turkey. For the rest of the trip, maps sold throughout Europe can be helpful (in London if in difficulty try Stanfords in Long Acre WC2) in estimating miles between towns and their relative positions, but they are not always up to date. In Turkey, all the tourist offices and the larger petrol stations such as B.P. and Shell sell road maps of the country.

In Iran, the tourist information bureau of Bazargan and Khosravi will give you the official map of the country with all the latest information about road conditions.

Mileage. London–Istanbul 1,950 miles, Ankara 2,050, Samsun 2,500, Trabzon 2,710, Erzerum 2,850, Bazargan 3,150, Tehran 3,630, Zahedan 4,230, and Quetta 4,710.

By car-train or boat. For those who do not wish to drive the entire distance, there are car-sleeper trains from continental channel ports to Vienna or Venice. The car ferry, *Truva*, of the Turkish Maritime Lines, goes once a week from Venice to Izmir (4 days). Ferries from the same company cross the Black Sea between Istanbul and Trabzon (two days by *Hopa Express I*).

If you want to go to Iran via the Soviet Union, you can put your car on a train in Moscow (it is obligatory to do so from Erivan to Iranian border) and pick it up at Jolfa, after having crossed the frontier. Information can be obtained at Intourist.

Driver's license. Although it is not compulsory, an international driving license is recommended. The *green insurance card* is not valid in Hungary or Bulgaria. You will be obliged to take out temporary insurance in these countries. In Iran, insurance will be required for the duration of your stay and must be obtained at the first large town inside the Iranian border (e.g. Tabriz, when coming from Turkey).

Customs documents. Auto papers (or a triptique) valid for one year are indispensable for crossing all frontiers in this area. The triptique is furnished by all national automobile clubs, on payment of a membership fee and a small guaranty deposit which is refunded after the trip with the return of the document.

ARRIVING IN IRAN

 CUSTOMS. Baggage inspection is only a simple formality for tourists. There are no restrictions on personal effects, including jewelry, one camera, one pair of binoculars, one musical instrument, one radio, a tent and camping equipment, fishing gear, a hunting gun (with compulsory carrying case), a pair of skis and poles, two tennis rackets, a canoe, one tape recorder and one typewriter. All the above material is listed on a written declaration and theoretically entered in the passport. Visitors are permitted to enter Iran with 200 cigarettes or an equivalent in tobacco products and a bottle of alcohol without paying any duty.

As exchange rates are liable to considerable fluctuations these days, we urge you to check on the current rates both before traveling and en route.

 MONEY AND EXCHANGE. The Iranian monetary unit is the *rial*, but in everyday life you count in *tomans*, an ancient money which has disappeared (one toman equals 10 rials). The value of banknotes is indicated also in Western numbers, but of coins only in Arabic. There are bills of 20, 50, 100, 500 and 1,000 rials, also of 5,000 and 10,000 rials, and coins of 20, 10, 5, 2, and 1 rials. As you will have seen already, rials is written "Rs".

Traveler's checks are the best way to safeguard travel funds. They are sold by various banks and companies in terms of American and Canadian dollars and pounds sterling. Most universally accepted are those of *American Express* and *Thomas Cook*, while those issued by *First National Bank of New York*, *Bank of America*, and the biggest British banks—*Barclays*, *Lloyds*, *Midland* and *National Westminster*—are also widely used.

In Iran, you can change your money either at a bank or at the Tehran bazaar where you obtain a slightly higher rate for banknotes, but not for traveler's checks. You can, of course, change money in all the big hotels, at airports, at the frontier posts of Bazargan and Khosravi and always at the official rate. Cash and traveler's checks can be exchanged for local money, also for Indian, Pakistanian, Afghanistan rupees, Turkish pounds, etc.

 LANGUAGES. The official language of Iran is *Fârsi* (Persian), which is of Indo-European origin. Therefore, we find many familiar-sounding words such as *padar* (father), *madar* (mother), etc. It is written in Arabic letters and numbers. Place names and the main streets are also indicated in Latin letters, but there is no standardized transliteration, not even on maps. Thus Alborz or Elburz; Ferdausi or Firdowsi; Meshad or Mashad; Qazvin, Chasvin or Kasvin; Qom, Qum, Ghom or Kum.

Most educated people speak English, but French and German are also understood. Yet it may often be difficult to find a foreign-language speaker when required, and in smaller towns foreign languages are rarely known. Turkish is understood in the northwest (around Tabriz) and Arabic in the southwest (Khuzistan).

To learn a few rudiments of Persian is not very difficult—the words are easy to remember. Otherwise, international sign-language is of great help. The key is *khoubé*—"that's good" or "that's fine", and *Inshallah* when it isn't—the latter means, loosely, "God willing" and is heard more often than anything else.

ISLAM, or submission to the will of God, is the name of the Moslem religion which claims to be the revelation of God to the world by his prophet Mohammed. It is very close to Judaism and Christianity; Moses, Jesus and others are accepted as minor prophets but Mohammed is considered the greatest of them all. The Moslem religion embraces only one God, Allah, and is based on the Koran (the book of revelations, divided into 114 *sourats*), on the words of the Prophet and on tradition—a collection of ancient Gospels. The Koran constitutes a code for the faithful, thanks to which he can perfect all that is best within himself. In this religion, the unity of God (there is only one God, God is one) is emphasized as opposed to the Christian Trinity.

Mohammed was born in Mecca around 575 A.D. Because of his monotheistic doctrines, he was forced to emigrate to Medina in 622 (Hegira) to escape persecution. He returned after 8 years, conquered his native city and died there two years later.

Islam makes itself strongly felt during the month of Ramadan when the Moslems fast between the rising and setting of the sun. Restaurants keep their curtains drawn and in the smaller towns some of them remain closed. Time schedules are completely changed: they open early in the morning in order to close during the difficult afternoon hours. At sunset, taxis, waiters, merchants and employees all disappear to break their fast. It is hopeless to attempt to find anything or do anything during the next half hour.

Shi'ism is the state religion of Iran; it split off from the Sunni religion (Kurdistan) due to differences arising after Mohammed's death. The Shi'ites regard Ali, Mohammed's son-in-law, as the legitimate successor to Mohammed and disregard the three caliphs who actually did succeed him and were supported by the Sunnites. The Shi'ites have developed a personal mysticism centered on suffering. Persecutions led them to practice *ketman* (mental restraint). The last Imam (religious head) having "gone away" in the 9th century, the Shi'ites believe that he will return at the end of time.

STAYING IN IRAN

CLIMATE. Iran's climate is continental, hot in summer and cold in winter, with considerable differences in temperature. For example, on the plateau, at Tehran (1,100 m— 3,600 feet), the temperature reaches +43° C (110° F) in July and August. The nights stay hot and everybody sleeps on roof-tops or terraces. In January and February, the night temperatures can go as low as −16° C (+3° F). During the day, thanks to the warm rays of the sun, the temperature climbs back to around zero. Isfahan, Shiraz, Meshed have similar climates, with a few variations. Tabriz (1,500 m—5,000 feet) is much colder and the victim of extremes, −25° C to +35° C (−13° F to 95° F). The weather along the shores of the Caspian is much more even, but the Persian Gulf ports have extremely hot summers due to the humidity as well as the heat. The winters are very mild. Seistan holds the record with an average temperature of +49° C (120° F) without interruption from April to November.

The Iranian climate is extremely dry, except for the Caspian provinces which never fail to receive their 1,200 mm (47 inches) of rain per year. Due to the thousands of newly planted trees, however, Tehran now receives some rainfall during the traditionally dry season between June and September. It rains a little in the spring and autumn, and in winter there are heavy snowfalls: approximately 250 mm (10 inches) in all. The wind usually blows from the Turkestan steppes in the northeast. Sand storms are not rare, and dust is the traveler's great enemy, especially in summer. In the eastern part of the country, the 120-day wind which blows up in June reaches speeds of 200 km (125 miles) per hour.

Temperatures in degrees Fahrenheit:

Tehran:	Jan.	Feb.	Mar.	Apr.	May	June	July	Aug.	Sept.	Oct.	Nov.	Dec.
Max.	45	50	59	71	82	93	99	97	90	76	63	51
Min.	27	32	39	49	58	66	72	71	64	53	43	33

Isfahan:												
Max.	47	53	61	72	83	92	98	96	90	77	63	52
Min.	24	29	37	46	54	62	67	64	56	46	37	29

 HOTELS. Despite the large number of Western-style hotels opened in recent years, you will do well to book in advance, especially in such tourist centers as Isfahan, Shiraz and above all Tehran.

In an Iranian-style hotel the food will often be more willingly brought up to your room than in a Western-style hotel where you may be forced to sit at formica-topped tables and subjected to music you could well do without. Therefore, if you have a table in your room, the greyness of the tablecloth may be compensated for by a telephone-intercom system to call the waiter. By the same token the lavatory facilities called "Turkish" are more likely to be clean and hygienic than those called "English" when they are public or shared conveniences. There seems to be no way to indicate establishments that would be sure to please both you and your pocketbook.

We have followed the official system of categories, though not necessarily the official ranking, because of the considerable variations in quality and price within these classifications. First of all there are the *deluxe* hotels: they exist only in Tehran, Isfahan, Shiraz, Abadan, and on the Caspian coast near Chalus. They are truly autonomous islands where you will find excellent service, very good local or international cuisine and everything to assure a pleasant stay—restaurants, shops, travel agencies, exchange office, hairdresser, post office, etc.

The four-star (****) hotels will offer you practically the same comforts but the variety of additional services is less extensive. The three-star (***) hotels are less well-equipped but are still comfortable. At the bottom of the Western style are the two-star (**) establishments which give satisfactory service and cleanliness, hot water, the possibility of a private bathroom, a restaurant and assured parking for your car. In the provincial towns, they are the only establishments capable of giving you satisfaction, although they are somewhat lower down the scale from hotels of the same category in the capital. The Tourism Ministry's *Inn* (or *meh-*

mansara in Fârsi) chain, some 50 hotels mostly 2 or 3 stars, will welcome you in many isolated places.

The first-class hotels, 3 stars and inns serve beer and other alcoholic beverages. They are equipped with central heating or air-conditioning, depending on the climate.

The hotels to which we give one star (*) may offer you reasonable accommodation. There is usually hot water and sometimes there are even private bathrooms available. Meals are served in the rooms if there is no restaurant. It would, however, be wise to look over the common bathrooms and showers before deciding to take a room.

For the student-style visitors, we will also suggest a few hotels without stars which can put them up for one night. They offer a roof, a bed, cold water, but not always in the room, and sometimes the possibility of taking a more or less hot shower.

Compared to Pakistani or Turkish hotels, Iranian hotels are rather expensive for comparable accommodation. In the first-class hotels, prices are posted in the rooms. The same is not true of more modest establishments where it is sometimes necessary to bargain and above all to stipulate that the heating and showers will not be added on to the bill as extras and to make sure that the hot water is not an illusion.

In a first-class hotel you will pay 1,000 Rs and possibly much more for a single room, 1,300 and upwards for a double room. In a 3-star hotel, a single will cost 800–1,100 Rs, a double 900–1,500 Rs. In 2-star hotels, the prices will be around 650 and 800 Rs respectively. In one-star hotels, you will pay around 300 Rs for one person, 450 Rs for two. In the knapsack-style hotels, it is customary to pay 120 Rs per person, but it is possible to talk the price down to 80 Rs. It will not necessarily be proportional to the comfort in this category.

RESTAURANTS. Our chapter on *Food and Drink* will give you information on local culinary resources. Insofar as restaurants are concerned, you will find international cuisine in Tehran and in all the big cities. It is also possible to find places with kitchens run by foreign cooks (French, Austrian, Italian, etc.) where you can enjoy savory dishes.

You will certainly come upon local-style restaurants, the most typical being the *Tchelo-kebabi* which, as its name indicates, specializes in tchelo-kebabs with half-a-dozen variations. Apart from chicken soup, you will have trouble finding anything other than basic rice preparations. One does find tea, carbonated drinks and sometimes beer. The tchelo-kebabis usually have a noisy atmosphere, the waiters rush around and the customers are as numerous at noon as in the evening. Even in the small towns, despite the rush at lunchtime, the presentation of the meal is appetizing and the food wholesome.

In the villages there are the *tchaikhanes*—teahouses—which are extremely simple and serve skewers of meat with bread or soup in an aluminium or enameled iron bowl. Although the exteriors are not inviting, the food there is as good as anywhere else. In Tehran and Tabriz, the Armenian eating-houses serve sandwiches and vodka.

Prices vary little from one establishment to another, and here is an indication of what you may expect to pay. The menu in a boarding-house in Tehran costs about 180 Rs. The tchelo-kebabs cost between 60 to 90 Rs, the tchelo-khoreshe from 40 to 50 Rs, soup 30 to 40 Rs, a plate of cheese, butter, jam 30 Rs, a carbonated drink from 6 to 10 Rs, tea (small) 3 Rs or (large) 6 Rs. The side-dishes—yogurt, salad, eggs, etc.—are counted separately.

TIPPING. Hotels, restaurants and nightclubs add a service charge of 15% to the bill; extra tipping depends on the quality of service; room service 10–20 Rs, barmen 10%. In the tchelo-kebabis, it is usual to leave some small change for the waiter, but there is no general rule. Tipping is not expected in teahouses or unclassified hotels.

Porters receive 10 Rs per suitcase; cloakroom attendants, doormen, parking place guards 10 Rs; barbers and hairdressers get 30–50 Rs. No taxi tipping required. The guard who shows you round a mosque or other site 10–15 Rs, especially if entry is free. The same sum is given to the young boy who takes you through the small streets of Isfahan, but none to the one who guides you to bazaars and hotels where he will get a commission. Give 10–15 Rs to the person who washes your car, 5 Rs to the one who wipes your windshield.

You will see beggars living like hermits along the roads; since begging is their "job" in a sense, you can give them a little something. They are very different from the beggars who importune only tourists.

CAMPING. There are several camping grounds in the vicinity of the large towns, and six well-equipped camps on the Caspian Sea, including a beach-front camp near Bandar Pahlavi; Chalus; Now Shahr; and Sisangan National Park. As a general rule, you are discouraged from camping in the countryside. Several towns have put aside land where travelers can put up their tents, near an airport for example. It is better to ask the local authorities (police) for permission to camp in the vicinity of their police station. This is usual in Persepolis where there is space set aside specifically for that purpose. For more information about this, contact the Ministry of Information and Tourism.

HUNTING. Shooting ranges from the birds of the Caspian Sea and Lake Rezaiyeh to bear, ibex, moufflon, and the protected Mesopotamian deer. Information, regulations and seasonal licenses (850 Rs for all birds, 170 Rs for game) available from the Fish and Game Department, 21 Shah Abbas Ave., Tehran. You must also have a carrying case for your gun, which is obligatory for passing through customs in any case. This permit will give you the right to hunt in parts of the country which are not reservations, outside the reproduction season, which differs according to game. Hunting is closed from March 21st to June 21st. To hunt in reserved regions, indicated in English on billboards along the roads, you must have a "special" permit issued by the Fish and Game Department for a specific region.

FISHING. An "ordinary" fishing permit can be obtained at the Fish and Game Dept. for 850 Rs per year. The "special" permit for trout fishing in protected waters can be obtained at offices located at these fishing spots. The shores and marshes of the Caspian Sea are protected, especially for salmon fishing. It is forbidden to fish at night. The fishing season begins on August 23rd and ends on March 20th.

SHOPPING. The chapter on handicrafts will give you an idea about rugs and other objects which you can find in small shops all over the country. For some time now the Iranians have over-estimated the value of their products as well as the buying power of the tourist. You must know how to bargain: in general, goods are worth half their declared price. Silverware—boxes, jewelry, place settings—are bought by the pound, the price varying according to workmanship. Silver is controlled and stamped (85%). A box eight inches square with very fine workmanship is worth around 3,000 Rs.

Turquoise is bought at Meshed, Nishapur or Tehran. The most valuable are dark blue, without blemish and rounded. Antique jewelry, especially Turkoman, is highly prized. Beware of cheap imitations. In the antique shops you will find old copper, arms and coins, miniatures, bronze from Luristan and prehistoric pottery, papier-mâché, painted wood, all more or less authentic.

As for souvenirs, *khatam* (inlay work) and *kalamkaris* (printed cloth) from Isfahan are very popular. So are the inexpensive *gelim* tapestries (used as rugs and blankets) from Fars province. More difficult to find are the engravings and embroideries done by tribal women (Baluchi, Turkoman, and Qashqai) for their own use. Do not be deceived by ugly ceramics, poorly engraved copper, badly enameled boxes and paintings on bone or plastic.

CLOSING TIMES. Iran had been using the Moslem calendar which reckons the years from the Hegira (A.D. 622). But in 1976, by official decree, the calendar now dates from the year Cyrus the Great founded the Persian Empire (559 B.C.). Therefore 1977 in Iran will be 2536! The ancient lunar calendar is still used for religious purposes, the year being 11 days shorter than the solar year, which means that all Moslem feast days are changeable. The weekly holiday is Djomeh (Friday), and the weekend therefore begins on Thursday afternoon. Working hours are from 8.30 a.m. to 1 p.m. and 4.30 to 8.30 p.m. The ministries, administrations and some banks are closed in the afternoon. In the country, the bazaars close at sunset.

The holidays are too numerous and too changeable to be listed. The following have fixed dates: the Iranian New Year, March 21–22; *Sizdah*, the 13th day of the year, April 2nd; Anniversary of the Constitution, August 5th; birthday of S.M. Mohammed Reza Shah Pahlavi, October 26th.

MAIL AND TELEPHONE SERVICES. Letters to the U.S.A. are 20 Rs for 10 grams, 30 Rs for 20 grams. To Europe 14 and 18 Rs respectively. Postcards 15 Rs to the U.S.A, 10 Rs to Europe; telegrams to Europe, 20 Rs per word. For a registered letter you must first buy the stamps and then go to another counter to have it registered. The central post office in Tehran (Sepah Avenue) is the best place. In the big towns, the postal service is well-organized.

FACTS AT YOUR FINGERTIPS

General delivery: At the central post office in Tehran, Tabriz, Isfahan and Shiraz. Ask your correspondents to write your *family name* in block capitals as the employees have trouble filing letters. You must show your passport. You can also have your mail sent to your Consulate or to American Express. Hours: 8 to 12 for all services; open until 6 p.m. for special services.

Note. You are warned not to make long-distance phone calls from your hotel room without checking very carefully what the cost will be. Hotels frequently add several hundred percent to such calls. This is an international practice, not one confined to Iran.

PHOTOGRAPHY. Films tend to be expensive. Care is needed once you start photographing anything except monuments. The Iranian does not pose willingly and can get touchy if you photograph a donkey, a peasant, or poverty under the illusion that it is local color; they would rather you took pictures of marble public buildings. However, there is no law forbidding you to photograph anything except military establishments and personnel. The police have no right to confiscate your camera; in case of trouble, contact the Ministry of Tourism. However do not forget that you are in an Islamic country and that extreme discretion should be exercised. Do not photograph women without permission. You can have your film developed in black and white and in color in Tehran or any large town; the price is rather high.

GUIDES-INTERPRETERS. You will have no trouble getting the cooperation of a guide-interpreter to visit the towns and countryside or for any other side-trip. There are guides who speak English, French or German. Do not hire one casually in the street. The Ministry of Tourism information offices or any first-class hotel will put you in touch with an authorized guide. The cost is about 1,000 Rs a day.

DRINKING WATER. Quite safe in large towns, especially in the first-class hotels. Tap water in Tehran is also safe, if you can bear the taste. Mineral water is not very tasty either. In rural areas, the water is *not* recommended and you should stick to tea, or carbonated drinks which can be found nearly everywhere—cheap and always served cold. Their only fault is that they are not thirst-quenching.

ELECTRICITY. The electric current in Iran is 220 volts (50/60 cycles). A European electric razor will work almost everywhere, but not American ones. Light sockets are the present European model. The current is subject to appreciable drops. In the countryside there is often no electricity at all. You would do well to take a battery-powered razor and a flashlight along with you.

NEWSPAPERS. Certain daily papers publish one edition entirely in English or French, for example the *Journal of Tehran* and *Kayhan*, which cost 10 Rs.

LOCAL TIME is G.M.T. plus 3 hours 30 minutes.

TRAVELING IN IRAN

BY AIR. *Iran-Air* has rather high rates for domestic flights. The aerial network covers all major tourist towns and provincial capitals. The lines which join Tehran to the large cities such as Tabriz, Isfahan, Shiraz, Meshed, etc. have several flights a day. The airplane is therefore an excellent mode of transportation in this country where distances between places are great.

Here are a few prices, but they may well be higher by the time you come to fly. Tehran–Isfahan: 1,600 Rs; to Abadan: 3,200 Rs; to Shiraz: 2,800 Rs; to Zahedan: 2,850 Rs; to Tabriz: 1,800 Rs.

BY TRAIN. The rail network is linked to Europe through Turkey as well as the U.S.S.R. via Tabriz in Azerbaijan, beside serving some faraway provinces such as Kerman, Khorasan (Meshed) or Khuzistan (Khorramshahr). The Caspian line ends at Gorgan.

The comfort of first class and sleepers is irreproachable and it is possible to spend a night on the train and arrive fresh and alert at your destination. There are two categories of trains: the expresses and the regulars. From Tehran to Khorramshahr you will pay 1,350 Rs, 660 Rs or 450 Rs for an express or 940 Rs, 565 Rs or 380 Rs for a regular, depending on whether you travel 1st, 2nd or 3rd class. For Tabriz, an express will cost 820 Rs, 520 Rs or 375 Rs and a regular 755 Rs, 450 Rs or 260 Rs. Even by express, the ride is always a bit slow.

BUS. There are companies whose buses are comfortable, rapid and frequent. They travel to the most deserted corners of Iran and it is the mode of transportation that most Iranians use, thus the cheapest. The comfort is proportionate to the distance the bus travels from the large towns, but in all cases of a reasonable standard. There are stops for rest rooms and refreshments. The main companies are *T.B.T.*, *Mihantour*, *Levantour*, *Iran Tourist*, *Iran Peyma* and *Adel*. From Tehran it is 12 hours to Tabriz, 36 hours to Meshed, 8 hours to Isfahan, 16 hours to Shiraz, 48 hours to Abadan, 3 days to Zahedan. Here are a few prices (always subject to change) from Tehran: Tabriz 250 Rs; Meshed 400 Rs; Hamadan 120 Rs; Gonbad-e-Qabus 200 Rs; Shiraz 300 Rs.

TAXIS. You will find taxis everywhere. The local custom is to pile 8 to 10 persons in these vehicles, although some of them have a rather unreassuring look, especially in the country. They will be your only means of transportation to places where there are no tourist offices such as Kermanshah and Susa. Prices are reasonable, but should always be settled in advance.

For traveling around the town, taxis are ideal as much for the convenience they offer in an unknown town as for their very reasonable prices. For an errand in town, it costs 5 to 10 Rs for one person, 20 Rs in Tehran; from 7 to 15 Rs for two or three people, 30 in Tehran. The black and yellow telephone taxis are much more expensive. These cars are also parked in front of the large hotels.

 MOTORING. *Don't,* unless you can cope with the law of the jungle (the roads are lined with wrecked vehicles). On no account neglect to take out personal liability insurance at the frontier posts of Bazargan or Khosravi, or you can contact the *Yorkshire Insurance Co.*, Amir Kabir Ave., or *Bimeh Melli,* Shah Reza Villa Ave., both in Tehran. Expensive at 2,300 Rs for a fortnight, 2,600 Rs for a month, but essential. In the open country it is difficult to foretell the reaction of an animal, a child or even an adult to an approaching vehicle. Those who make the law on the roads are, as everywhere else, the large trucks. When two of them try to pass each other, both equally stubborn, it can be troublesome. Take your foot off the accelerator when you see one coming, just to be on the safe side. The Kazvin–Tehran run is the most dangerous in the entire country. There is heavy traffic on this straight road and everyone drives very fast.

As for the road at night, beware of the fact that obstacles are not always indicated and loom up at the last second. Since most truck drivers ignore signal lights at crossings you are at some risk. A system used by truck drivers about to pass each other is to flash their lights.

In case of any accident, the foreigner is always in the wrong. In cities and large towns, there will be a police station to handle the formalities; in the villages and distant areas, do not waste your time in useless conversation. If the accident is serious, go to the provincial capital, or to the nearest administrative district, and ask to see the governor (*ostandari, fermandari*). Be sure to inform your Consulate. Avoid signing any paper and do not let your passport be taken away from you.

In town, drivers tend not to use any directional signals, which means that great attention must be paid at all times. Cars pull out in traffic and change lanes whenever they feel like it. A turn in the middle of the street seems to be current practise, despite all the blowing of horns and sudden braking this imposes on other cars. In short, the Iranian cares little about driving rules.

Condition of the roads. Under the Fifth Development Plan to 1978, the Iranian road network is being greatly expanded, not only by asphalting an ever larger proportion of the present 25,000 km of all-weather roads, but also by constructing technically ambitious shorter road links.

As far as dirt roads and tracks are concerned, we can only say that they are of uneven quality, depending on whether they have been leveled or not and on the good or bad weather of the preceding days. Some of them suffer from corrugation caused by the wind which makes it impossible to exceed 25 miles per hour. You must not be afraid of fords, bumps, jolts and steep inclines. We shall give you regional details in each section, though before venturing off the beaten track it might be as well to check with the *Touring and Automobile Club of Iran,* 37 Varzesh Ave., Tehran. From one season to the next, the condition of the roads can change entirely.

The road which crosses the desert area between Naïn and Gonabad by way of Tabas is not impossible for a sturdy car, but it is not advised and is extremely uncomfortable in summer. Furthermore it does not hold much interest for tourists.

Finally, it is not necessary to have a Land-Rover or Jeep to visit the whole of Iran. In our chapter on itineraries we will indicate what type of cars are needed for the different stretches of road.

Road signs. Iran has adopted the American system. There are little yellow square panels on which the usual signs are painted in black. In the urban centers all the panels are white and everything forbidden is indicated by a black sign in the middle of a barred red circle. What is permitted is printed in a black circle. The signs indicating location and kilometers are totally insufficient. They are only found on the main roads. The signs written in Arabic letters are naturally more numerous but can only be read by the initiated. Distances are indicated in kilometers, but in the countryside they still speak of *farsak*, an old measure equal to about 6 kms.

Repairs-spare parts. You will always find a mechanic able to help you to get your car started again but not sufficiently competent to adjust your car perfectly since the necessary tools are often not available. Spare parts for assembly-line cars can be found in Tehran and the large provincial towns but stocks are seldom complete. Citröen, Renault, Fiat, Volkswagen, Mercedes and Opel are well-represented. It is useful to carry along a few spare parts. Labor is inexpensive (50 or 60 Rs an hour). If you have time, it is better to superintend the repair of the car if only to prevent the mechanic from exploring an unknown vehicle. It is also advisable to bring along an instruction book.

Tyres are often the weak point in a country whose roads provide ample cause for trouble. Carry along a puncture repair kit which will help you to avoid the nightmare of two successive flats. You will find garages almost everywhere but, if you break down in some remote region, the truck drivers are helpful and are geniuses at improvisation. The custom of the road in Iran requires one to stop for cars in trouble. Do not forget to do this; perhaps you will benefit in turn.

Maps. The maps furnished by the Ministry of Information and Tourism are good enough for your holiday in Iran. They are not always up-to-date but they are useful in the major cities and will enable you to find the principal monuments. These remarks are also true of the maps and plans you will find in this guide.

The maps drawn and sold in Europe indicate the position of towns in relation to each other, but they are only good for that. The roads indicated very often exist only on paper.

Car Hire. You will have no trouble renting a car, with (strongly recommended) or without a chauffeur, in Tehran or in the provincial capitals. Hertz and Avis have their agencies in Iran and you can reserve a car through their offices abroad. Otherwise the receptionist at the big hotels will provide you very quickly with a car plus driver at 6 Rs per km on paved roads, 10 Rs on unpaved. Remember that it is possible to hire seats in cars to almost any destination.

Gasoline (petrol). You will not find any of the foreign gasoline trade names in Iran. The NIOC (National Iranian Oil Company) operates surprisingly few filling stations for one of the greatest oil-producing countries in the world; they are indicated on the official maps. Only about one half sell the excellent and very cheap super, 7.50 Rs per liter, about 34 Rs per gallon; the others sell only normal, 6 Rs per liter, 27 Rs per gallon. Motor oil costs 18 to 29 Rs per liter.

FACTS AT YOUR FINGERTIPS

LEAVING IRAN

 CUSTOMS. It is forbidden to export antiques that are older than 100 years old. Make certain that the word "modern" is put on the bill of sale of all your important purchases, if necessary having it certified by the Chamber of Commerce in the town where you buy the items or by your Consulate.

CUSTOMS ON RETURNING HOME. If you propose to take on your holiday any *foreign made* articles, such as cameras, binoculars, expensive timepieces and the like, it is wise to put with your travel documents the receipt from the retailer or some other evidence that the item was bought in your home country. If you bought the article on a previous holiday abroad and have already paid duty on it, carry with you the receipt for this. Otherwise, on returning home, you may be charged duty (for British residents, VAT as well).

Americans who are out of the United States at least 48 hours and have claimed no exemption during the previous 30 days are entitled to bring in duty-free up to $100 worth of articles for bona fide gifts or for their own personal use.

The $100 duty free allowance (years ago, it was $500!) is based on the full fair *retail* value of the goods (previously, the customs' estimation was on the whole-sale value). You must now list the items purchased and *they must accompany you when you return.* So keep all receipts handy with the detailed list, and pack the goods together in one case. The $10 mailed gift-scheme (see below) is also based on the retail value. Every member of a family is entitled to this same exemption, regardless of age, and their exemptions can be pooled.

One quart of alcoholic beverages and up to 100 cigars (non-Cuban!) may be included in the exemption if you are 21 years of age or older. There is no limitation on the number of cigarettes you bring in for your personal use, regardless of age. Alcoholic beverages in excess of one quart are subject to customs duty and internal revenue tax. Approximate rates are (1/5 gallon); brandy or liquor, $2–$3; champagne, 90c; wine, 15c. The importation must not be in violation of the laws of the state of arrival.

Only one bottle of certain perfumes that are trademarked in the United States (Lanvin, Chanel, etc.) may be brought in unless you can completely obliterate the trademark on the bottle, or get written permission from the manufacturer to bring more. Other perfumes are limited by weight or value.

American rates of customs duty may change, so it is best to check the regulations with the American Embassy during your visit.

You do not have to pay duty on art objects or antiques, provided they are over 100 years old. Remember this and ask the dealer who sells you that Sheffield plate or that 17th-century Dutch landscape for a certificate establishing its age. But when you buy, remember also that some countries regulate the removal of cultural properties and works of art.

Gifts which cost less than $10 may be mailed to friends or relatives at home, but not more than one per day (of receipt) to any one addressee. Mark the package: Gift/Value less than $10. These gifts must not include perfumes costing more than $1, tobacco or liquor, however, they do not count as part of your $100 exemption.

Do not bring home foreign meats, fruits, plants, soil, or other agricultural items when you return to the United States. To do so will delay you at the port of entry. It is illegal to bring in foreign agricultural items without permission, because they can spread destructive plant or animal pests and diseases. For more information, read the pamphlet "Customs Hints", or write to: "Quarantines", Department of Agriculture, Federal Center Bldg., Hyatsville, Maryland 20782, and ask for Program Aid No. 1083, entitled "Traveler's Tips on Bringing Food, Plant and Animal Products into the United States".

British residents, except those under the age of 17 years, may import duty-free from *any* country the following: 200 cigarettes or 100 cigarillos or 50 cigars or 250 grams of tobacco; 1 liter of spirits over 38.8% proof or 2 liters of other spirits or fortified wine, plus 2 liters of still table wine. Also 50 grams of perfume, ¼ liter of toilet water and £10 worth of other normally dutiable goods.

Returning from any *EEC country*, you may, *instead* of the above exemptions, bring in the following, provided you can prove they were not bought in a duty-free shop: 300 cigarettes or 150 cigarillos or 75 cigars or 400 grams of tobacco; 1½ liters of strong spirits or 3 liters of other spirits or fortified wines plus 3 liters of still table wine; 75 grams of perfume and ⅜ liter of toilet water and £50 worth of other normally dutiable goods.

Canadian residents: In addition to personal effects, the following articles may be brought in duty free: a maximum of 50 cigars, 200 cigarettes, 2 pounds of tobacco and 40 ounces of liquor, provided these are declared in writing to customs on arrival and accompany the traveler in hand or checked-through baggage. These are included in the basic exemption of $150 a year. Personal gifts should be mailed as "Unsolicited Gift—Value Under $15". Canadian customs regulations are strictly enforced; you are recommended to check what your allowances are and to make sure you have kept receipts for whatever you have bought abroad. For details ask for the Canada Customs brochure, "I Declare".

THE IRANIAN SCENE

FACTS AND FIGURES

To begin with a short geographical sketch. The Persian Empire covers a surface of 1,645,000 square kilometers (628,000 square miles) which is not quite as large as Mexico but six times the size of Colorado and almost seven times the size of Great Britain and Northern Ireland. Wedged between the Caspian Sea to the north and the Persian Gulf to the south, it constitutes a natural route between the steppes of Asia and the plateau of Anatolia, an open door to all Europe. This situation explains the succession of invasions that Iran has endured in the course of its history.

The center of the country, which is simply a desert-like basin, is surrounded by high mountains. To the north, the Elburz mountain chain stretches from east to west, from Khorasan to Mt. Ararat. The volcanic peak of Demavend rises to an elevation of 5,700 m (18,700 feet) there, but other almost as imposing peaks surround it: Mt Alamu, 4,850 m (15,900 feet); the Elburz (which dominates Tehran) 4,150 m (13,600 feet); the Shahzadeh-Kuh, 5,600 m (18,370 feet). The Khorasan mountains, however, rarely rise to a height of over 3,000 m (9,840 feet) and have never been serious obstacles to invaders coming from Central Asia.

To the west, the Zagros belt starts at Lake Van in Turkey, reaches the Persian Gulf, then slants towards the east. Wild landscapes in which from time to time the steep cliffs and rocky barriers give way to beautiful forests, are quite breath-taking. Several summits rise above 4,000 m (13,100 feet). The Fars mountain mass links up with the Zagros range. The volcanic summits of the central chain, doubling the Zagros to the east, reach a height of over 4,000 m (13,100 feet).

Framed by these mountainous ranges, the central plateau has an average altitude of 1,000 m (3,280 feet). Most of the population is settled on its periphery, while the center is barely inhabited. It would be difficult to say which of these two regions is the worst: the vast salt desert or the great sand desert (Dasht-i-Kavir, Dasht-i-Lut). The swamps of Naïnaq Sar, to the east of the Lut desert, slope to only 300 m (984 feet). These hollows are filled by *kavirs*, the last traces of an inland sea, completely dried up today. Sometimes after a rainfall, the kavirs become marshy but they do not take long to dry up and crack, and the stagnant water left in their bottoms is too salty to be of any use. Surrounded as it is by massive mountain ranges, the Iranian plateau seems like a world closed in on itself, lost in the contemplation of a vast and empty center. History has proved that it has served more often as a crossroad rather than as a barrier.

To the north, Iran opens onto a closed sea, the Caspian, whose water level is some 50 m (164 feet) less than that of open seas. Its shores are sandy and scattered with dunes, and its sole ports are Bandar Pahlavi and Bandar Shah. They only serve for trade with the Soviet Union. To the south, along the Persian Gulf, the shore has accumulated alluvial deposits filling it up with silt. The head of the Gulf extends 3 km (1.8 miles) forward every hundred years, which explains why the site of ancient ports is today some 200 km (124 miles) inland. The shores of the Oman Gulf are somewhat unhealthy due to the relentless heat and humidity.

Water is rare in Iran. Few rivers have uninterrupted courses. Only the Karun, which originates in the snowy heights of the Zagros, receives enough water along its course to be navigable before emptying into the Persian Gulf, and even its flow is very irregular. None of the other rivers flowing towards the southern coasts are worth mentioning, because in fact they surge with water only on maps.

The Caspian basin is richer since it boasts at least four rivers with uninterrupted courses: the Safid Rud whose delta forms the province of Gilan, the Chalus, the Talar and the Gorgan. Most of the rainfall never reaches the sea. A land of enclosed basins, Iran has a number of lakes. The largest is Lake Rezaiyeh, situated in the center of the Azerbaijan plateau, whose waters contain up to 25% of mineral salts. The rivers of the Elburz mountain ranges which flow towards the central desert, if they do not dry up en route, empty into Lake Namak to the south of Tehran. The Zayendeh Rud, Isfahan's river, vanishes into the swamps of Lake Gavkhane to the southeast of the city. The rare waterways of Fars feed several rather large lakes. Baluchistan and Khurasan also have their brackish marshes. To the east, in the Seistan, Lake Hamun, fed by the waters of the Helmand which flows all through Afghanistan, furnishes water to the driest area of the country.

The Kurds, who live in the north of western Iran, have given their name to the region—Kurdistan—predominantly barren chains of mountains and hills, with occasional forests and mountain pastures. Towards the south, Luristan, inhabited by nomadic tribes, is potentially rich but somewhat underdeveloped. The Fars, Persia in the strictest sense of the word, provides the link between Luristan and the Persian coast; like the latter it is particularly dry and barren. At the foot of the Fars mountains, rare winter rains provide enough vegetation to sustain cattle on the Khuzistan plains. Meager palm groves grow along the banks of the Karun. Ever since the discovery in 1901 of oil-bearing veins at the feet of the mountain ranges, the ancient cities in the area have become industrialized. At the top of the Persian Gulf Bandar Shahpur is the Trans Iranian railway terminus while Khorramshahr is the country's most important port.

The coastal plains along the Oman Sea are unsuitable for cultivation as they are devoid of fresh water and afflicted with abominable weather. Several thousand fishermen lead a difficult existence there. Until the 17th century, the vital center of this coast was the port of Ormuz. Bandare Abbas shared its activity later, and today it has been supplanted by Bushire which is as much Arab as it is Iranian.

Azerbaijan, in the northwest corner of Iran, lies between Turkey, Iraq and the Soviet Caucasus. Like its neighbor Armenia, it has been profoundly marked by volcanic eruptions and has been subject to frequent earthquakes. Around Lake Rezaiyeh, the orchards and vineyards prosper and the greater part of the province is fertile, particularly because of the water provided by the melting snow. Tabriz, the capital, was an important commercial center for a long time, and although its economic role has diminished, its cultural prestige is still considerable.

Further east, between the Elburz mountain ranges and the plateau, the towns and villages form a high road joining Zagros to Khorasan. Kazvin has been supplanted by Tehran, the capital. Other important centers in this region are Isfahan and Hamadan. On the banks of the Caspian Sea, the Gilan and the Mazanderan regions group together a fifth of the country's population over a territory of about 30,000 square kilometers (11,600 square miles), which does not cover more than 2% of its total surface. There are very few towns, with a multitude of small hamlets and farms scattered around them, hidden in the greenery. The plains are rich with orchards, cotton and tobacco. The climate is also mild enough for the cultivation of tea. The sea and fresh waters abound in fish and in the spring the fishermen catch sturgeon at the mouth of the rivers. The jungles of this region are still alive with wild game.

The most eastern province of the Persian nation is Khorasan. The east and south are the domains of the nomads. The non-migratory agricultural population of the north, for centuries the victim of Turkoman raids, has, since the take-over of these neighbors by the Soviet Union, enjoyed a better existence. Fruits and the opium poppy are the best known natural resources of this region. A few of the main towns are Tus (the birthplace of Firdowsi), Nishapur with its turquoise mines, and Meshed, the religious capital which shelters the sanctuary of Imam Reza.

The Seistan region is at the heart of the Iranian desert. Life there is only possible because of the few rivers that reach it. The Afghan Helmand river pours thousands of cubic meters of water into Lake Hamun, the surplus spilling over into Lake God-i-Zireh further south. In fact, Seistan is but a vast naked steppe peopled by wandering shepherds. The Helmand Delta is one large, low jungle where some 20,000 people eke out a difficult existence. This was not always the case but it has been caused by dam and canal destruction and climatic changes.

Climate

On the whole, the climate of Iran is continental—dry and hot in summer, harsh in winter. Fortunately, the altitude is responsible for some happy corrections to this picture. One of the characteristics of the Iranian climate is the extreme dryness of its summers. Even during the winter, rainfall is rare. The differences in temperature, however, are rather remarkable. The thermometer can easily read −4° F in January and 112° F in July–August at an altitude of 4,000 feet. The differences in latitude and topography are responsible for certain nuances in this case. Bordering the plateau, at comparable altitudes, Tehran, Isfahan, Shiraz and Meshed reach a maximum temperature of 104° F in July–August and a minimum of +5° F in January–February. On the Persian Gulf the temperature is never more than 95° F in summer but the humidity makes the climate very uncomfortable. Seistan is hotter than all the rest with an average temperature from April to November of 120° F which nevertheless does not prevent the temperature from falling to freezing point in winter.

The exterior slopes of the northern and western mountain ranges receive great quantities of rain and snow in the cold season. On the other hand, the eastern and southern sides, especially those along the Oman Sea, are sterile and arid. The plateau weather is even more varied than that of the mountains. Tehran, at the foot of the Elburz chain, receives about 300 mm (12 inches) of rain each year, but the central hollows and basins, surrounded by interior secondary mountain chains, are totally deprived of rain.

Two types of winds blow in Iran: the southwest wind which blows from Arabia and the northeast wind which passes over the Turkestan plains from June to October.

Vegetation and Wildlife

From the Caspian jungles to the central deserts, from the peaks of the Zagros to the stifling heat of the Persian Gulf, Iran runs the gamut of tropical plants. Many familiar species crowd its forests: the oak, the walnut, the maple, the pine and the white poplar of Tabriz. The chinar (plane) is the favored tree and adorns the streets of the capital. In many mountainous regions, particularly in the Fars, the forests have become moors. Some shrubs are of important economic value, furnishing indigo, madder, henna and the gum used in certain dyes and paints.

We may assume that the lilac and water lilies come to us from Persia. Roses are much less characteristic of the country than tulips which bloom suddenly here and there during the brief spring season. We find them again, along with carnations and peonies, on the faience of the Qajar monuments.

In the mountains, man has willingly ceded vital living space to the wild animals. During the winter in Zagros, one meets marauding wolf packs and frequently deer leap across the road. The lion no longer exists—ages ago he took refuge on the bas-reliefs of Persepolis and on the national flag. One region which remains particularly interesting because of its wildlife is situated in the north of Iran around the Caspian. Here the forest is lush and dense and shelters a great variety of species. In default of the lion, the tiger, the leopard and the cheetah sow terror among the ibex and wild sheep. Wild boar prowl around the fields. The ducks, swans, geese and other migratory birds swoop down on the ponds. The pheasants, partridges and hares add to the rice planters' habitual diet. And let us not forget the jackal—another Persian name—who howls to the moon during the icy desert nights.

Population

There are certain entities which cannot be denied or carved up without causing serious injustice to historical and scientific truth. The Iranian plateau, which includes present-day Iran, Afghanistan and

West Pakistan, is one of these. This region is bordered by two basins, cradles of ancient civilizations: to the east, the Indus valley where the ruins of Mohenjodaro and Harappa were discovered and to the west, Mesopotamia watered by the Tigris and the Euphrates, with such names as Sumer, Ur, Babylon and Nineveh. Asians, Semites, Aryans and, later, Greeks, Arabs, Turks and Mongols all penetrated these lands, peopled them, fought over them and created vast empires for themselves, such as those of Alexander, Genghis Khan and Tamerlane. During the course of the centuries, the people became divided up, re-grouped around diverse capitals, evolved according to their own particular genius and reacted more or less happily and successfully to Occidental ascendancy over them. It is only lately, through the dictates of international policy, that frontiers have been strictly drawn and the populations fixed within well-defined territorial limits. This has not always gone hand in hand with their deepest aspirations.

Actually, the Iranian as such does not exist and it would be wise to remember this basic truth if you wish to get along well with the inhabitants. Remember that the people you meet are Persians but that this name has many nuances which we will explain a little further on. No more than elsewhere can the man from Iran be the preserved fruit of a pure race, and yet he cannot be confused with any other. Persian unity is psychological and cultural and we shall try to define it.

How can one be Persian? Nearly 27 million human beings share this privilege. Since the beginning of time, the Iranian plateau has existed as a path between central Asia and Anatolia, so it is not surprising that today it is inhabited by widely varied races. Historically, Iran existed before the arrival of the Iranians, and the Elamites of Zagros are well known to historians. They belong to those races which we group under the name of Asiatics. During the last two thousand years B.C., they were invaded by Indo-Europeans from Central Asia (first the Hittites and then the Kassites, the Medes and finally the Persians). The Iranians—*irani* or *aryani*—therefore imposed their religion, their language, their customs and their name on a primary race and yet one from which they drew a cultural and certainly ethnic heritage; therefore, the Persian does not resemble only the Indian or the European. In the edicts proclaiming their victories, the Achaemenids asserted themselves to be "Persians, sons of Persians, Aryans of Aryan stock," which leads us to suppose that a good many of their vassals were not. In the following centuries the arrival of other Aryan populations, the Scythians and the Parthians, reinforced the supremacy of this group on the Iranian plateau.

Later, it was the Sassanid stronghold which, for a while, withstood the pressure of the Turkish-Mongolian tribes from Upper Asia. The missionary raids of the Arabs and the establishment of their empire marked Iran less than did the successive waves of horsemen, natives of a far distant Asia, who overflowed little by little into Asia Minor (Turkey) and southeast Europe, leaving behind them dynasties and entire peoples along the way. This occurred between the 10th and the 15th centuries, from Mahmud of Ghazni to the end of the Timurids; but the importance of the Turkish element can be seen in that up until the end of this period a dynasty of Turkish origin occupied the throne of Iran (the Qajars) and that even today there are large Turkish minorities in Azerbaijan and in the heart of the country, the Fars region.

Not all of the people who crowded the great highway from Meshed to Tabriz stayed there; perhaps the barren earth couldn't feed them all. In fact, the population seems to have varied greatly during the passing of the centuries and the results of certain census counts are surprising to us today. There were 50 million inhabitants in the Iranian Empire during the time when it included Iraq, Armenia, Caucasia and Afghanistan. At the end of the 19th century it was estimated that there were eight million Persians; today this figure has risen to 27 million, thanks to the progress of modern medicine. This means that there are 15.6 inhabitants for every square kilometer, a rather meager figure compared to European densities. This population, half of which is under 20 years of age, is very unevenly distributed. Certain fertile provinces, such as those near the Caspian, have a tendency to be overpopulated; the central regions remain deserted and the southern coasts are unable to nourish more people, except for the oil towns which spring up in the desert. It is safe to say that half of the territory is uninhabited. Towns and villages have been established on the edge of the desert plateau, at the foot of mountains, as well as on the banks of large lakes. The villages resemble ports of call and supply where journeys across hostile expanses are organized.

Ethnic Groups

Many Iranians do not consider themselves to be Persians and, even among those who do, ethnologists have considerable trouble isolating the different groups. The differences the Iranians discern among themselves are based on distinctions of language and customs rather than on ethnic concepts. The foreigner will have even more trouble distinguishing between the various groups since in 1936 Reza Shah imposed on everyone, townsmen and peasants alike, the wearing of European clothes (though this is not strictly observed in the remoter provinces, especially in Kurdistan).

The Persians of Persia, in the strictest sense of the word, call themselves Tadjiks and their native tongue is *Fârsi* (Persian). They constitute the basic group of Fars. Farmers or merchants, we find them everywhere on the Iranian plateau, in the Seistan region and as far away as Central Asia where Soviet Tadjikistan has regrouped them. We can distinguish two types, one with dark skin and wavy hair, the other with very white skin.

Two other groups of Indo-European origin live in the Zagros, the Lurs and the Kurds. These are mainly nomadic sheep herders, grouped into tribes and more concerned with quarrels between clans than in the interests of a nation towards which they feel little affinity. This is true of the Kurds in particular, spread out as they are between Iran, Iraq and Turkey.

Azerbaijan has a great many Turks, closely related to the Turkish Ottomans. The Qashqai tribe which settled in Fars during the 18th century was also Turkish. The central Asian races are still represented by the Turkomans on the Caspian and in Khorasan. As for the Hazaras, with their slanted eyes, coming from the Oriental mountain chains, nobody knows if they were left there after Mongolian invasions or if they were perhaps the first inhabitants of those mountains.

The Arabs of the Persian Gulf settled there peacefully and were good neighbors, as did the Baluchis who were nomads and wandered over the south or settled along the banks of the Oman Sea. The remainder are minorities left there after invasions or as a result of more or less ancient deportations. Armenians are numerous in Azerbaijan, more numerous still since in Persia they found a welcome which had been refused them by the Turks. At the beginning of the 17th century, Shah Abbas transferred the entire Armenian town of Jolfa to the outskirts of Isfahan to insure the cooperation of these clever and skilful workmen. In the large towns they represent a very active part of the population—merchants, jewelers, restaurateurs and garage owners. They do not mix with other groups and have their own language, newspapers and churches. There are also 50,000 Jews who engage in comparable activities with equal talent.

The Social System

Eight million Iranians can be qualified as city dwellers, living in towns of over 100,000 people: Tabriz and Meshed, two large centers; Tehran, Isfahan and Shiraz, the capital cities; Rasht on the Caspian, Ahwaz and Abadan, the oil cities; Hamadan and Kermanshah on the road to Iraq. The rapid increase in the urban population is proportionate to the speed of the country's industrialization: the mushrooming towns of Khuzistan have attracted a large working population. The same is true of Tehran which has grown from a population of 300,000 in 1950 to now almost 4,000,000.

The peasant class is still the largest throughout the huge Persian territory. The whole life of a peasant centers around water. Nobody can equal him in finding it, even in the driest climate. He preserves with great care the network of *kanats*—underground canals—which his fathers bequeathed to him. He has a long past full of uncertainty and misery behind him. His future is precarious, even in the rich Caspian provinces. The land usually does not belong to him, and of the tons of rice he harvests, he keeps only the bare minimum to ensure his and his family's subsistence. But since the 1960s, he has for the first time become the owner of the land on which he toils (see discussion of agrarian reform under *Agriculture*).

So much for the rural sedentary population. There are still some nomads: the Kurds, the Lurs, the Qashqais and the Baluchis, soon to disappear under a comprehensive settlement program.

The old aristocracy, the "thousand families", formerly owned all the land and alone used to enjoy the goods of this world. But Reza Shah confiscated the lands of his rebellious subjects, which made it possible for his son to portion out immense estates, thus starting the desired agrarian reforms. Until recently, landed property was the sole base on which fortunes were founded. Thanks to them, industrial enterprises have been progressively created. In well-to-do circles there are women who are emancipated and who work.

The traditional middle class, the bazaar merchants, enemies of any innovations which might endanger their system which is still based on notions of hierarchy and guilds; and the *mullahs* (monks), the only ones to still wear the turban and the robe and to veil their wives more severely than with the innocent *chador*; is now swamped by a new professional class of doctors, economists, engineers, civil servants, teachers, and bank employees, in commercial and industrial enterprises. The acceleration of the development program, due to the quadrupled oil revenue, provides unprecedented opportunities for the educated few, who are intelligent and politically aware, especially in the cities.

There remains the Army: recruited from various social strata, the officers represent an educated elite receptive to new ideas.

Agriculture and Fishing

Almost 40 percent of the active population still lives by farming and cattle raising. It may seem paradoxical in this arid part of the world which is mountainous and waterless and where desert lands predominate—only a small part of the country's total surface is arable (11 percent) and only four percent is exploited.

The northern provinces, which receive the most rain, comprise the greater part of arable land. We do find here and there a flourishing oasis but of small dimensions (Isfahan, Shiraz, Kerman, etc.). What is cultivated in Iran? Wheat, which constitutes the basic crop: 5 million tons of it are harvested each year, mostly in Azerbaijan. One million acres are planted with barley with one million tons harvested. The northern provinces provide 90 percent of the total rice crop (1,000,000 tons). As far as cereals are concerned, Iran produces enough for its own use and sometimes even exports rice. The same does not hold true for tea, as Iran consumes a great deal of it. The beet, imported in 1935, is an increasingly important crop, especially in the Khorasan. The 600,000 tons of sugar extracted from the beet each year more or less cover the national sugar consumption. The same is true of tobacco, cultivated at Rasht and Rezaiyeh (small leaves) and in the Fars (special tobacco for the water pipe). In the Fars, the poppy is also cultivated (30,000 acres) and destined for opium production. (The Iranian courts inflict capital punishment in cases of illicit drug traffic.)

Now for the fruits: grapes are grown in Kazvin, Shiraz and in the Zagros valleys: apricots in Marand and Meshed; peaches in Meshed and Maragheh; oranges in the northern provinces; dates in the Khuzistan and at Bam; apples and pears in Meshed and Quchan; cherries in Shahrud. To all this add the crops of the market-gardens which surround every large town—tomatoes, squash, cucumbers, chick-peas and the inevitable white melons and watermelons. The industrial crops are cotton and the mulberry tree of Mazanderan and Gorgan on whose leaves the silk worm is fed.

We cannot continue without a few words on agrarian reform, which came about with the confiscation of land from large property owners. Indeed, the peasant problem required a serious change in attitude on the part of the government leaders. Agrarian reform was thus begun in January of 1951 with the distribution by the Shah of royal lands: 100 heads of families received their property titles from the hands of their sovereign. Furthermore, a law formulated in 1962 forbids a proprietor to own more than one village—wealth was measured according to how many villages were owned—and more recently the maximum size of an estate has been limited to between 30 and 200 hectares, depending on the crop and the region. The new proprietor, however, left to his own resources or at the mercy of his leaders, would often mismanage his land and fall into debt. So teams were sent into the countryside to teach the farmers the fundamentals of agricultural economy. Cooperatives were created, the financing insured by a 10 percent tax levied on the farmers. In 1968, two agricultural societies were founded, which have effectively assisted agricultural modernization, industrialization and mechanization. Let us also point out the creation of Equity Houses where the arbitrators are not chosen by the government but elected by the villagers. To be sure everything has not yet been done, but a good start has been made.

Cattle raising is carried out by tribes (around 600,000 people) on the endless wastes and meager grazing lands. The national livestock comprises 30 million sheep, 15 million goats and five million horned cattle. A few horses are raised in the northern provinces and in the Zagros. Camels are increasingly being replaced by trucks and railroads. The raising of pigs is an Armenian speciality. The annual amount of caviar from the Caspian varies between 150 to 200 tons. About ten thousand tons of fish are caught every year and are canned at Shahi and in the Khorasan. Tuna and sardines are handled at the Bandare Abbas fish canneries on the Persian Gulf.

The Water Problem

Lack of water is responsible for the limited agriculture of Iran: 90 percent of the land is unsuited for farming without artificial irrigation. The problem is an old one. The early settlers of the plateau had been hindered by underground water pools which inundated their tin and copper mines. The Persians and the Medes took advantage of this situation to acquire the precious liquid and forced the conquered to dig kanats, an underground network of canals.

The second stroke of genius was that of Shahpur I, who forced his Roman engineer prisoners not only to build bridges and trace roads but also to make water barriers with movable sluice gates to irrigate the plains of the Khuzistan; the Kaju bridge at Isfahan (17th century) works on the same principle. This is not all: during the 14th century, the Iranians invented the vaulted dam. Proof of this can be seen in the ruins of the Kebar, 25 km (15 miles) south of Qom. It is 50 m (165 feet) long and 26 m (85 feet) high.

Today, the Ministry of Water and Electricity uses more modern techniques but it is still faced with the same problem: how to provide water when needed and how to store it until it is used. The ancient system of kanats continues to be used, improved and perfected by means of deep drilling and pumping stations.

The construction of dams solves the second problem while also providing electric energy. The Mohammed Reza Shah Dam (Dez) and the Farah Pahlavi Dam (Safid Rud) were the first of ever larger dams all over the country, simultaneously assuring the water supply of the rapidly expanding towns. The building of an atomic plant for desalination of the Persian Gulf waters is in progress.

Industry

We cannot broach this subject without first mentioning oil, providential manna which gushes from the ground. Iran is one of the chief producers in the world. The adventure began in 1901 when a prospecting monopoly was given to William Knox d'Arcy. The first drillings began in 1908 at Meidan-e-Naft. During this period it was estimated that there were five billion tons of oil reserves. In 1919 this figure had doubled. New agreements were signed in 1933 reassessing and augmenting royalties and in 1949 a national company was founded to prospect, exploit and refine the product of new wells. Temporary nationalization of the Anglo-Iranian Company in 1952 was resolved two years later by the formation of a consortium consisting of seven major oil companies. But the National Iranian Oil Company increasingly exploited new fields, and today production stands at close to two hundred million tons a year. When oil prices more than quadrupled in 1973, prospecting was further speeded up. The largest wells are in the Khuzistan, near the Iran-Iraq frontier. The biggest oil refinery is situated at Abadan. Other refining centers have been installed at Kermanshah, Isfahan, Masjid Suleiman, Naft-e-Shah and very recently at Tehran to treat oil from wells discovered in the Elburz region. Large quantities of natural gas are piped to the Soviet Union, while that from the southern fields at Sarajeh and Gachsaran (in the Khuzistan) is liquefied and shipped abroad. The subsoil of Iran also contains coal, chromium, copper and magnesium. At Anarak, antimony is mined as well as nickel, lead, zinc, cobalt and even gold. Steel mills have gone on steam and plans for fertilizer plants are being realized.

Among other industries, textiles are in the lead, principally cotton and wool. And then there is the silk factory at Chalus which treats 350 tons of cocoons each year. The food industry takes second place with sugar refineries, flour mills and tea factories. The cement manufacturers produce nearly two million tons a year for use throughout the country.

Iran is open to all foreign industries and favors investments, but a great many enterprises are public and managed by representatives of the state.

Infra-Structure, Commerce and Economy

In such a vast country, communications have been one of the major preoccupations of its sovereign. The Achaemenids invented the postal system by using relays of fresh horses; they would carry the sovereign's orders from one end of the empire to the other. The trails used by horsemen and caravans, marked with stops, teahouses and inns, are unfortunately no longer adapted to modern traffic. The new roads have lost in charm what they have gained in convenience. The present network consists of 50,000 km (31,750 miles) of roads, one half of them passable all year round; about 10,000 km (6,300 miles) are paved, and numerous road projects are under way. The Trans-Iranian railroad was the first public interest project carried out under the aegis of Reza Shah. Of a total of 4,000 km (2,480 miles) of tracks, the 1,500 km (930 miles) which link the Caspian to the Persian Gulf have a symbolic value. It boasts 200 tunnels, 3,800 bridges and viaducts and reaches an altitude of 2,000 m (6,550 feet). The Tabriz–Tehran–Meshed line is now completed. It is planned to join Kerman to Zahedan, where the Pakistan railway has a terminus.

Iran has some important ports: Bandar-e Abbas, Bushire, Bandar Shahpur, Abadan and Khorramshahr on the Persian Gulf; Bandar Pahlavi on the Caspian Sea. The last four have pipelines connecting them to oil wells. There is also another oil port on the island of Kharq.

There are more and more buses and trucks in Iran, likewise privately owned cars, especially in Tehran. The national airline company, Iran Air, joins all the main provincial cities and links Tehran with a number of other national capitals. Several provincial airports can accommodate large aircraft. Tehran will be able to receive planes such as Concorde on which Iran Air has taken out some options.

Thanks to oil—90 percent of the export in absolute value terms—the Iranian commercial balance has a huge surplus. Iran is the fifth exporter of crude oil in the world, its principal clients being Western Europe and Japan. Zinc, lead and chromium ores have been vigorously exploited during the last 10 years. Leathers, animal skins, dried fruits and cotton are sold in Eastern and Western Europe and caviar interests gourmets everywhere. West Germany buys half of the rugs exported.

Imports consist above all of heavy equipment and basic industrial materials. Imported finished articles are slowly being replaced by locally manufactured products.

The economy is regulated by Five Year Development Plans. The fifth plan, which became operative in March 1973, was based on an allocation of $32 billion. As the oil revenue in 1974 alone equaled that foreseen for the entire five year period, this amount was raised to $68.6 billion by the Ramsar Conference in July 1974. An annual growth rate of 25 percent at constant prices is now envisaged, leading to a doubling of the per capita income from $810 in 1973 to $1,600 in 1978, again at constant prices. As the Shah declared on this occasion: "Money is no longer a constraint, only the lack of skilled workers", estimated at some 400,000 for the expanded projects. Iran has entered the international capital market as an important lender and is acquiring participation in American and European industries such as the German Krupp steelworks.

The Language

The official language is Fârsi, or Persian. Fârsi is a dialect from the Fars, the region around Shiraz. Under the Sassanids it became the language of the civil servants and soldiers. Today it is understood by everyone, although there are ethnic minorities who continue to use their own special idioms. Therefore, don't be surprised in Tabriz and all over Azerbaijan if the waiter who takes your order for two teas, "do tchai" in Persian, yells "equi tchai" in Turkish to the cook. A few Turkish words would be useful in this region and even more so with the Turkoman of the Caspian and the Khorasan who have their own local dialect. A few Arab words would be helpful in the Khuzistan region on the Persian Gulf.

Persian descends from Pahlavi—the language of the Sassanids and the Avesta, the sacred book of the Zoroastrians. In other words, barely changed, it is the language of our common ancestors—the Aryans. Everything becomes clear: padar (father); madar (mother); doktar (daughter); etc.

Persian is spoken in Iran and in Afghanistan, and for a long time it was the language spoken in the courts of Bukhara and Delhi. It has a significant cultural importance. A great many Asian languages have borrowed from its vocabulary. Even English-speakers use words such as *azure, bazaar, shawl, lilac, orange*, etc., without even knowing that they are of Persian origin.

Reza Shah removed many foreign words from the Persian dictionary and introduced the new words necessary to modern life. He was unable to change the writing of Persian which closely follows the Arabic alphabet and is not very convenient for recording the Persian phonetic system with its rich vocalism—Arabic has only three vowels, Persian seven. But the Persians are very attached to their calligraphy, which shines on their faiences and gives perfect form to their poems. When in contact with foreigners, they speak mainly English and a smattering of French.

Character

Judgements on the Persian character by Westerners are so diverse and so contradictory that sometimes we wonder if they are talking about the same people.

In fact, the intelligent, cultivated and refined Persian possesses the defects of his virtues. He has a critical sense which makes him a sceptic, a person who understands the value of things, of life, of death ... and of great causes. Five thousand years of history mean 5,000 years of often painful experience for him and have made him wary. Iran is becoming more Westernized but Iranian thought is Oriental and has every intention of remaining so. From this stem all the misunderstandings, for in order to understand the Iranians, one must think as a Persian.

Literature

At the origin of Persian literature we find the Avestas, the sacred books of Mazdaism. They were written between the 10th and fourth centuries before Christ. Zoroaster (around 660–583 B.C.) described the struggles between good and evil and conversations between man and Ahura-Mazda, his God. During the time of Alexander, 12,000 bull skins were needed to transcribe these texts. It was, however, the Sassanids (third–seventh centuries A.D.) who gave us the Avestas in their present form. A number of anonymous poems handed down to us are proof of Persian brilliance in letters during this dynasty.

The Arab conquest imposed its language for several centuries on the schools and universities. Through the channel of popular poetry, the Persian language was reestablished at the beginning of the 10th century, first in the court at Bukhara where the Samanid princes encouraged its renaissance. Although Ar-Razi (Rhazez) and Abu 'Ali b. Sina (Avicenna) still wrote their universally important scientific and philosophic treatises in Arabic, Persian was used in purely literary works. Rudagi (10th century), the "father of Persian poetry", composed numerous *ghazals*, both lyric and bacchic. Daqiqi was commissioned to celebrate the glory and virtue of the ancients.

Firdowsi (around 940–1020 A.D.) carried on Daqiqi's undertaking. He worked on the modern Persian version of the "Book of Kings", the *Shah Nama*, a traditional theme which he reinvigorated with descriptions of adventures, battles and love stories. It was an ambitious work, but while waiting for glory, one must go on living. The Samanids were overturned and Firdowsi took refuge with the Buyid princes, their rivals, and offered them the 7,400 couplets on the life of Joseph, son of Jacob. It was the first interesting try at a romantic epic. Alas! it was only in his final hour that the poet finally received the long-awaited praise and fame.

At that time, all the poets, historians and intellectuals who were important in Persian literature lived at the court of Ghazni: Unsori, "the prince of poets", author of panegyrics, rival of Firdowsi;

Suzani, a precursor of Verlaine; Sanaï, the first mystic poet (1070–1140 A.D.); etc.

The best-known protegé of the Seljuks is without doubt Omar Khayyam, the poet, mathematician and philosopher who died in 1123. The translation in 1859 of his works by Fitzgerald familiarized all of Europe with the wisdom of his famous quatrains (*Rubáiyat*).

The 13th century witnessed the blooming of mystical poetry. The greatest representatives of this genre are Jalal-ad-din Rumi, called Maulana, founder of the Order of the Dervishes, and Attar, the "Apothecary of Khurasan", who went still further into mystical experience. The roads leading to fusion with God are explained by Maulana in 25,000 verses. Besides these two great *sufis* (poets), Mizami invented the "court cycles" with *Khosrov and Chirine*.

Another great figure of the 13th century is Sa'di. After a turbulent youth—he was even taken prisoner during the Crusades—Sa'di returned to "live the rest of his years" at Shiraz, his native town, where he died a centenarian (1292 A.D.). The *Golistan* (Garden of Roses), a mixture of prose and verse, is a collection of moral anecdotes; the *Bustan* (Garden of Fruits) is a book of poems. The facility, the delicate yet warm feeling and a sense of proportion make this work a great classic.

Hafiz (who died in 1388 A.D.) was also from Shiraz. He left posterity over 500 ghazals but this abundance does not detract from the profundity of his work. Perfect form joined to rigorous thought render his works extremely difficult to translate. Goethe tried with some success. Hafiz is the most popular of the Persian poets; everybody is familiar with his verses and they have become part of everyday language and conversation. We cannot pretend to know the Persian if we are not familiar with at least a few stanzas. Zakani introduced satire in the 14th century; he was as sharp and cutting as only his fellow citizens could be. Jami (1414–1492) wrote lyric poems during the Timurid epoch in Herat. It is astonishing that the brilliant court of the Safavid dynasty had very few poets of note.

Music

Persian music is closely linked to poetry and religion. It was Herodotus who provided the first evidence on this subject. He described the rites of the Achaemenids in which a large part of the sacred texts are sung recitations. Instruments are mentioned only later on under the Parthians and the Sassanids who played the harp, the lute, the mandolin, the flute and the oboe. Music was already codified: modulations, rhythms, "modes" which condition the general tonality of the piece. They had seven different modes, depending on the sentiment they wished to express. History has handed down the name of a famous singer, Barbedh, an intimate of Khosroés II (sixth and seventh centuries A.D.). He gave a melody to each day of the year and combined it with modulations corresponding to the 30 days of the month. Musicians joined the kings in all their activities, including hunting, where they played the harp as accompaniment to the rhythm of the chase. Bahram V (421–438 A.D.) did not stop there but also imported musicians from India. Therefore it is not surprising to find certain similarities between Indian and Persian music.

Generally, we don't understand these exotic resonances and we classify all of them under the generic title of Oriental music. It is important first of all to define the difference between the popular song which is lively and rhythmic, and classical music which has a more intellectual approach. The basic idea is the melody line and not the harmony. Instruments are usually played in unison. Characteristic themes for particular hours of the day and for certain moments of the year give the artist a definite frame within which he is allowed to improvise. From one day to the next it is impossible to hear a piece played exactly the same. Initiative plays such an important part that the singer is not only a mere performer but the real creator of his song. The transcription of a piece onto paper gives only a vague idea of what was played on a given day by a certain artist. From generation to generation, themes and melodies have been handed down but nothing comparable to the monuments of Occidental classical music. Young musicians are now trying to put all of this heritage down on paper.

A concert piece unfolds in five movements. First the *taksim*, an introduction improvised by the violin and sustained by the other instruments. This is followed by an instrumental prelude, the *pichrau*. At this moment, the chosen theme is taken up by the singer, first without accompaniment to familiarize the audience with it, then it is developed following different rhythms. The circle is closed by once again taking up the theme of the pichrau.

There are as many different instruments as there are provinces. The Târ family—from which our guitar undoubtedly originates—gave birth to the *do-târ* (2 strings), and the *sé-târ* (3 strings). These are not to be confused with the zither which resembles more the *soutour*. The *kétmanché* is similar to a violin. Among the wind instruments, there are the *neï* made of reed, the *sourneï* made of ebony, and many ingenious, sometimes splendid, instruments in between. The *soutak* made of baked earth and filled with water imitates the nightingale, the ox-horn is called a *nefir* and the *boug*, which is made of copper, announces feast days with great pomp. The *dool* with two surfaces and the uneven *tabli* are large drums which are played with the finger-tips.

Education

Education, which at the beginning of the century was the prerogative of the mullahs, was secularized by Reza Shah. Only religious instruction is still given in the *madresseh* (plural: *madares*). Islamic methods, considered out-of-date especially in the scientific field, have been replaced by an Occidental teaching style. University courses are given by Iranian professors. Foreign experts are sometimes invited to hold seminars. Technical teaching is carried on in several institutions. Many students obtain scholarships for specialized studies in the United States, France, Germany, etc.

The great innovation since 1963 is the establishment of the "Education Corps". Until a few years ago, 70 to 90 percent of the rural inhabitants were illiterate due to a lack of primary schools. Education of the peasants and agrarian reform are now carried on simultaneously. Today, at the end of their secondary studies, young people are enrolled in the Education Corps: four months of training give them adequate military and pedagogical instruction and the *sepahis* are then sent to villages to teach. In five years, 1,250,000 children and 450,000 adults have learned to read and write with the help of 40,000 recruits. After their military service, half of the sepahis choose to make the teaching profession their career; as a result, illiteracy has been greatly reduced.

Education is free through the eighth grade and at vocational schools; and at universities, provided the graduate will undertake to work for the government after completion of studies.

Public Health

Iran has made a great effort in the domain of public health by improving hygienic conditions and fighting epidemics. Malaria is almost extinct in the provinces of the Caspian where in the past it affected 90 percent of the population. Effective sanitary measures are taken at the eastern frontiers whenever there is a threat of cholera, a disease which is endemic with certain neighbors. Smallpox vaccination is obligatory.

Private and semi-official organizations, such as the Iranian version of the Red Cross and the Royal Pahlavi Foundation, endeavor to instal necessary sanitary equipment and to educate the people in its use. Since 1954 the "Health Corps" (modeled along the lines of the Education Corps) has traveled through the villages nursing, vaccinating and giving advice on diet and hygiene. Infant mortality is now diminishing.

Tehran has excellent hospitals and the doctors are products of the best medical schools in the West.

FACTS AND FIGURES

Press and Radio

The Iranian Press is almost entirely oriented towards the Tehran public. The two principal daily papers, *Ettela'at* and *Kayhan*, along with their regional editions, never sell more than 80,000 copies. *Peyghame, Emrouz, Poste Tehran* and *Bam Shad* have a total of 25,000 readers taken all together. The French-language *Journal de Teheran* is published daily as well as the English-language *Tehran Journal* and the *Kayhan International*. A weekly newspaper in French, *Orient-Panorama*, publishes political and economic news. Each provincial capital has its own newspaper with a small circulation. Some minority groups, such as the Armenians, publish newspapers in their own language.

Radio Iran broadcasts every day from Tehran with news bulletins in Persian, French, English, Turkish, Arabic and Russian. Television has three channels, one of which was organized by the Americans and is in English.

The Modern State

Iran has been a constitutional monarchy since 1906. The first constitution has been revised several times—in 1925, 1949, 1956. The Parliament is made up of two houses: the Lower House, or National Assembly, which has 200 deputies (the Majlis) who are elected every four years from districts throughout Iran; and the High Chamber, or Senate, which has 60 members (six-year tenure), half of whom are chosen by the Shah and the other half elected by the people. The Lower Chamber wields the budgetary power. Legislative power is held by the Shah and Parliament who have the right to initiate new laws. When new laws are drawn up, they must win the approval of both houses and also receive the royal seal. Executive power belongs to the Shah—who also disposes of important constitutional powers—and to his cabinet ministers. The latter are appointed and dismissed by the Shah and are responsible to Parliament. As to judiciary power which is exercised by the courts of justice, it is separated from the legislative and executive domains. The judiciary is modeled along French lines and so has been profoundly influenced by the French system.

As far as administration is concerned, the country is divided into 14 *ostans* or provinces, subdivided into 141 *shahrestans* (towns and urban districts), which in turn are made up of 448 *bakhs* (wards). At the head of each province and shahrestan is a governor representing the central power. The reforms in recent years have been turned towards decentralization with the aim of granting more power to the local communities.

55

Today's sovereign is Mohammed Reza Shah Pahlavi, who also bears the title of Shahanshah Aryamehr. He succeeded to the throne on September 16, 1941 but was not crowned Emperor until October 1967. The throne is hereditary by order of male primogeniture and custom has it that the coronation does not take place until after the seventh birthday of the heir apparent. In crowning the Shahbanou Empress of Iran, the Shah, as monarch, conferred upon her all the authority necessary to assume an eventual regency.

The role of the founder of the dynasty was to open his country's doors to modern times and his son's reign will be remembered for the realization of the famous "White Revolution". This event was announced by the Shah on January 26, 1963 and was approved the next day by popular referendum with a 98 percent majority. The White Revolution includes six basic points: the abolition of serfdom by way of agrarian reform; the establishment of the "Education Corps"; the sharing by workers in the profits of companies; the nationalization of the forests; the revision of the electoral laws; the selling of state-owned factory stocks to help finance agrarian reform. Two years later, three other reforms were added: the organization of the "Health Corps"; creation of the "Army of Development" to assist the farmers; and the establishment of "Equity Houses" for the settling of accounts in the different rural disputes. In 1968, the Shah announced the nationalization of water rights and educational reform. His tremendously ambitious program has been largely realized. Iran, in the forefront of the OPEC countries, is assuming an important regional and, at least economically, also international, part.

The personal activity of the Empress is quite important. She has especially promoted the emancipation of the Iranian woman. The electoral reform law of July 1967 gave civil rights to the women: marriages and divorces are now governed by the same legislation for both sexes; the right to work has been given to wives and the first women's unit in the Education Corps has been formed. The Shahbanou is also interested in the work of national renovation. Her visits to the poorer quarters of the capital are well-known. It was she who took the first steps toward improving sanitation in these quarters.

THE IRANIAN WAY OF LIFE

Complicated, but Relaxed

Sir John Chardin was one of the famous 17th-century travelers who visited the court of Shah Abbas twice. A French Protestant jeweler who eventually settled in London and is buried in Westminster Abbey, he wrote in his *Travels in Persia and the East Indies* that the Persians lived in harmony with the soil from which they had sprung, utilizing to the fullest the sometimes meager gifts of nature. They had not waited for the invention of refrigeration to have cold drinks all summer long, thanks to the snow supply which the villagers knew how to store underground during the winter. They had not waited for air-conditioning to protect them from the heat but made use of their basements during the day, the terraces at night, and enjoyed the gardens through which cool streams flowed. Since the time of Darius, water ran down from the mountains by means of invisible canals. In a word, the "Barbarian from the West" came to know a civilization as ancient as it was refined.

After Sir John Chardin, and during the next two centuries, all sorts of travelers, merchants, soldiers and writers, visited the Persian Empire. They have left us with widely varied impressions. In this second half of the twentieth century, how would we now describe a "homo persicus"?

Persians believe hospitality towards foreigners to be a duty, and their prescribed etiquette is so complicated that foreigners are often confused by it. Do not forget to use their polite forms for welcome and thanks, as they will appreciate your efforts to behave according to their standards.

At first glance the people in Tehran look like any others living in cities throughout the world. Since Reza Shah's decrees regarding modernization, they dress in Western fashion. However you will notice that older men wear their coat thrown over their shoulders, like their fathers wore their robes, and that at the entrance to the mosques there are a great number of European shoes with flattened heels so that they may be slipped on like Turkish babouches.

The Hammam

Perhaps you have passed 20 times in front of these doors outside which large squares of red and black cotton are drying and have glanced inquisitively down the tiled corridor that seems to disappear into the bowels of the earth. Or else, from the top of a minaret, you have seen a roof adorned with earthen cupolas surmounted by a large skylight: you have been looking at one of the most lively popular institutions of Iran: the hammam.

Although we call it a Turkish bath, the hammam is an Iranian invention which slowly spread throughout the Orient. It is no more reserved for princes than are the Scandinavian sauna or the Roman thermal baths. It is a place of relaxation available to all and it offers a far more important service than do public baths. The hammam is a part of everyday life, of marriages and churchings (thanksgiving service for a woman after childbirth); in short, one doesn't go there merely for hygienic purposes but also to renew the body by way of a purification rite. To tell the truth, one also goes there to pass the time, to see one's friends and to chat.

Let us enter a hammam, but take care, as certain hours are for men, others for women. You undress and put on a *long* which is a red and black loin cloth. You enter a large steam room, furnished with a big tiled platform heated from below, in which you sweat copiously.

Then the client takes a thorough shower and calls the *karegar* who gives him a vigorous massage, cracking the joints and kneading the back and chest with an expert hand. After this operation, the bather lies on a low bench, the merciless attendant takes a rough glove filled with a special clay and begins to "erase" dead skin and rub off any other impurities. You then get soaped with special foam, which is rinsed off with buckets full of very hot water, and emerge from this experience feeling beautifully relaxed and airy.

There is no mixing of the sexes here. Male attendants take care of the men and female attendants take care of the women. Mothers really appreciate the hammams and go there accompanied by all their children. They remain for hours, meet their friends, drink tea and eat sweets brought to them while they gossip.

The Tchaikhane

If the women meet each other at the baths, the men meet at the tchaikhane, the teahouse. They go there as much for the brew, a golden tea served boiling from a samovar, as for the atmosphere. They stay for hours, fingering their prayer beads and listening to the latest gossip. From time to time, a glass of tea is brought, a piece of sugar is put in the mouth, the burning liquid poured into the saucer and its fragrance inhaled before drinking. A traveler arrives with a watermelon and the waiter immediately rushes for a tray and place settings.

If a client wants to smoke, the *kalian* or "hookah", a water pipe, already lit, is brought to him. This instrument formerly played a large role in etiquette: people of high standing were never separated from their pipe and offered it to all visitors. The Persian kalian is composed of a metal or cut-glass beaker half full of aromatic water with a mouthpiece and tube fitted into an earthen pipe bowl. A special tobacco is humidified, pressed like a sponge, then placed in the bowl and lit with the help of charcoal. Servants are responsible for lighting their masters' pipes. They can be smoked by several people at once, and it is a good way to pass the time among friends.

Sometimes the calm of the teahouse is disturbed by the appearance of a dervish, a religious wanderer who comes to prophesy disasters and to beg for his living. When he has finished amusing the clients, he is shown the door.

The Tales

Sometimes a story-teller enjoys the limelight. These professional minstrels go from teahouse to market-place, from town to village, telling stories and legends and singing songs. Each region has its favorite themes and we often recognize transposed or rearranged episodes from the *Shah Nama* (Book of Kings) or *A Thousand and One Nights*. Love, magic, voyages, death and disaster; all are fascinating subjects for the story-teller. Tales get mixed up but good always triumphs over evil.

Some of these tales are interspersed with the singing of lyrical verses, followed by a refrain. These interludes are part and parcel of the art of the story-teller and increase the listener's pleasure. Other tales resemble fables, like the story of the three school-masters whose excess of imagination wins them the prize for stupidity; or that of the fake prophet who sees his oracles come true and is frightened out of his wits.

Popular poetry called *bazari*, in the "language of the bazaar", is always sung or chanted. There are cradle songs, children's roundelays and love couplets. Bazari differs from classical poetry in that it adheres to syllabic meters, while the latter borrows from Arabic poetry's metric system. This alone suffices to prove its extraordinary antiquity.

Religion

Numerous religions are practiced in Iran and, although we know a great many of them, we cannot be sure to have named absolutely all. Persians have always been fervent devotees of theology and philosophy. The majority of them are Moslem Shi'ites (15 million). The orthodox Moslem Sunnites number only one million and are located in Azerbaijan, Kurdistan, Khuzistan and Gorgan. There are minorities distinguishable also by their race and language. Along with Shi'ism, which has been the State religion for a long time now, there are some more or less related sects. The Ismailians recognize in their Imam, the Aga Khan, a divine emanation. For the Nossaayris, Ali is the representative of Allah, while for the Alialahis, Ali is Allah himself.

The Persian is inclined to flee from doctrinal rigidity by way of mysticism or Sufism. In principle, the kind of mystical knowledge represented by Sufism has no place in Islam because Allah, who is totally transcendental, can have no direct communication with man. Its emphasis on imagination and sensibility is suspect in the eyes of the orthodox. Nevertheless, Sufism has had an enormous following in Persia from the ninth century. Its end is rapture, intimate union with Allah, in accordance with the ritual laid down by those who have received *baraka* (grace). The Sufi Brotherhoods are extremely numerous and still very active in Iran.

Christianity embraces about 120,000 faithful who are divided into Chaldeans, Nestorians and Armenian Catholics. They are especially numerous in Azerbaijan and in the large cities. The ranks of the Orthodox have been augmented by Russian refugees who have now become naturalized Iranians. American missionaries watch over 6,000 Protestants, Roman Catholics are rare and there are 50,000 Jews.

Baha'ism has its followers (120,000, perhaps more). Its founder, the Bab, martyred in 1850 by the Moslems for criticizing their mullahs, sanctioned monogamy and the suppression of the veil. Despite persecutions, the Baha'i multiplied in Anatolia and Persia and some writers have pointed out that the first Islamic reforms were carried out there.

The Mazdaites, fire worshippers, faithful to the ancient Persian religion, have not totally disappeared. After the Arab conquest, many of them fled to India, settled particularly in the area of Bombay and took the name of Parsee (Persian). Those who remained in Iran (50,000) are active and intelligent, call themselves Guebres or Zardutchis, and live in Tehran, Shiraz, Kerman and above all in Yazd. These distant disciples of Zoroaster leave their dead exposed in the Towers of Silence in order not to contaminate the earth, water or fire, and birds of prey come to eat their corpses, thus becoming their living tombs. Finally, in the Kurdistan mountains there still exist a few devil worshippers, the Yazidis.

Shi'ism, the national religion, was born when the Moslems gave the Caliphate to the Arab Omayyad dynasty rather than to Hassan and Hosein, sons of Ali, son-in-law of the Prophet. Ali is venerated by the Shi'ites in his own right, and he and his descendants are regarded as the only rightful caliphs. On the other hand, the caliphs are dishonored in memory, above all Omar, conqueror of Persia. Shi'ism has made it possible for the Persians to preserve their originality and the bases of their thousands-of-years-old civilization. Persecuted, they learned what suffering meant, and have continued to commemorate the tragic death of the Imam martyrs, Hassan (poisoned) and Hosein who with his faithful companions was encircled in the Karbala desert by the Omayyads before being assassinated. In memory of the terrible thirst they suffered, an animal, a lamb or chicken, is never sacrificed without first being given a drink of water. During the 40 days of mourning to commemorate this tragedy, large processions are held, the crowds shout "Hassan, Hosein", beat their breasts and hammer their heads with swords symbolically in manifestations of despair. Out of respect for the blood of the Prophet from whom the twelve Imams came, the Shi'ites have created the equivalent of saints. They are represented by hierarchical religious leaders who, contrary to the spirit of the Koran, are the only ones to be granted the right to read and comment on the Holy Book. It is in this that the Shi'ite doctrine differs considerably from the orthodox one. "Allah, eternal and all-powerful, has established the laws by which the world lives. The Koran has always been. Mohammed has thus personally contributed nothing to it."

Either because of the necessity for secrecy due to persecutions, or perhaps from a desire to protect holy places from the eyes of the unbeliever, certain important religious sanctuaries, notably at Qom, Meshed and Shiraz, are strictly forbidden to anyone who is not a Moslem. But it must be made clear that a mosque is quite unlike a church or a catheral. The *mihrab*, a niche indicating the direction of Mecca, does not imply a real presence of the divinity and, if shoes are removed at the entrance, this is done both as a sign of respect and to avoid damaging the rugs on which the faithful prostrate themselves during the hour of prayer. Outside, the taps and basins which adorn the courtyard are for the faithful to wash before praying; the porticos and rooms surrounding the courtyard are used for study, contemplation and conversation among friends. The Iranian mosque offers spiritual refreshment, peace, shade, water and the restful color of its ceramics in a land where nature is not always so generous.

The intolerance of the Shi'ites, especially towards the orthodox Sunni Moslems is evident in some places, but does not reflect the Persian mentality in general. Metaphysically curious, but not bigots, they have always had a horror of State religions, imposed beliefs and ready-made solutions. Submission to a religious leader does not at all exclude freedom of expression and thought. Listen to this joke, for example: A dog enters a mosque. Scandalized, the faithful chase it out with sticks. A passing mullah intervenes—"Why are you hitting that animal? He has neither common sense nor intelligence. I who am intelligent never set foot in a mosque."

This anecdote may well be considered as simply a family joke, limited to the faithful, but it also shows a profound non-conformism which sometimes goes so far as scepticism. During the time of the Sassanids, the Persians became tired of being oppressed by the Mazdaian priesthood, and this certainly played a part in helping along the Arab invasion. Today we may very well be surprised by the official support given to the Shi'ite religion which is incompatible with the demands of progress. Reza Shah understood this: the spirit of Persian genius existed before the Moslem religion and will outlive it.

Muharram

The month of Muharram is of particular importance in the Shi'ite religious calendar. It is a month of mourning, a time when each believer relives more or less intensely the painful drama at the center of the Shi'ite mystique, the Karbala massacre. The martyrdom of Hosein and his followers is the theme of the various ceremonies that take place during this month. Dramatic moments are not wanting. It was Abbas who tried to give water to Hosein and his companions. The moment he plunged his gourd into a stream an enemy cut off his right hand. He seized his sword, but his left hand was also severed. This legend explains the metal hands which adorn the tops of Shi'ite monuments.

For the first nine days of the month of Muharram, all public life in the country is suspended. The faithful are invited to attend continuous sermons and recitations which take place in private houses or in sanctuaries. The houses have a black flag hanging at the door. Sometimes there is nothing more than an awning with a platform in the middle of a courtyard. Alcoves decorated with symbolic objects complete the decor and emblems of the different trades and neighborhoods are present. Three people share the task of stirring up the public: the orator, the panegyrist and finally the preacher whose sermon ends in a mournful chant. The audience participates in the drama of Karbala by weeping and wailing.

These seances have given birth to the *Taziya*, or passion play, frowned upon by the mullahs but actively supported by the faithful. It portrays episodes from Hosein's life, many imaginary, and is performed before a public that often becomes hysterical. There is stark realism as well as beautiful poetry. The Karbala plain is represented after the battle, with mutilated corpses covered with desert sand (actually chopped up hay) and the costumes are lavish. The leader hands out the roles and also directs; the text is read as often as it is recited. It is a fascinating mixture of spontaneity and stylization, the actors playing their role with truly mystical passion. The Taziya has unfortunately become rare today, and it is almost impossible to attend one that is done on a large-scale.

On the ninth day of the month of Muharram, the faithful dress in black and parade in the streets, beating their breasts and crying "Shah Hosein". The 10th day, Ashura, is celebrated with processions in which in the past men stripped to the waist and flayed themselves with thongs. These public manifestations were forbidden by Reza Shah and are rarely allowed to take place now so as not to shock modern sensibilities.

Forty days after the Ashura, the mourning of Hassan is observed; and later, the death of Ali. The annual cycle is thus marked with painful mysteries that focus religious thought on the fact of suffering and the virtue of compassion.

Norouz

The Persian New Year is a feast day which goes back to the days before the Moslem conquest, perhaps even further back than the Sassanid rulers who gave it its luster. The year begins at the spring equinox, fixed on March 21st. Several days before, all kinds of dervishes and buffoons converge toward the towns. Families prepare new clothes and sometimes new dishes are used. The last Wednesday of the year is Red Wednesday, on which two ancient rites for the expulsion of evil are observed. Three brushwood fires are made and are cleared in one single leap while saying: "My pallor and my evil for you, your rosy cheeks and gaiety for me."

New Year's Day is announced by cannonfire. In private houses, the preparation of the meals of *haft sin* is in progress. There must be seven dishes beginning with the letter *S*. They are chosen among *sib* (apple), *siah daneh* (fennel-flower), *senjed* (olive), *sir* (garlic), *serkeh* (vinegar), *sabzi* (herbs), etc. The table is set with a mirror, a candelabra with as many candles as there are children in the house, a copy of the Koran, bread, a bowl of water with a green leaf floating in it, rose water, sweets, fruits, a fish, *mast* (yogurt) and colored hard-boiled eggs.

On this day, the king gives a large reception during which he offers his visitors the ritual meal. Thirteen days later, the "thirteenth outside" occurs. The house is left for the day to the spirits who will then leave it in peace for the rest of the year. It is the occasion for joyous family picnics in the lovely spring-touched countryside.

Zourkhane

The Iranians regard polo as their traditional sport, but, since the only people who still play it are a few officers, we prefer to talk about the *zourkhanes*, the "houses of strength", which exist in every town, no matter how small it may be. Every evening from 5 to 7, the *pehlevans* (the athletes who take part) go there to train for the good of their bodies and souls.

The precise ritual followed by the athletes is evocative of some of their religious practices. Sufism, the mystical doctrine of Islam, has in fact strongly marked the spirit, hierarchy and even the architecture of the zourkhanes. The dome covering the square or hexagonal pit is copied from the tombs of Ali and Hosein. The ground is of mud to remind the strong that they should be humble. The leader sits on a chair and beats time for the exercises with a drum and bell. Throughout the performance he offers encouragement, based on themes from the Shi'ite faith: "Oh Allah, help, Ali, by the martyrs of Karbala . . . Oh! Imam Reza . . ." The audience participates in the spectacle by giving ovations to the efforts of the champions.

The athletes are dressed in embroidered leather pants laced under the knee. The leader gives the signal and the gymnastics begin. Each athlete has his own well-defined place in the arena, established according to his rank in the Brotherhood. The *Seyyeds*, descendants of Imams, are given special places.

**The King's Mosque in Isfahan, started by
Shah Abbas in 1612; one of the most
impressive achievements of Safavid art**

The Madresseh of the Shah's Mother, built
in 1710 and a "triumph of delicacy"

The athletes begin with a performance of "land swimming": holding on to a board, the pehlevans imitate the motion of ocean waves, flexing their arms 220 times in a row. The more inspired sometimes reach 1,000. Following this collective exercise, comes the *seng*, or weight-lifting, which is reserved for the outstanding athletes. Lying on their backs, they lift two large wooden shields weighing about 130 pounds apiece, keeping perfect time together. The number of lifts is chanted out in a litany. Then come the physical exercises involving dexterity with Indian clubs. The final juggling requires great self-confidence and faultless reflexes. In the next phase, the pehlevans spin like a top, arms extended horizontally, somewhat like the whirling dervishes. Religious exaltation is expressed by a stamping of feet. The movements executed with an iron bow (whose cord is a chain) are in a more warlike vein. They are manipulated in unison, the athletes finish up by spinning the bow and chain downwards around their bodies and jumping out of the circle thus formed around them when the bow reaches the ankles. On official occasions, the session is terminated by a wrestling match. After 10 minutes, the adversaries rise, embrace each other on the forehead and leave the arena.

Finally there is a massage. The novices massage their elders and are in turn massaged by a professional. After a last ritual of thanksgiving, the pehlevans leave the gymnasium, feeling closer to Rostem, the mythical hero. One last detail: there are 21 zourkhanes in Tehran alone.

The Women

In order to understand the situation of women in Iran, you must remember that the society is in the process of undergoing enormous changes: what common measure can there be between the ex-nomadic Bakhtiari woman, the wife of a provincial of high-standing and a worldly society lady living in Tehran? Despite the evolution in customs and legal status, the Iranian woman has kept the mannerisms of her ancestors in many areas. Her world is a universe somewhat different from ours; it has always fascinated travelers because of its mystery. However from Sir John Chardin to Pierre Loti, the Western witnesses were men whose curiosity was not satisfied and therefore it changed into compassion. If a Western woman onlooker had been admitted into the circle of female family life, she would have better understood what was going on.

From one end of Iran to the other, but in cities and towns more than in the country, the women go about their work wearing the traditional chador: an ample, light veil of nondescript color, crossed in front and knotted behind the neck. Children of 5 years are very proud of this accessory. For the older girls, it is an excuse for infinitely subtle coquettishness: it can more or less hide the face, can be worn higher on the head or is used as a wall to hide behind. For the poor, it serves to hide their shabby garments—the worn-out sweater and formless dress can barely be seen beneath the folds of this cloth. This veil is not considered as a punishment, or oppressive. It is simply that an Iranian woman would not venture out without her chador, just as you would not go into the street wearing a swim suit. In short, it is a question of propriety. However, this reflex is tending to disappear, especially in Tehran.

The veil is a symbol of respectability still adhered to by many people more than a precaution taken by jealous husbands. In small restaurants the women are sometimes asked to sit upstairs. In the tchaikhanes in the country, low benches are installed in the gardens for this purpose. They are put there for the convenience of the clients; to avoid mixing with the crowd, the mullahs prefer to install themselves in these quiet corners.

The Home

The arrangement of the house reveals the same preoccupations. Half a century ago, the *biroun*, the master's apartment, was completely separated from the *anderoun*, the women's area that was guarded by eunuchs in the homes of the upper-class. These special servants no longer exist but the division of the house remains the same in the poorer homes, where a curtain preserves the woman's privacy. In general, the rooms do not have a specific purpose, and each can be used in turn as bedroom, dining room or living room. If the family is large, a room is set aside for each household in it. The furnishings are simple: rugs cover the floors and walls, sometimes serving as doors. Large cushions and pillows placed on the rugs and decorated chests serve as the basic furniture. This "on-the-ground" comfort is rejected by the well-to-do people of the cities who nowadays prefer European furnishings with a tendency to the massive and ornate.

There is no style or refinement in the choice of knick-knacks or ways of lighting. The poor have only one room that is heated in winter and it becomes the refuge of the entire family. The Iranian *korsi* is an original appliance which allows everyone to endure the difficult cold season. Imagine a low table placed over a brazier, the whole covered with a large quilted cloth. The feet are slipped under the wooden structure, a blanket is pulled up to the chin and the back is supported by cushions. The housewives manage to cook, it seems, without ever leaving the warmth of the korsi! An inconvenience does exist, however: one has no desire to leave it. A sign of the times: the oil stove is slowly replacing the korsi and its fire built of sun-dried cow dung.

On the other hand, corrugated iron is not replacing the *qagel*, a layer of mud and chopped straw which makes the roofs and terraces water-tight. Moreover, a whole chapter would be needed to describe these roofs and terraces where Iranians play, chat and sleep during the hot weather.

Children and the Family

Children remain under the exclusive authority of the women until the age of seven, and nothing much is asked of them. When they reach the age of reason, they are considered to be small adults and faced with situations which seem to us to have little connection with their capabilities. However this may be, it is clear that the Iranians adore their little ones and that the parents go to enormous trouble to assure their education and well-being.

In the country, a child is regarded as a gift from heaven, since he is a future work-hand. A boy is doubly welcome because it is assumed that he will bring a wife into the patriarchal household. The girl is provisionally a stranger. When she marries, the fiancé pays his mother-in-law a "milk fee" to repay her for the care she has taken of her daughter. In this respect, too, changes are taking place. Numerous sons are no longer so heartily desired. Poorer families in Tehran limit themselves to one or two children, so as to maintain a standard of living acquired with difficulty. The prominent families do the same so as not to deplete their heritage. Nevertheless, in the eyes of the great majority, sterility is still considered a grave defect and innumerable women use pious methods to ward it off.

The family remains important to the Iranian. Think of it as a basic unit, grouped around one older member and often living under the same roof.

If you travel by plane or by bus, you will notice crowds at the airports and stations, awaiting the arrival of family members who are returning, and consisting of parents, brothers, but above all sisters and cousins, wearing their chadors, delighted with this chance for a promenade. They crowd to the tune of 8 or 9 into a taxi, without counting the small children, and they scream with joy. There is no doubt that there will be a celebration at the house that night. To-morrow, the neighbors and friends will call to greet the traveler who will then return the visit.

The individual is never isolated but is connected by a group of duties and rights to this rather large community in which everyone has a feeling of solidarity. Our individualism would make us revolt against this threat to our liberty. Like many Orientals, the Iranian thrives on it. Since the women cannot be involved in public life, familial distractions are of great importance to them. Fêtes, marriages, family walks and picnics are their only possibilities for outings. But they do entertain each other, gossip, drink tea, eat candy and sweets and sometimes play music together.

Marriage

Marriage surrenders the young girl to a new family. After transactions, about which the young people have not a word to say, the date of the contract is set. The fiancé has paid the "milk fee" and has given his father-in-law part of the guaranteed deposit which will take care of his wife if he repudiates her. The bride's father has contributed financially and with great effort to the installation of the young couple. A ceremony takes place at the bride's home. Hidden behind a curtain with her attendants, she waits for the mullah to ask for her consent. After many purely conventional hesitations, she accepts. The marriage is then performed by proxy, without the couple ever seeing each other. The customary festivities follow. But this is only the beginning of the performance. Many months may pass before the *arouci* is celebrated, after which the husband will come for his wife and solemnly unveil her.

Until the last few years, young married women lived in dread of being repudiated. The husband had only to pronounce the sanctioned formula for the unhappy woman to find herself deprived of her children and of financial support. Since the 1967 law regarding the protection of the family came into effect, marriage and divorce are regulated by laws which are the same for men and women alike. Divorces are relatively frequent in Iran and this is nothing new because authors during the last century claimed that many women were married three times before their 25th birthday! Polygamy is also part and parcel of their customs: it is considered unlucky to have a co-wife, but this is often deemed preferable to divorce. However, polygamy is not widespread, mostly because of the financial means it requires.

Empress Farah's influence on the subject has been considerable. She has fought alongside many women in different organizations to change the standing of women. Princess Ashraf founded the Supreme Council to help coordinate their activities. Since 1963, the right to vote has been granted to all women. In 1967, they were granted civil rights and now can even work without the consent of their husbands. The *Women's Organization of Iran* offers vocational training and legal advice in more than 70 welfare centers, to which family planning clinics are attached. There are now many careers open to Iranian women and artistic endeavors seem to attract them in particular. They are intelligent with a great deal of temperament but this is nothing new and Persian tales are full of examples in which the cleverness and tenacity of women triumph.

In earlier times, the poet sang of the round moon-face, languorous gazelle eyes and milk-and-honey complexion of his beloved. The qualities to be admired have changed now and chic is measured in terms of conformity with Occidental standards. Happily, the niceness, vivacity and simple friendliness of the pretty girls in the countryside and among the tribes counteract a tendency to the other extreme sometimes seen in the cities.

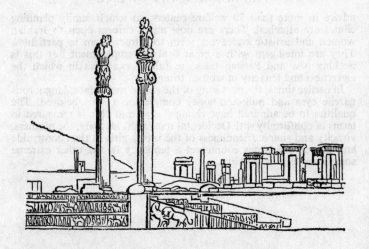

HISTORY OF IRAN

Persian Perseverance in Good Times and Bad

The first traces of prehistoric Iran are to be found in the foothills of the Zagros mountains on the edge of the Mesopotamian basin and near ancient Sumer. Only the archeological excavations at Susa and Luristan give us glimpses of those distant times. The earliest strata take us back to the Neolithic period, some 4,000 years before Christ. Copper was already known and the raised decorations painted on pottery show us that the people were shepherds and farmers. The cuneiform of Mesopotamia replaced the ancient pictorial writing but linear writing did not appear for another thousand years. This was prehistory, the Bronze Age was at its peak, and iron, which was to become an everyday material, had been discovered. Successive invasions were doubtless one of the causes of these changes. The diggings at Tepe Hissar, near Damghan, which brought to light Scythian jewelry typical of the art of the steppes, prove that a new people had invaded the area. If we needed new proofs of the mixing of races, the tombs and vases with Mycenaean decorations at Tepe Giyan provide them. The Semites came from the west and the Aryans and Turanians from the east and the north to intermingle with the people already there.

70

The population having been pinpointed, it is important to describe its surroundings which differ slightly from today. In comparison with the present-day coastline, the Persian Gulf had penetrated some 200 kilometers inland, transforming Lagash, Ur and Eridu into coastal towns and allowing ships to sail in as far as the outskirts of Susa. The Caspian Sea also stretched out further to the north and to the east, where it joined and merged with the Aral Sea, thus receiving the waters of the Oxus (Amu-Darya) and the Iaxartes (Syr-Darya). As for Seistan, today a desolate region, during those ancient times it was a prosperous country, carefully irrigated and cultivated.

Elam and the Medes

The history of the Iranian plateau begins with the Elamites. Their eighth king, Luhi-Ishan, and the ninth, Hishep-Ratep, in a succession of 12 kings, were contemporaries of Sargon the Ancient, king of Akkad, around 2400 B.C. Settled in Awan, slightly to the northwest of Susa, they provoked the all-powerful Sargon with their warlike raids. Therefore Sargon, as well as his successor Rimush, undertook expeditions against the Elamites pushing as far as the Guti country in the north of Kurdistan. They established their yoke so firmly over Babylon and around their kingdom that Helu, 10th king of Elam, ruled only over the southern part of this territory. It was not until the reign of Silhac-Inshushinac (1165–51) that the Elamite kingdom reached its zenith with frontiers extending from the lower Tigris to Persepolis. After the death of Inshushinac, Elam fell again under the sword of Babylon, then governed by Nabuchodonosor I (Nebuchadnezzar) (1146–23). A long silence covered the following period from 1150 to 742.

At the end of the eighth century, when Assyria extended its hegemony from the Zagros mountains to the Mediterranean under the rule of Sargon, six Median tribes decided to organize themselves into a nation and to entrust their destiny to the fairest and most enlightened of their chiefs, Deioces. He chose Amadana, now Hamadan, as his capital and ruled for 53 years, from 708 to 655, keeping up friendly relations with Assyria. His son Phraortes (655–633) continued this wise policy and then, having conquered the Persians who had settled in the Fars, turned against Assurbanipal, the Assyrian. This was a disastrous idea which cost him his life in the early days of the war. The experience served as a lesson to his successor Cyaxares (633–584) who re-organized his army and modeled it on that of the enemy. He also put to use the ancestral equestrian talents of the nomads, which gave the cavalry a decisive superiority in battle. This, however, did not prevent him from being beaten by the Scythians sent against him by the Assyrians, after his attack on Nineveh. He saw them devastate Media with the ardor of mercenaries. The Scythian troops continued to pursue their systematic ravages and until 615 Cyaxares was busy trying to rid the country of small groups of Scythian troops which had remained behind. Then, with the help of the Babylonians, he once again laid siege to Nineveh. Assyria was now on the decline and the storming and destruction of Nineveh in 606 completed its defeat. The Assyrian Empire was then divided between the king of Babylon, who inherited the Mesopotamian plain, and the Median king, who received Armenia and the sources of the Tigris and Cappadocia. As a result, the kingdom of Lydia, successor of the Hittites and homeland of the famous Croesus, became their neighbor. At the death of Cyaxares, Astyages, the new ruler of the Medes, married the daughter of the king of Lydia. Until 558, he reigned over a peaceful and prosperous state which extended from Afghanistan to central Asia Minor.

The Achaemenids

The year 558 B.C. saw Kurach II on the throne of Susa which he governed in the name of Astyages. Kurach II is none other than the Cyrus of Greek history, founder of the powerful Achaemenid dynasty, its name taken from the tribe to which it belonged. Eight years after attaining power by means of intrigue and revolt, Cyrus overthrew his sovereign and brought all of Media under his control. Croesus, father-in-law of Astyages, joined the battle but was quickly defeated in his own capital of Sardis. Cyrus then pushed on against the Greek colonies of Ionia. There he ceased his western conquests, returned home and immediately left for the east where he extended the limits of his kingdom to the Indus and the Iaxartes. From India to the Aegean he was the uncontested ruler, except in Babylon. Weakened, it was conquered in 539 but, and this was a new development, the city was not pillaged or destroyed and the temples were respected. Even more important, the statues of gods from other cities held by the Babylonians were returned to their rightful owners. In this way, Cyrus the Great inaugurated a policy of tolerance for which he became famous. He died in 529, having conquered an immense empire.

Cambyses, his eldest son, succeeded him and decided to extend his father's empire. He left for Egypt but first had his brother assassinated to ensure his own sovereignty. The conquest of the Nile valley was easy. Egyptian power was undermined by the interventions of the priesthood. The interference of foreigners in national matters paralyzed the government. Defeated before Pelusa, Pharaon (Pharaoh) was put to death. Cambyses, following his father's example, protected

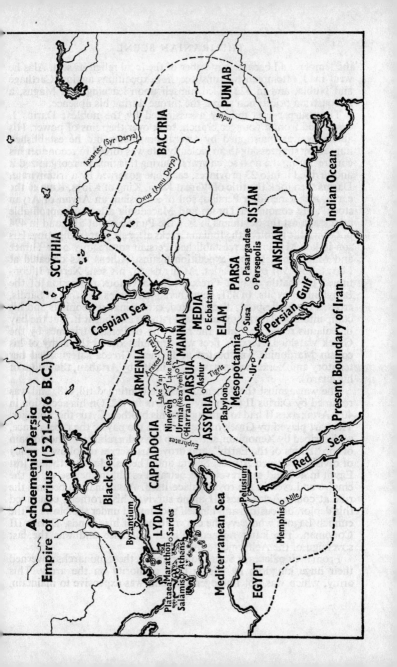

Achaemenid Persia
Empire of Darius I (521-486 B.C.)

the temples and became a member of the local religious sect. Alas he went mad, attempted two unsuccessful expeditions against Carthage and Nubia, and in 522 killed himself upon learning that Magus, a Zoroastrian priest, had seized the throne during his absence.

The usurper was quickly assassinated by the nobles; Darius I, descended from a younger branch, took over the reins of power. His authority was questioned by several pretenders but he established himself by suppressing them violently. He was forced to reconquer his empire during the next seven years. During this time he reorganized it and divided it into 23 provinces, each one governed by a triumvirate. Darius then took the title of "Great King, King of Kings, King of the earth, Achaemenid, a Persian, son of a Persian, an Aryan of Aryan stock". He conquered Thrace and Macedonia after an unprofitable attack against the Scythians in 515, the Punjab about 512, and in 494 put down the revolt of the Ionian Greeks after six years of fighting. His son-in-law Mardonius reestablished Persian sovereignty over Thrace and Macedonia, but an expedition against Athens was defeated at Marathon (490) by Miltiades. At his death, his son, Xerxes I, continued the battle against Greece, after a vicious repression of the Babylonian revolts. In 481, he gathered his troops together at Sardis, crossed the Hellespont, disembarked, exterminated Leonidas and his companions at Thermopylae, seized Athens and burnt it. But the bay of Salamis resounded with the ramming of Persian triremes by the Greek warships. Xerxes's fleet was annihilated and the army of his cousin Mardonius was beaten at Plataea. Greece safeguarded her territory and Xerxes was assassinated in 465 by Artaban, the leader of his guards.

The war against the Athenian League continued till 448, and was resumed by Darius II as an ally of Sparta in 412. On his accession in 405, Artaxerxes II had to fight against his brother, Cyrus the Younger. The part played by Greek mercenaries, in the pay of the rebel prince, as described by Xenophon, showed up the vulnerability of the domain of the "Kings of the Earth", and drove Artaxerxes to follow a policy of division between Athens, Sparta and Thebes. He nevertheless lost Egypt in 400 and saw revolt and betrayal establish themselves in the empire and even in the royal palace itself. Assassination became the rule at court. Artaxerxes III alone survived his brothers, continued this deplorable custom and himself succumbed under the blows of the eunuch Bagoas who gave the crown to one of his friends, Darius III Codoman. The latter reigned without brilliance and was the last sovereign of the Achaemenid dynasty.

From their palaces at Susa and Persepolis, these monarchs governed their huge kingdom by basing their authority on the army. This army, which was not homogeneous and was expensive to maintain, forced the provinces to pay heavy taxes. The incompetency of the last rulers and the revolts and foreign wars the empire had to sustain against Greece and Egypt, sufficed to weaken the power of the "Kings of Kings" and to demolish the Persian colossus.

Alexander the Great and Successors

Master of all Greece at 20, Alexander pitted his army against the Persians with the firm intention of driving them out of the Mediterranean. The Macedonian phalanxes won the first victory at Granicus in 334, thus liberating all the Greek cities of Asia Minor. Crossing present-day Turkey, Alexander restricted himself to the realization of his primary objective: to prevent the Persians having access to the Mediterranean. To accomplish this, he inflicted a second defeat on them near the Gulf of Alexandretta and invaded Phoenicia and Egypt, where he founded Alexandria. In the spring of 331, Alexander refused Darius' offer to divide the empire and began the conquest of the eastern part. He marched on Mesopotamia and crossed the Euphrates and the Tigris on whose left bank the army of Darius III awaited him. This army was completely crushed and routed. Then came the capture of Babylon and Susa and the burning of Persepolis. This senseless act may have been an accident as Alexander had the murderer of Darius executed and honors rendered to the royal remains, thereupon proclaiming himself the successor of the Great King. The triumphant march continued to the Punjab across the regions which today have become Afghanistan and West Pakistan. In 324, the conquest of Asia was accomplished, but Alexander did not have time to organize his empire. He died in Babylon a year later at the age of 32.

An embittered war began immediately between Alexander's generals over the rich legacy. Eventually Greece went to Antigonus, Egypt and southern Syria to Ptolemy and Asia to Seleucus. The latter, known as Seleucus Nicator, is the only one of interest to us. He founded the Seleucid dynasty, settled in Babylon and then on the banks of the Tigris at Seleucia, founded new towns in Susiana and kept peace in all his states. If Seleucus coveted India, King Chandragoupta had an eye to the west and even succeeded in gaining the territories today forming Afghanistan and Baluchistan. On his side, Seleucus received 500 elephants from the Hindu king, which assured his victory at Ipsus against the army of Antigonus (301). Finally, marriages between members of the two royal families sealed the peace.

Seleucus, however, now saw his states reduced to Syria, Mesopotamia, Persia and Bactria. His successors, never at rest from incessant attacks leveled against them by their neighbors to the east and to the west, were unable to avoid the decline of the Seleucid Empire. The Gauls fell upon Asia Minor and created Galatia, while Syria remained a cause for friction with the Ptolemys. In 250, Bactria declared its independence. A short time later, the Parthians started a movement for emancipation from the Greeks. In 223, Egypt took possession of Asia Minor and in 200 Rome entered the scene and occupied Greece under the pretext of protecting it. The Seleucids were forced to abandon their territorial pretensions and gave way before the legions of Scipion the African. They ruled over Syria for one more century, before ceding their place to the Romans and the Parthians. The latter were highly reputed horsemen and archers and had shown their unfriendly intentions since 247. Installed in their capital, Hecatompylos, somewhere between Tehran and Meshed, they appropriated Gorgan and Mazanderan, and their chief Tiridates (248–214) then took the title of "Great King". His son engaged in open warfare against the Seleucids, and Mithridates (174–136) conquered Media, Fars, Elam and Babylonia. The Romans, who had inherited the kingdom of Pergamon, arrived in Cilicia and the invaders met each other on the Euphrates in the persons of General Pompey and Phraates III around 69 B.C. During the next two-and-a-half centuries, the Parthians and the Romans engaged in constant battles over an ill-defined frontier. Meanwhile, quarreling became constant in the Parthian camp, rivalries exhausted these poorly organized and greedy warriors and finally internal anarchy destroyed them. Rome was no less harassed, for the fighting was taken over by a new Persian dynasty whose founders claimed kinship with the Achaemenids.

The Sassanids (224–638 A.D.)

The founding of the Sassanid Dynasty goes back to Babek (Bapek) (208) or Ardashir (225), his youngest son. In fact, both settled in the Fars and worked to awaken Persian nationalism by revolting against Artabanus V, the last Parthian king, whom Ardashir killed in 224 during the course of a decisive battle. The latter, crowned "King of Kings of the Iranians", dreamed of reestablishing the Achaemenid Persian Empire. He already possessed Babylonia, conquered Media and took up once again the fight against Rome. Shahpur I (241–272) relentlessly pursued this effort, took Armenia and Mesopotamia and captured the emperor Valerian as prisoner. He signed an alliance with the Queen of Syria, in vain alas for she was deposed shortly thereafter.

However, far-reaching internal reforms took place in every area. Contrary to Achaemenid eclecticism, a close-knit unity, national as well as religious, occurred under the Sassanids. Administration was centralized and the exceedingly hierarchical church succeeded in

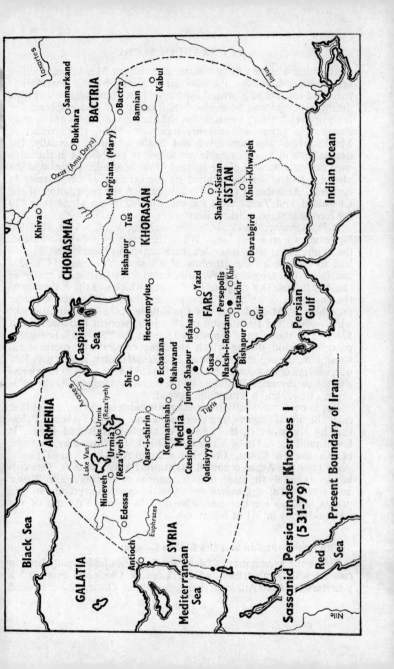

Sassanid Persia under Khosroes I
(531-79)

------- Present Boundary of Iran

establishing a state within a state. Zoroastrian Mazdaism, codified and annotated, became the national religion. Shahpur nevertheless remained tolerant as is proved by the fact that Manichaeism was born during his reign and he shielded its founder. He also respected the faith of his Christian subjects, but the doctrinal pressure of the great Zoroastrian priests affected his successor. Mani, the prophet of Manichaeism, was persecuted and finally crucified. Actually, the descendants of Shahpur could not afford to be tolerant in the same way, not only because of the attitude of the Mazdaian priesthood but also due to the dismay aroused by the increase of Christianity in Armenia. Ardashir II (379–383) inaugurated the persecution of the Christians, and Yazdegerd I was assassinated by the Maguses in 420 for having granted religious liberty.

It is, however, in Persia, under Bahram V (421–438), that the Nestorian Church was born. When this ruler ascended the throne, the White Huns had succeeded the Kuchans in Bactria and he also had to deal with their attempts of invasion. Yazdegerd (438–457) continued the religious persecutions and even massacred many of the Armenians. This religious intolerance, which was the real cause of the Sassanian downfall, did not prevent the rise of a new doctrine preached by Mazdak: he was the founder of a communistic sect which advocated the sharing of all goods, women included. From 531 to 579, the reign of Khosroés I, called the "Blessed", brought a peaceful period during which time the empire was reorganized. Ctesiphon, the capital, became an intellectual center. Roads were laid out, surveys undertaken, a budget estimated on the basis of a progressive tax on revenues. Painting and the minor arts (especially the goldsmith's trade) had a remarkable revival.

But in conformity with the mysterious swing of the pendulum that rules the life of empires, and despite the conquest of Syria and Palestine by Khosroés II, the decline of the Sassanids had begun. It lasted until the death of Yazdegerd III in 651, followed by the flight of his son to China. Ctesiphon fell into Arab hands in 637; some years later the Arabs occupied the entire Iranian plateau. This collapse was largely the result of four centuries of warring against Rome and Byzantium, aggravated by dynastic quarrels, tyranny by the priests, and palace intrigues. The final blow was the rout of the Sassanid army in 641 at Nihavand.

The Arab Invasion and the Shi'ite Schism

Before the appearance of Islam, the Sassanids had already been in contact with Arab tribes and the kings of Ctesiphon even had a Secretary for Arab Affairs in their government. Omar, who succeeded

Muhammed in 634 as Caliph, was master of Arabia, Syria and Southern Mesopotamia. There was also nothing standing in the way of his invasion of Persia. He invaded it and subdued it from 637 to 642. The country ceased to exist as an independent state and Zoroastrian Mazdaism was persecuted in turn. Persia, now an integral part of the Arab Empire, fell under the domination of the Caliphs, the spiritual and temporal leaders of Islam, Osman in 644 and Ali in 656. The latter was assassinated five years later and the question of succession was posed once more. The Omayyad family, Arab aristocrats and governors of Syria, seized the Caliphate despite the claims to it presented by the sons of Ali, Hassan and Hosein. The latter were arrested and killed in the middle of the desert, and this is the origin of the Shi'ite schism. In fact, the Persians used this as a pretext (Hosein had married a daughter of Yazdegerd III) not to recognize the Caliphs of Damascus, past or future, and to contest their authority as Leaders of the Faithful. The mullahs first established the Shi'ite doctrine and then spreading their own interpretations of the Koran, moved further and further away from orthodoxy, giving birth to new sects such as Sufism. Utilizing the disorders, the hitherto hunted-down Mazdaites reappeared as well as the Jews and Christians. Newcomers made their appearance: the Druzes, the Yazidis, who venerated the devil, and the Ismailians. The Omayyad family ruled until 750, but made the mistake of disregarding the heretics. Another Arab line, the Abbasids, made use of the discontent of the Persians to take the Khurasan and overthrow the Caliph of Damascus. The Abbasids were not recognized as legitimate by the Shi'ites either, but they nevertheless were able to govern without coming up against too much. There are two famous names in this dynasty which lasted from 750 to 870: El Mansour, the founder of Bagdad, and Harun al-Rashid, whose magnificence dazzled the ambassadors of Charlemagne. This was the era of the Bagdad of *A Thousand and One Nights*.

Meanwhile, as of 820, Persian emancipation began. The rulers of the Khorasan enjoyed great independence and when their throne fell to the Samanids, the latter, who were Persians, fought for freedom from the Arab yoke. They ruled over eastern Persia during the 10th century, using only the Persian language in their city of Bukhara. From Shiraz, the Buyids worked for the liberation of Iraq Adjemi, from Media to Fars. Adod el Addaula (949–982) even annexed Mesopotamia and had himself crowned "King of Kings". In the year 1000, the Arab nightmare had disappeared. The Caliph of Bagdad was nothing more than a Sunnite spiritual leader. Persian genius was reborn, encouraged and supported by the courts of the Samanids and Buyids.

These two dynasties yielded to Mahmud of Ghazni (997–1030), a

Sunnite ruler of Turkish origin from Afghanistan, pillager of India, who nevertheless surrounded himself with an enlightened court where Firdowsi, "the Persian Homer", wrote his verses. Then, the Ghaznevids crumbled before the Seljuks who swept through all Persia and governed it from 1040 to 1220. From 1072 to 1092, Malik Shah ruled an empire, including Asia Minor and all of Iran, which reached its zenith. He founded a university at Bagdad, protected artists and poets, among them the illustrious Omar Khayyam. At his death the empire was once more divided up and the Seljuk Sultans of Iran were unable to forestall the onslaught of the northern Turks, who were themselves being harassed by the Tartars and Mongols. And so in 1194, the Turkish sultan who ruled from Khwarizm to Turkestan, deposed the Seljuks and replaced them, but not for long. The silhouette of Genghis Khan cast its shadow on the gates of the Caliph's kingdom.

The Mongols in Persia

After the submission of China, Genghis Khan launched his troops in 1220 against Transoxiana and eastern Iran, overturned the dynasty of the sultans of Khwarizm and died in 1227. Ogodii, his son, continued the advance towards the west and with his brothers Tului and Jagatai, organized an empire. In 1260, the title of Great Khan passed to Kubilai, son of Tului, who entrusted the governing of the Iranian provinces to his brother Hulagu. Hulagu captured Bagdad, established his capital at Tabriz and ruled his lands with a firm but liberal hand. A Buddhist, he granted both the Christians and the Moslems religious liberty. By the time his third successor, Ghazan, came to power the Mongols had absorbed the Persian way of life and Ghazan was converted to Islam. Although the Mongols held full power until 1316, Persians were granted high administrative posts and became patrons of the arts and literature.

The role of these eleven Khans—Kings of the World, as they were called—encompassed more than military and administrative areas. They developed trade and the sciences. Architecture used a new technique for the first time, that of enameled bricks, so characteristic of Iranian monuments. Although local dynasties divided the power of the Mongols among themselves a peaceful era ensued. Next the Muzaffarid dynasty of Kerman sought authority over Fars and most of western Iran. Although of Arab origin, it was purely Iranian at that time.

The new conqueror was Timur-leng, Timur the Lame, or Tamerlane. Related to Genghis Khan but a Turk and Moslem, he carved himself out a kingdom in Transoxiana and in Turkestan. He attacked

Persia in 1380, subdued a revolt in Afghanistan, then conquered Armenia, Georgia, Fars and Syria, began the invasion of Muscovy, stopped at the entrance to the Don, retraced his steps, laid waste to India and returned to Samarkand to prepare the conquest of China. Death overtook him in 1404, at the age of 71.

Shah Rukh, his son, consolidated the empire and founded a library at Herat. After his reign, Persia once again was divided up. The eastern part remained under Timurid domination while, from Shiraz to Tabriz and from Trebizond to Bagdad, power fell into the hands of the Turkomans. The Timurids continued to patronize the arts which produced work reflecting the influence of China. Now a new external factor came to change the face of the world: the discovery by the Europeans of the maritime route to the Indies. It meant the immediate ruin of Iranian transit routes and the future interference of foreign powers in the internal affairs of Iran.

The Safavids (1502–1722) and Persian Renaissance

The powerful Brotherhood of the Safavids lived at Ardabil, in Azerbaijan under Turkoman domination. Anxious about the Brotherhood's growing influence, the Turkomans persecuted it, thus provoking one of its members, Shah Ismail, to revolt. He seized Baku and Tabriz and became the champion of national restoration, extolling a Persian Persia, Moslem and Shi'ite, freed from Arabs, Turks and Mongols. The idea was not new, but its very persistence shows how dear it was to Iranian hearts. The young Ismail had no trouble at all in augmenting his possessions. Kazerun, Kerman and Yazd fell in turn and finally, in 1505, Isfahan also. To the east, the Uzbegs overturned the Timurids and threatened to subdue the newborn state. Shah Ismail decimated them, killed their leader and took Meshed. After this he came to an agreement with a Timurid from Afghanistan, Babur, to maintain the Timurids' authority in Transoxiana. The organization of Persia was begun by Tahmasp I (1524–76), but the battle against the Sunni Turks continued and it was Shah Abbas (1587–1629) who finished the work of his predecessors by chasing the Uzbegs out of Khurasan and the Turks out of Azerbaijan and Bagdad.

This prince then realized the dreams of the ancients by bringing about the Persian renaissance and carrying it to its peak. He became Shah Abbas the Great, the builder of the scintillating domes of Isfahan, the renewer of art and handicrafts. He created national unity, enriched his country and began a skilful policy of dealing with European countries. (France was allied with the Turks against the Austrian ruling house which in turn negotiated with the Persians.)

All in all this remained a minor preoccupation compared to the fears aroused by the first Portuguese arrivals who wanted to mark the maritime route to the Indies with their presence. They occupied the Hormuz Strait and the Hormuz and Bahrein islands and an agreement gave them a monopoly over Persian commerce. The British intervened in 1598 when Essex sent Anthony and Robert Shirley to enter Shah Abbas's service and induce him to make common cause against the Turks and develop trade. Shah Abbas sent Anthony to Europe as his envoy. Robert was appointed Master General of the Persian army. In 1608 he was sent to Europe in his turn by Abbas. Five years later he was knighted and later returned again to Persia where he died at Kazvin in 1628.

In the meantime a battle took place between the English and the Portuguese. The English took Hormuz and gave it back to the Shah. In return the English were given permission to establish a commercial base at Bandar Abbas and the right to maintain a navy in the Persian Gulf to ensure its security. The Dutch were also in the picture and Abbas had to safeguard himself by maintaining a careful equilibrium between the rival forces. He improved his kingdom, laid out roads, built caravanserais, irrigated the countryside and distributed drinking water across the country. New tapestry workshops were opened in Isfahan. It was a golden age.

Though the successors of the Great Shah Abbas did not enlarge or improve their kingdom, they did at least maintain it. Externally, they could only observe the growing covetousness of their Western friends for the Indies. The entire 17th century was dominated by this fact. The Dutch succeeded the weakened Portuguese but their wars in Europe prevented them from taking advantage of these circumstances. The English Company was master when France appeared on the scene. Commercial expeditions were sent to the court of Isfahan and failed only because of their clumsy diplomacy. And while the Europeans were becoming lost in the intricacies of Oriental trade on the shores of the Indian Ocean, another power was looming on the horizon. The Russia of the Romanovs, established on the banks of the Caspian Sea since 1556, was becoming a vast empire whose proximity would never cease to disturb the days of future Shahs.

In 1772 the Safavids still held power over Afghanistan and then an Afghani chief assassinated the Persian ruler of Kandahar and preached the holy war of the Sunnis against the Shi'ites. His tribes attacked Persia but this Afghani dynasty lasted barely ten years. Once again a Turkoman from the tribe of Afshars, a certain Nadir also a Sunni Moslem, organized the battle against the Afghan invader and chased him out. Embellished with the title of Shah Nadir, he sat on the throne of the King of Kings (1736), attacked Afghanistan, seized

Kandahar, and sent a sacking and looting expedition to India. He brought back the famous Throne of the Peacocks from Delhi. After a raid of the Uzbegs, he returned armed with the submission of the Khans of Bukhara and of Khiva. For several years Shah Nadir reconstituted the domain of his predecessors, turned by his successes into a cruel tyrant. One event of his reign is worth pointing out, for we will meet with the victim again a little later. Aga Mohammed was taken as hostage and castrated after his father, chief of the Qajar tribe, had been killed. Such heinous crimes and persecution of the Shi'ite faith were the cause of the assassination of Shah Nadir, immediately followed by the breaking up of his empire. Under the impetus of Ahmad Khan of the Durani tribe, Afghanistan regained its independence. As for Persia, it fell into the hands of a governor of Shiraz, Karim Zand (1750–79). He ruled over it peacefully, beautified Shiraz, his capital, restored the ancient monuments and kept the dangerous eunuch Aga Mohammed as a prisoner.

Externally, the international situation had evolved. Peter the Great of Russia had already attacked Persia during the Afghan invasion and had appropriated Gilan, Mazanderan and Gorgan. But these provinces were handed back by his niece, Anna Ivanovna, who ascended the throne in 1730. In India, England had successively ousted all its rivals: Portugal, Holland and France. England and Russia now fought each other for the upper hand and Persia painfully suffered the backlash from this state of affairs.

The Qajars (1786–1925)

The Turkish dynasty of the Qajars marks perhaps the most painful and unhealthy period of Persian history. These unstable rulers were more preoccupied with their personal problems than with the destiny of a country whose boundaries were slowly being reduced. Foreign interventions became more numerous and more pressing, the intelligentsia was divided and the religious quarrels once again aggravated the situation.

We must return to the eunuch, Aga Mohammed, to explain the ascension of this disastrous dynasty. Mutilation had not reduced his ferocity. Escaping from Shiraz at the death of the regent, Karim Khan, he went to his compatriot Qajars, raised troops and undertook the conquest of Persia. This resulted in 20 years of atrocities, including the gouging out of eyes of the male population of Kerman. Such conduct brought hatred upon Aga Mohammed and his successors. There was now a great rupture between the ruling classes and the people. Between 1797 and 1925 six sovereigns succeeded the tyrant, none of whom made the slightest attempt to right these wrongs. These years only confirmed the greed of foreign powers and the incapacity of the national leaders. Here are a few striking events which occurred during this sad period.

Fath Ali Shah (1797–1833) was the contemporary of Napoleon, with whom he signed the Treaty of Finkenstein. This was the moment when the Russians acquired Georgia, Mingrelia, Dagestan and Cherran, thus gaining possession of what was to become the oil fields of Baku. An expedition, sent to investigate the area, reported in these terms: "Oil is a mineral liquid that is totally useless. By nature it is sticky and smells bad. It cannot be used in any way."

Mohammed Shah (1834–47) tried to attack Afghanistan, in spite of warnings from the English. His reign might have prided itself on the birth of Baha'ism. This new religion was led by Mirza Ali Mohammed who came from Shiraz. He attempted to reconcile all religions and preached universal peace. His disciples hailed him as "Bab" or "door" between the world of flesh and the spirit. He had a large and influential following and denounced religious corruption. The people responded and hoped to see the Shah affirm his authority over a priesthood which no longer pleased anyone. Shah Mohammed ignored the new faith and disorder arose. Civil war and massacre occurred under his successor, Nasir-ud-Din-Shah (1847–96). He had the Bab tortured and then executed him personally but this did not restore the situation. A new Bab was appointed and took refuge in Bagdad. The Baha'i were persecuted but they persisted in advocating the abolition of the veiling of women, polygamy and the death sentence.

England and Russia continued to quarrel at the expense of Persia, which did not prevent the Shah from visiting Europe, thereby emptying the national treasury. The constant need for money was solved by the Shah ceding to foreigners anything they asked for: mining concessions, monopoly of the forests and fallow lands, levying of customs, etc. Foreign banks were established in Tehran. In 1896–1906, Muzaffarid-Din-Shah, son and successor of the previous Shah, demonstrated a lavishness equal to that of his father. He gave up the Caspian fisheries, the forests of Mazanderan and the turquoise mines of Nishapur. The Germans joined the dance by opening several banks and the Russians borrowed from France at 3.5% to lend to Persia at 5%. In 1905, William Knox d'Arcy obtained oil prospecting and exploitation rights. But, things began to change. The "Young Turk" movement began to spread, creating agitation against the Sultan and finding many sympathizers in Tehran. The young Persians rioted and the police retaliated. On the fifth of August 1906, the Shah did at least grant a constitution and swore on the Koran to respect it. He died shortly thereafter.

Mohammed Ali Shah (1906–09) came to the fore. This resulted in a reign of three years of anarchy, riots and terror. Parliament discussed, made speeches, wanted a charter and a declaration of the people's rights (following the lead of the French Revolution). In 1908 the Shah dissolved Parliament and restored calm to Tehran by force. Tabriz became the capital of the resistance and red flags flew from the roofs of the bazaar there. The army gave way. Rasht and Isfahan joined the rebels, Tehran was seized, and Mohammed Ali abandoned his throne to his son, Sultan Ahmad Shah. But the boy was only 12 years of age and so there were a series of regents who governed in his place. Confusion and corruption flourished, the country was in the hands of the Europeans and the First World War exploded. In spite of the desire to be neutral, Persia was transformed into a battlefield and ravaged as much by the foreigners as by local vandals; the two hereditary enemies, the Russians and the Turks, had a marvelous time in a free-for-all, on Persian territory. England kept well out of it, instituting itself protector of Persia, offering to help and advise. Indeed we must give England her due here for she was the only country to offer compensation, even if only minimal, for the devastation inflicted on Persia. The man in the street emerged from this period dazed, bewildered and with a morbid dislike of all foreigners.

Reza Shah and Modern Times

In 1920, Reza Khan, the future inspired dictator of Iran, was but a Persian officer still involved in the war against the Russians. On the 22nd of February 1921 he entered Tehran, staged his coup d'état, imprisoned all the ministers, but did not yet take over power. He was first War Minister and then, in 1923, Prime Minister. Sultan Ahmad Shah left to visit Europe and never came back. In 1925, Parliament reassembled, deposed the Qajars and offered the throne to Reza Khan, who became Reza Shah Pahlavi. This word Pahlavi, which designates the language spoken under the Sassanids, expressed his desire to return to Persian beginnings and his hostility towards Islam increased, which caused him to pursue and harry the mullahs right into the mosques themselves.

A contemporary of Ataturk, the builder of modern Turkey, Reza Shah did the same for Iran, following his reforms step by step, planning national industrialization, removing the people's feeling of degradation, and forcibly opening their eyes to the modern world. He reestablished security in the state, reorganized the army, made amicable pacts with Afghanistan, Iraq and especially Turkey. Mills, cement factories, sugar refineries and electricity generating stations were installed, although production was not always profitable. At least, however, the money remained in the country and the budget was not burdened with excessive foreign expenditures. The first national undertaking was begun, the construction of the Trans Iranian railway, paid for by the revenues acquired from the sugar monopoly and royalties from the Anglo-Persian Oil Company. It is true that foreign technicians were involved, but the work remained Iranian. This lack of industrial specialists prompted the Shah to reform the educational system and, above all, to secularize it. Faculties of law, medicine, literature and science, and technical schools were opened. An Iranian Academy rewrote the dictionary, removing foreign words which modernism had introduced into the vocabulary.

As far as agriculture was concerned, much effort was put into reforms but less progress was made than in industrial development. With the confiscation of seignorial lands the Shah became the greatest landholder in the country which gave him elbow room to attack agrarian reform. The peasant class remained miserably poor and uneducated. He suppressed polygamy, also set up civil courts and granted equality of rights to both sexes, instituted the compulsory wearing of European-style clothing and prohibited the veiling of women. A big step forward had been taken which opened up the country to a future geared to the needs of this century. Iran was remolded as a secular state, not anti-religious but independent of religion, and was on the march.

In the years which preceded the Second World War, Reza Shah Pahlavi, the "Old King", as all of Persia called him, had shown a certain sympathy for the fascist regimes, perhaps somewhat understandable at the time. This attitude raised the suspicions of the English and the Russians. Forced to abdicate in 1941, Reza Shah died soon after in South Africa. His son, Mohammed Reza Shah, came to power at the age of 22, in an atmosphere of crisis. He chose neutrality and concentrated on keeping his country free of foreign occupations. The Allies agreed to maintain the independence of Iran and promised to remove their troops the moment hostilities ended.

If the Old King had paved the way to progress and modernization, his son opened up, perhaps prematurely, the road to democracy. Political parties entered upon the scene, among them the *Toudeh*, a party representing the extreme left. The constitution of an opposition brought with it several uprisings and created incidents, but an essential principle was recognized—the right of the people to self-determination and control over their destiny.

In the confusion of the years following the war, the figure of General Ali Razmara, who had studied at St. Cyr in France, emerged as Chief of the General Staff of the Army. After having brought peace back to Azerbaijan in 1946 after the departure of the last Russian troops, he was commissioned by the Shah in 1950 to lead the government and became Prime Minister. He expressed his opinion forcefully: ". . . All around us we see nothing but the poor and hungry, while a group of wealthy people export their capital to foreign countries." However, he was suspected of having favored English interests in the Anglo-Iranian Oil affair and was assassinated in 1951 by a fanatical Shi'ite.

In 1952, with the nationalization of Persian oil which so stirred the political and economic world, the Mossadegh affair occurred. Later the picturesque "doctor in pyjamas", an accomplished litigant and a moving actor (if we recall his interventions at The Hague), fell into disgrace but received the Shah's personal thanks for his work.

During the 1960s, the second of the Pahlavis established himself firmly on the throne, imposing radical reforms against the opposition of the formerly predominant landowning class. By the mid-1970s, largely due to the vast oil revenues, the Shah has begun to fulfill his avowed desire "to see unity reign among the various classes of Iranian society, in both speech and action and to fight against poverty".

ARTS AND HANDICRAFTS

Bronze, Sculpture, Tile and Carpet

The art of ancient Iran—by which we mean pre-Achaemenid, Achaemenid and Sassanid—is not original. It is inherited from Sumer, Mesopotamia, Akkad and Assyria, and later it came under the strong influence of Greece and Rome. This being said, Persian artists did stamp their works with a personal touch that made it impossible to confuse them with those which inspired them. Their themes, which are peculiar to them, permit their work to be identified and even dated.

It would require too much time and space to describe in detail all that this art has produced. First of all, we must relegate to the background certain works of an anecdotal nature which have no other end than to celebrate the glory of the great sovereigns. Under this heading would come the victory of Darius I over the Magus Gaumatas, sculpted in the rock at Bisutun, or that of Shahpur I over Emperor Valerian, immortalized in the caves of Taq-i-Bostan. These works reveal the spirit of the era but not the true genius of their creators.

In all forms of decoration, whatever they may be, sculpture, bas-relief, gold and silversmith's work or painted pottery, there is a constant preoccupation with the stylized representation of animals.

Pre-Achaemenid Art

The first manifestations of pre-Archaemenid art can be seen at the Tehran museum where it is represented by objects found at Tepe Sarab, Tepe Sialk and Susa (fourth millennium). Usually, they take the form of pottery decorated with friezes representing a series of animals, often goat-like. Some vases, on the other hand, confine bodies within linear motifs. Another example, a goblet, discovered at Susa, is adorned with an ibex whose horns sweep in a wide and graceful curve all the way to the end of its spine. Or there is a wild boar in terra cotta, treated in a crude way but animated with a certain vitality. A certain number of animal motifs continue until the Sassanid period, for example that of two goats facing each other with a plant between them. This persistence of the same motif has made it possible to follow the evolution of a style and the continuity of certain fundamental characteristics. One such familiar theme has been found on a cylinder seal from Susa. These seals, made of limestone, marble or soap-stone, give evidence of primitive urban civilizations and, thanks to the vogue of certain of the motifs, their profusion has made it possible to determine the taste and the subjects in favor at a given epoch.

The period of the Akkad dynasties (2340–2180 B.C.), which marked the end of the city-states in Mesopotamia, has also given us a collection of seals and ceramics dealing with themes identical to those of preceding epochs. Only a specialist can properly date them. More important is the appearance of monumental sculpture. A rock sculpture in relief at Darband-i-Gawr (23rd century), in Kurdistan, would seem to be the ancestor of those at Sar-i-Pul (21st century), of Bisutun (Parthian era) and even of Naqsh-e Rustam in Iran (third century A.D.). The Sar-i-Pul relief depicts the triumph of King Anubanini over his enemies. To the right, the goddess Inanna hands over to the king a ring, symbol of power, and this gesture resembles that of the god Ahura-Mazda offering a beribboned circlet to the Sassanid sovereigns.

Elamite Art

Again, a great number of cylinder seals discovered in the vicinity of Susa makes it possible to distinguish three periods in Elamite art. Ancient Elamite art, dating from the beginning of the second millennium B.C., is characterized by the use of heads and bodies of animals modeled in the round: a kneeling ibex adorns the legs of a receptacle, a ram's head forms the handle of a cup, the head of a bird or of a serpent decorates the end of a flag pole, etc. It is interesting to note how fur is rendered by small cuts in the stone, and how the eyes are made to stand out considerably and are accentuated by sea shells.

A series of terra cotta statuettes of Rubenesque women, evoking fertility goddesses, makes the transition to the middle Elamite period. From this time (about the 13th century) dates one of the oldest Iranian architectural accomplishments: the palace and the ziggurat of Choga-Zanbil. It rises up like a mountain and once formed a pyramid of successive stages with outside staircases, at the top of which was a shrine dedicated to the god Inshushinak. A sacred enclosure served to lodge the priests and servants of the sanctuary. On the façades of the different stages, there were alternately projecting and receding members, a type of construction in sun-dried brick since the fourth millennium. Painted enamel tiles (green, white and blue) decorated the entrances to the ziggurat. In the palace, five crypts were found in which reclined a skeleton and the remains of incinerated bodies.

As to sculpture, we are familiar with remarkable statues and statuettes in bronze, gold and silver from the middle Elamite period. They represent kings and their wives in noble and dignified attitudes. In the tradition of animal motifs, there is a lion's head, almost in the form of a cube, decorating the end of a whetstone. There are also some rock sculptures in relief from the middle and late Elamite periods. The late period (10th and 9th centuries B.C.) saw a decline in the art of enameled tiles and the appearance of faience caskets sometimes adorned with human or animal figures. One of them, for example, is composed of two heads modeled in the round, as well as a griffin and a winged bull with a human head. Small cylindrical bronze vases, conical at the bottom, are also representative of the late Elamite period.

The Bronzes of Luristan

These bronzes, discovered in the mountains of Luristan, to the northwest of Elam, are still Elamite art. They represent, in fact, one of the most highly perfected techniques of the Elamites. The only scientific excavation that has brought some of these bronzes to light was done at Surkh Dum, and all the results have not yet been published. The objects dug up are of all kinds—hatchets, daggers, halberds, seals, rings, bracelets, horse bits, emblems, idols, quivers, receptacles, pins, belt buckles, etc., They are the work of the Elamites, the Kassites, Cimmerians and the people of the Zagros. This extremely original production covers a period going from the 15th to the 7th century B.C. It is becoming possible to establish a chronology—difficult to achieve amidst such a profusion of output—and it suffices to remember that those in the most independent style are from the latest period. It is believed that all these objects were cast by a lost wax process.

The beginning of the first millennium B.C. saw the blossoming of several civilizations, creators of finished and perfected works of art. They are worth noting, if only to date them correctly. They include gold cups from the northwest, discovered at Hassanlu in Azerbaijan and at Kalar-Dasht in Mazanderan; terra cottas and very modern animal forms, belonging to the Amlach civilization in Mazanderan and Gilan; pottery with spouts for pouring liquid, from Tepe Sialk; grey ceramics of the Manians, to whom we also owe a single silver goblet and wall tiles adorned with raised knobs; the treasure of Ziwiye with its ivory statuettes and a collection of miscellaneous objects of different origins. Animals and demons are the dominant motifs of the items in these magnificent collections.

Achaemenid Art

The art of the Medes is practically unknown, and what we do know of it shows it to be one of transition that had borrowed extensively from preceding civilizations. Scythian and Greek influences are also apparent. Several tombs, sculpted in rock, have half-columns reminiscent of Ionic columns. The tomb of Cyrus at Pasargadae, which takes on the form of a Greek or Urartu temple with a triangular façade, reveals Median architecture's intermediary position between the ancient traditions and Achaemenid art.

We come now to the masterpiece of Iran's ancient architecture: Persepolis. Nothing can better explain Achaemenid architectural art—that brilliant and grandiose synthesis of all that was being built throughout the civilized world of that time—than this inscription of Darius describing the construction of the palace at Susa: "The workers who cut the stone were Ionians and Sards, the goldsmiths who worked the gold were Medes and Egyptians, the men who manufactured the burnt brick were Babylonians, the men who decorated the walls were Medes and Egyptians." This was something absolutely exceptional and gave birth at Persepolis to buildings in a classic style. This gigantic architecture remained harmonious and uniform throughout, while the decoration in low and high relief was powerful in its overall conception and animated in its detail. Its realism was kept within the limits of the essential, but was sufficient to give an impression full of life. The sculpture remained subordinate to the architecture and perfectly fulfilled its decorative and functional role. The capitals of the columns, formed by the fronts of two kneeling bulls or griffins, are a perfect illustration of this. A space was provided between the heads of the animals in which the main beams were imbedded, while between the horns the secondary beams passed, perpendicular to the main ones. The perfection of this style can be better grasped if we compare it to that of Pasargadae of which there are only a few remains. The bas-reliefs of the palace of Cyrus are carved like two-dimensional silhouettes, recalling the Assyrian style where the details are simply cut into the surface.

We do not know of any Achaemenid statuary created separately from architecture, except for a series of small metal statuettes representing animals, generally lions or goats. They have a certain uniformity of style, a tendency towards abstraction and depersonalization of the model, which does not exclude diversity in the treatment of the same subject: either done in compact forms and clearly defined, in a circumscribed space, characteristic of Oriental art in general; or, on the contrary, in free forms, decorated with wings or other appurtenances. Unhappily for the traveler and for the Iranian museums, the most beautiful pieces of goldsmith's work are in Paris, New York or London, so that a visit by the art lover to the Louvre, Metropolitan or the British Museum is a valuable preamble to the discovery of Iranian treasures.

Parthian and Sassanid Art

In the artistic domain, there are only very few traces of Alexander's passage and the occupation of the Greek Seleucids. In any case, they are of only minimal interest to us. As to the Parthians, if their art is better known, it is above all thanks to the ruins of Ctesiphon and of Hatra in Iraq. In Iran, we only know the cities of Darabgird, Takht-i-Suleiman and Firuzabad. Although the latter was founded by Ardashir I (227–241), the first Sassanid sovereign, it still belongs to the Parthian period. Parthian architecture is characterized by the appearance of the iwan, a sort of square construction comprising a monumental portal covered by a high barrel-vault. The palace of Asura contained four, open on each of the sides of an interior courtyard. This plan constituted an important step in the evolution of Iranian architecture. It was found again later on, notably in the conception of the mosques. The façades are modeled on those of Roman monuments. They are made up of arches and niches, recessed between the rows of columns which give a rhythm to the surfaces, somewhat in the same way as the flutings on the wall slabs of Babylonian ziggurats.

Parthian sculpture shows the personages full face, standing firmly upright. The bronze prince of the Tehran museum is the most handsome example of this. In the domain of the minor arts, there are the curious receptacles whose handles represent gracefully shaped cats.

If, by the size of its palaces, Sassanid architecture perpetuated the taste for the gigantism of the Achaemenids, it reveals its Parthian and thus Greco-Roman origins. The iwan is still used, but, with the multiple annexes attached to it, it is no more than an entrance hall; as to the façades, they still have a succession of recesses, of semi-circular arches, of half-pillars and half-columns. And this without concern for organization, equilibrium and overall harmony that was of prime importance to the Greeks and Romans. It seems rather that the Sassanid architects were only concerned with a practical system of exterior decoration. The elements that compose and adorn the walls can be repeated and extended indefinitely, thus making it possible to increase the size of the constructions at will. This orna-mentation does not yet appear at Firuzabad, in the massive palace of Ardashir I, but it is found in that of Ctesiphon of which there remains, alas, only one side of a façade, due to the earthquake of 1880.

The palace at Bishahpur is interesting because it acquaints us with the lay-out of the interior decoration of royal Sassanid residences. The throne room was in the form of a cross and surmounted by a cupola. It has 64 recesses whose stucco frames were decorated with acanthus and palm leaves all painted red, yellow and black. A Hellen-istic influence is clear; the same is true for the mosaic found in a courtyard. Fragments of column capitals in the form of bulls were discovered and attest to the presence of Achaemenid architecture as well.

In addition to the fire temples, mention should be made of sacred towers encircled by a corridor or platforms and capped with a cupola resting on four arches supported by pillars. But the remains of these sanctuaries have been found only in Mesopotamia. As to rock carvings in relief, they continued to evoke with gripping realism the glory of the sovereigns and hunting scenes or equestrian battles. The refined and dynamic art of the sculptors of animals expressed its mastery here.

This skill and competence in describing epic combats between man and beast were called into play at the Sassanid court on gold and silver plate whose sumptuousness was proverbial. Most of it has gone to the United States or the Soviet Union, but the museum at Tehran possesses some beautiful reproductions. One of the most remarkable pieces shows King Peroz on horseback, chasing two rams, while two others have already been overrun. In this composition, the sovereign and the hunted beasts stand out in gold against a silver background and are inscribed in an unusual way on the inside of the cup following its curves perfectly. The goldsmith was able to strike a perfect tonal balance between the two metals, setting them off by the inlaid enamel work of certain details, such as the horns of the rams, the bow or the decorations of the quiver. In the fourth and fifth centuries A.D., the goldsmith's trade seems to have acquired an increasingly pictorial character.

Among the most typical examples of Sassanid art are the molded and sculpted stucco slabs that were used to cover over the masonry. In general, they represent abstract or symbolic motifs, rosettes or emblems, sometimes accompanied by inscriptions.

Islamic Art

With Islam, the entire world of fantastic animals created by the Iranian sculptors, goldsmiths and silversmiths gave way to a more abstract inspiration, while their techniques spread as far as the limits of the Arab world. The conquest of the Caliphs put Persian art in suspended animation for some time. Artistic activity sank into a half-sleep, from which it awoke several centuries later to give birth to a new estheticism, in conformance with the Moslem canons that architects and artists had assimilated in the meantime. It should not be forgotten that religion dictated its laws or rather its taboos in artistic matters. The Koran is categorical: all representation of human beings and animals is forbidden.

Shi'ism permitted the Iranians to get around this rule, but they did not produce anything of esthetic value. Like all the other Moslems, they invented an abstract art, made up of ornamental foliage, rosettes and interlaced designs from which the plant element disappeared little by little, becoming stylized in the extreme.

It is in the mosques that we find the clue to a better understanding of the development of this art. There we may follow the evolution of their decoration of faience, in the form of tiles or mosaics. This system of wall facing comes from a very old tradition in Iran since it was a Mesopotamian architect who had the idea, even then, of enameling the exterior bricks so that they might resist even the worst weather and last through the centuries. Remember the frieze of the "Immortals" discovered at the palace of Susa, in which there already existed the blue so beloved of the Seljuks and Safavids. It was the Mongols who reinvented this technique. The tomb of Hulagu Khan's mother (1260) at Maragheh, and that of Oljaitu (1316) at Soltanieh, are the oldest known monuments to be decorated with enameled terra cotta tiles.

Starting in the 10th century, Kashan also was famous for its bluish faience, and eventually its name was attached to the painted tiles adorned with garlands, foliage and flowers (*kachis*). Blue and yellow to start with, they ended, after many variations, as the peonies and tulips of the Qajar monuments. It may be that, among numerous other constituents, the Friday Mosque at Isfahan contains some fragments of mosaics of Seljukid faience, dating from the beginning of the 10th century. However, this ceramic work, with its angular designs, did not influence the Persians who tended rather towards rounded forms. The Blue Mosque at Tabriz, built in the reign of Shah Jahan (1465), shows a more characteristic aspect of the utilization of faience mosaic. It stands out against its base of bare brick, forming large lozenges of color against the ocher of the brickwork. This new technique was from then on to be an essential feature of all Iranian monuments. The artists covered the mosques with faience mosaics, whose arabesques and varied geometrical forms follow the curves of the cupolas and cast a multi-colored mantle over the domes of Isfahan.

Safavid Art

If Persepolis is specifically Achaemenid, Isfahan is Safavid, and it is there better than anywhere else that we can study and admire Iranian art of the 16th and 17th centuries. In architecture, a new idea, urbanism, arose, although the term did not exist at that time. A quick glance at the Royal Square gives evidence of this preoccupation. This vast quadrilateral, some 500 m (1,640 feet) long by 75 m (246 feet) wide, was situated in the heart of the city, where commercial life was at its height and where the people indulged in merrymaking on festival days. The most beautiful monuments of Isfahan encircle it: the Mosque of the King, the Mosque of Shaikh Lutfullah, the Royal Palace, and the Imperial bazaar. The Mosque of Shaikh Lutfullah, a low building with an earthen cupola encircled with volutes, forms a contrast with the immense and majestic Mosque of the King, whose entrance is flanked by two minarets. Its dome is also larger, its form more ample, and it seems to float above the horizon of arcades that surround the square.

Contrary to the Turkish mosque, especially Ottoman, whose architecture concentrates on its exterior aspect, the Iranian mosque is turned inwards. It is composed essentially of three iwans surrounding a closed courtyard, the fourth side being constituted by a main building where the entrance is found. This is a basic plan, already fairly advanced, sometimes completed by different annexes, madares (religious schools), lodgings, vestibules, etc.

The interior of the cupolas, the arches, and the vaults which cap the iwans, are decorated with ceramic stalactites. Moreover, all the surfaces, walls and framework, domes and minarets, are covered with faience tiles or mosaic. Not all of them have simple abstract or floral decorations, but some moldings are adorned with inscriptions (white on a dark blue background) quoting verses of the Koran or the name of the prophets.

Non-religious buildings do not have the same architectural unity. There are reminiscences, sometimes very remote but irrefutable, of the ancient Parthian iwan to which have been added pillared rooms, verandas, galleries, in a word all that could embellish and adorn a royal dwelling.

Despite the Koran's prohibition against making human or animal figures, some exceptions are found, even among the most orthodox, for example the portraits of the Ottoman sultans Mehmet II and Suleiman. The Persian painters did transgress the law, especially when they became influenced by the Italians in the 17th century. A series of frescos hidden under a thick coating of paint has been brought to light in the Chihil Sutun pavilion at Isfahan. There are two types, both executed between the 17th and end of the 18th centuries. Some of them, of large dimensions, picture important historical events, while the others, smaller, depict love scenes in artificial landscapes, which recall the miniatures, that refined and mannered art so characteristic of the resplendent Persian Renaissance. Particularly successful miniatures, executed in the styles of the 16th and 17th centuries, can be seen at the handicrafts museum in Tehran, and all the meticulousness and the detail work can be savored thanks to the existence of several rough sketches in which the preparatory work appears. This was not the debut of Iranian painting. The Persian painters, who lived in the 15th century in the court of the Shaibanids at Herat (Afghanistan), were already talented artists, more influenced by the Chinese than by the West.

The eras following the Persian Renaissance of the Safavids brought nothing better and could not produce any artistic renaissance worthy of interest. On the contrary, with the penetration of European ideas, and the disorder reigning in the central government of the country, a rapid decadence began from which contemporary Iranian artists have had a great deal of trouble in extricating themselves.

Persian Handicraft

On the other hand, the popular genius is not dead, and Foundations have created training centers to safeguard the traditions of the Iranian. The abundance, variety and quality of objects produced by craftsmen are immediately evident when you visit Iran. There is still no segregation between curios for tourists and articles destined for local consumption, even in the most inexpensive category. Poor relations of the luxury industries, small handicrafts, limited to the production of everyday articles, are still lively and active. At Isfahan, the "Qalam Kar" is once again in vogue. It consists of gaily-colored cotton fabric handprinted with wooden blocks to depict animals, trees or abstract figures, often in the form of a frieze.

Traditional transport and traditional dress.
Two country scenes

A 19th-century palace nestles in the luxuriant
gardens of Bagh-e Eram, Shiraz

Also a spectacle from another age are the streets where copper is worked, the artisan seated on the ground near a fire of glowing embers kept alight by a child. Held on its wooden forming-block with the help of the artisan's big toe, the metal takes its form to the rhythm of the mallet's beat, while on the door-step an assistant meticulously puts the finishing touches on a bowl, scalloping the edges with a chisel, or, with a nail, piercing holes in a basin. Already a good number of these rustic forms are to be found in the shop windows of the antique dealers.

Other techniques demand a greater delicacy of touch. For example the khatam, a kind of inlay work made up of tiny spots of color, set in with great regularity and precision. It is used on box lids, different kinds of frames, table legs, panels of all sorts, repeating a star motif or tracing a sinuous design on a uniform background. Brilliant compositions which once mixed gold and silver with ivory and sumptuous oriental woods, today are made of brass, camel bone, dyed orange wood, teak and ebony. These materials are first filed down into slender rods of triangular cross-section and are highly polished. They are then assembled into thick bundles of about an inch in diameter, depending on the design desired. After this, they are glued and thoroughly bound together, and they form a cylinder on the cross-section of which is the star or rose motif which is to be indefinitely repeated. The artisan cuts off thin slices from the cylinder, glues them between two flat pieces of wood, fitting them together and filling in the spaces between with small triangular pieces. After drying, the pair of thin planks is split down the middle with a saw, half the thickness of the veneer adhering to each of the two parts. This forms a meticulous piece of inlay work which sets off the miniature that it is used to frame.

The Art of Rug-Making

A simple object for domestic use in the nomad's tent, a luxurious article when placed between the thousand cedar-wood columns of the palaces at Persepolis, the Persian rug has spanned the centuries, thanks to its utilitarian character and to the symbol of wealth attached to it. Decorative motifs were already firmly disengaged from figurative forms, the principles of abstraction established and, above all, the various techniques involved—dyeing, weaving and knotting—sufficiently developed for it to survive during the first period of Islamization. But, it has come down to us remodeled by the trends in Islamic culture that flourished in the 16th century under the stimulus of the Safavid kings. Shah Abbas the Great installed a carpet factory in Isfahan, where he engaged the best artists and weavers of the kingdom.

The Chinese influence, which refined the designs of that time, occurred there. This brought about a brief flowering that atrophied under the Afghan domination, only to surge up again later under the reign of the Qajars.

It is then that the reputation of the Persian rug spread in Europe and America, enriching the foreign merchants, who were in fact responsible for its decadence because of their hurry to satisfy the demands of a too-numerous clientèle. The governmental organizations founded by Reza Shah tried to restore the original quality to this craft if not a new creative impetus. It has become stabilized today in a judicious compromise between the ancient methods and a form of mechanization applied above all to the treatment of raw materials. Traditional dyeing processes are being used once again, such as natural coloring matter procured from madder root, nut rinds and the euphorbia plant.

Immediately after being washed, the wool is graded because it will be the primary determinant factor in the quality of the rug. Carded, spun and dyed, it is then placed on the loom of the weaver who will knot it on the vertical threads of the warp, inserting a horizontal woof of cotton between each row of knotted strands.

The artisan can proceed according to several different methods. Using a needle or a crochet-hook to close the knots or, alternately, using only his bare hands, he will allow one or two strands to become visible on the right side of the rug, the value of which will increase in proportion to the number of stitches to the square centimeter. Tightly knotted stitches will serve to ensure the delicacy and refinement. There is little inventiveness in recent creations, but that does not really much matter since the old designs suffice in themselves, with a wide choice of motifs already existing, so that there is an extraordinary number of possibilities in the different sets of combinations available.

The modern rug is priced according to its delicacy, the refinement of its design and its decorative value. Many criteria are to be considered where old rugs (from 30 to 100 years) are concerned. Period rugs (over 100 years old) are much sought after by collectors. First of all, the state of preservation must be taken into account, then the age of the rug, how interesting the composition is, the origin and, last, finesse. Only a specialist can appraise the balance of these different elements.

Persian rugs are designated by the place of their geographical origin. They are called for instance a Kerman, or a Shiraz, which does not mean that the rug was made in that city but that it was sold there. The affair becomes complicated where the factory borrows a pattern from the traditional repertoire of another province, for example, an Isfahan rug may have been woven at Meshed, and this sometimes causes a certain confusion. The method used in the fabrication of the rug affects its quality still more than does its origin. In the cities and towns, the rugs are knotted in private or royal mills. Vertical style weaving is used. The patterns are derived from those created under the Safavids and are more or less modified to conform to international taste. These factories produce very large rugs, which are perfect from the technical point of view. The worker sometimes uses a grid in order to follow his model. More often, the sketch's directions are dictated by a supervisor who goes over the pattern point by point. The smaller establishments work in a similar manner.

In the villages and tribes rug making is women's work. In principle, their output is designed to be used for domestic purposes, but for a long time now their sale has become an important source of income. The nomads use the horizontal method exclusively, as it is readily separated into pieces. The formats are necessarily smaller (3 to 6 feet on average). As to the motifs, they are extremely varied, and because they have escaped from fashion's influence, they have a freshness of inspiration that is extremely attractive. The quality depends on the wool and the dyeing methods used.

The dyes used today are generally fast. If there are any doubts, a moist rag rubbed on a corner will make the colors run. Some nomad rugs have bands of variegated hues, but this is not a defect. It is simply due to the fact that the wools come from different batches, or that migration from one place to another interrupted the work.

Here are the principal varieties you will hear mentioned. *Afshar*: a tribal rug, first-rate wool, medallions, roosters, stylized animals. *Bakhtiari*: very sturdy tribal rugs, trellis-work, small medallions in a check pattern, or a central medallion with triangular corner-pieces. *Baluchi*: fabricated in the Khorasan; extremely diverse designs and varying degrees of excellence. *Shiraz*: this market is supplied by the nomads who camp in the vicinity, Qashqais, Basiris, Arabs, etc.; naive personages, stylized and geometric figures in warm colors. *Hamadan*: this type is supplied by the factories of Malayer, Sanandaj (Senneh), Bijar and by Kurdish tribes and is very hard wearing. *Isfahan*: factories at Isfahan and at Yazd, medallions, triangular forms and flowers. *Kashan*: roses, vases and arabesques. *Kerman*: decoration consists of medallions and triangular forms; very well-balanced compositions. The Kerman-Laver is incomparable, of excellent quality. *Naïn*: famous for their delicacy and refinement. *Qom*: the best contemporary workshops; fields of stylized cypresses, vases, flowers crowned with birds; beautiful modern silk rugs. *Tabriz*: Turkish knotting, often described as the finest in the country, with medallion and triangular forms. Tabriz is also said to be renowned for its ability to copy designs from other areas.

Silver Work

Whether we arrive in Iran via Tabriz or via Kermanshah, the silver attracts our attention: the trays, the caskets, the forks and spoons, the cups and the goblets gleam in the shop windows. They are embossed or chased objects whose reliefs draw the light; delicate, sparkling, metal lace-work or motifs modeled in the round on a background of silver.

We must return to the faraway days of the Sassanid and Achaemenid sovereigns to see the art of the Persian gold- and silversmiths at its peak of perfection. They had acquired such mastery that embossing and chasing was an everyday art. Most of the lovely Sassanid bas-reliefs seem to be the work of engravers.

The alloy used today contains 85% silver and 15% copper, a standard approved by the museum-workshop of the Beaux-Arts at Tehran. The ornamentation draws its inspiration, or takes its pattern, from a wide range of subjects for which several cities have become renowned: the birds of Shiraz; the strawberries and thistles of Tabriz; the flowers and cherries of Isfahan, generally stylized. The lids of the boxes are sometimes enameled, recalling the appearance of miniatures.

In Iran it is easy to find choice pieces whose workmanship is without parallel. It is remarkable that there are still masters capable of keeping to the high standards of past centuries and we can only hope that they will persist in maintaining this perfection.

IRANIAN FOOD AND DRINK

Rice, Yogurt and Caviar

by

ROBIN HOWE

(*The author, a noted expert on foods around the world, has written several definitive books on cuisine, including that of the Far East and an entire volume on soups alone.*)

In Tehran at first glance it does appear easier to find a glass of draft beer than one of Iranian wine, or a *Wiener schnitzel* than a *Fesanjan*, an Iranian dish of chicken in a walnut and pomegranate sauce. But a good second glance soon belies this false impression. Apart from the restaurants in which the local people take their meals, there are several international-style hotels and restaurants that specialize in national as well as international dishes.

Isfahan has every kind of Iranian restaurant, from the elegant serving traditional dishes to small hole-in-the-wall food bars offering snacks, i.e., two eggs on a plate, *do tokhme morgh nimrou*, or omelets, *kuku*, flavored with chopped herbs or eggplant. Incidentally this town is famous for *gaz*, better known to the West as nougat. Shiraz has a number of good restaurants, and it is here during the hot days of summer that those who know seek out the *palude* parlors, modest establishments dispensing a local specialty, palude, a thick cornstarch concoction like an ice-cream, flavored with rosewater and fresh lime juice.

Those traveling in the country will welcome the straight-forward kitchens of inns or motels, also the noisy, large restaurants catering to bus and coach passengers, as well as locals, who arrive in droves at all times demanding plates of *Istamboli polo* (rice and tomato), *tchelo-kebabs* (rice with kebabs), or *shashlik* (kebabs served without rice), or *luleh kebabs* (rice with meat balls). Any of these dishes will be served with a salad and a bottle of *abdug*, diluted yogurt, bottles of which are clustered on every restaurant table throughout the country.

Tchelo and Polo

Rice is the staple food of the people, whether rich or poor, in town or country. It is long grain rice which the Iranians cook superbly. Thus there are two important words a foreigner must learn, *tchelo* and *polo* (*polow*). Tchelo is rice that is cooked separately then topped with a sauce, *khoreshe*, when it becomes *tchelo-khoreshe*, or *tchelo-kebab* when served with kebabs. Polo means *pilau* or rice cooked with other ingredients. There is *polo sabzi*, a vegetable pilau; *polo noranj* or *polo chirin*, sweet-sour, saffron-colored and flavored with raisins, almond, orange etc.; *albalu polo*, also a sweet-sour pilau with mutton, black cherries and rice cooked in layers in a casserole. *Adas polo* is rice and lentils with meat, spices and raisins; *bagoli polo* is rice with beans, while *morgh polo* is a chicken pilau. There are many other polo dishes but these are the most usual.

No one can avoid tchelo dishes, in particular tchelo-kebabs served only at lunch time and with a certain ritual. The kebabs are either chicken or lamb broiled on a flat skewer over charcoal. The rice is piled in a heap on a platter, a well made in the center into which is stirred a large chunk of butter, one or two raw egg yolks, and mixed together. The kebabs are then added and sprinkled with *sumac*, a local reddish spice. Abdug is always served with this dish.

After tchelo-kebabs, the most important dish is tchelo-khoreshe, or rice with a thick ragout-like sauce made from meat, vegetables and fruit, often with nuts added, or combinations of all these ingredients. No matter how many dishes are served at lunch in the home, there will always be a tchelo-khoreshe. The bottom of the tchelo rice is deliberately allowed to burn and this is scraped off and served separately as a titbit.

There is plenty of good meat in Iran, mainly lamb but also goat and kid; every scrap of the animal is used, including the testicles, considered a delicacy. Much of the meat goes into the preparation of kebabs, large or small, or *köfte*, pounded meat which is made into meat balls like hamburgers or rolled round the skewers, looking like cigars, and broiled. But köfte can also be meat loaf, *köfte gusht*, or breaded meat patties, *kotlete* or *köfte kubideh*, or rich and highly spiced *köfte Tabrizi*, claimed the finest of the köfte breed. Small köfte are used to garnish soups, also sauces.

Next come stew-like dishes called collectively *abgusht* and made with lamb. The name means "water of the meat" giving a hint of the flexibility of this dish. If guests arrive unexpectedly, water is added to the pot which explains why anything from a thin soup (too many guests) to a thick stew is called abgusht.

Other dishes likely to be met are: mutton and eggplant stew (*khoreshe badinjan*); lamb and chick-pea stew (*yakh-nat humous*) and dozens of similar stews. Of the chicken dishes, one of the best is *jouje kebab*, broiled chicken previously rubbed in lemon juice and spiced. Chicken Kiev, *jouje kievsky*, crumbled butter-stuffed rolled chicken breasts, is superbly cooked, as is another dish taken from neighboring Russia, beef stroganoff, which is slivers of tender beef cooked in a sour cream.

Fish and Fish Eggs

In parts of the country, mainly along the Caspian Sea, fish is a staple food but on the whole the quality of fish is not too good. In the Caspian region cooked rice is called *kateh*.

The best caviar in the world comes from the Caspian, from the sturgeon caught under government license. Caviar is not cheap, even in the Caspian towns or in Tehran but it is possible to order a portion large enough to eat with a spoon, the correct way, plus a hint of squeezed lime. And do not be surprised if as you walk along the streets of the capital you hear a hoarse whisper in your ear, "phsst, fresh caviar?" For there is a flourishing black market since the sale of caviar is also government controlled. Incidentally, the sturgeon is a good eating fish, especially when broiled as steaks or kebabs on a spit.

The Iranian word for soup is *ash*, and for a cook *ash-paz*, thus indicating the important place of soup in the Iranian menu. Many are rich and complicated, but others are a simple chicken or mutton broth garnished with chopped vegetables or noodles, even a type of ravioli, and lightly flavored with lime juice. In Azerbaijan they serve borsht and cabbage soup and a curious but pleasant dried fruit soup, *gushe barrek*. Yogurt is the basis of several soups, a favorite is *ash mast,* iced and flavored with finely chopped mint and garnished with chopped cucumber and raisins.

Although the Iranians are meat eaters, they deal fondly with their vegetables, combining them with meat to make side-dishes or sauces and stews, or with yogurt to make interesting salads. There are some appetizing vegetable casserole dishes, alas seldom seen outside an Iranian home.

However, like their neighbors the Turks (from whom they borrowed the recipes) they stuff eggplants, cucumbers and peppers, also large apples and quinces, with a savory meat stuffing. Such dishes are all called *dolmeh.*

Bread is an important food and there are four main types, most of it is served hot: *nane lavashe,* baked in a pit oven, comes in large thin rounds, folded into a triangle like a napkin; *nane sanjak,* just as thin but baked on hot pebbles—and look out for the odd pebble which sometimes sticks to the bread; *nane barberi,* thicker and baked in long bat-like slabs, and finally *nane taftaan* which, when propped up to dry, looks like cane chair backs. In the larger cities French-type bread and rolls are also baked.

Local dairy products are good, the butter, milk and cream is rich. The yogurt is thick and sold by the bucket or in a large bowl. The uses of yogurt are many and varied. It is used in salads, in soups, and to make sauces, also to marinate meat. It is served as a snack between meals or to finish off a meal; it is eaten with compotes, preserves, honey and jams. Diluted with water or soda it makes the cooling summer drink, abdug, probably the national drink of Iran. It is made in the home and also sold on the street where the vendors parody Omar Khayyam as they cry: "A jug of abdug and thou."

There is not much variety in cheese and the most usual is a white goat cheese which is invariably served with onions and radishes at all meals. Street vendors sell a snack of bread and white cheese, *nane ve panir.* It is also served at breakfast with bread or grapes, or sprinkled with chopped mint or tarragon.

Sweets and Drinks

Soft drinks include many fruit and vegetable juices, squeezed by the street vendors as their customers wait. Carrot juice is sold throughout the year but there are other seasonal drinks, orange and lemon and pomegranate, the last a startling purple color. Its somewhat tart flavor is popular and it is also used to make sherbets, jellies and sauces. (There is a Caspian fish dish with a stuffing of nuts, prunes and raisins, and moistened with pomegranate juice, and a well-known soup *ash-anar,* with pomegranate juice and lentils.) There are sparkling mineral waters and local beer, also a sherbet of mixed fruit juices to which water and ice are added. This is thick and eaten with a hollowed-out carved spoon.

Fruit, which is good and varied, is served at all times of the day. Try some fruit with a cooling drink, or a glass of wine with a bowl of grapes or peeled and quartered apples. Iranian dates literally ooze juice when fresh, while nuts are sold by the bushel. No self-respecting Iranian would set out on a journey without a handful of nuts in his pocket.

One thing is certain, the sweet tooth must be an Iranian characteristic, otherwise how can one account for the prodigious number of cake and confectionery shops. Tehran has hundreds of such shops, with the sweetest, stickiest possible pastries, many of the baklava type or oozing cream. There is a fascinating array always of cookies, *nane shirin*, and one particularly fine shop specializes in big black cherries filled with vodka and dipped in chocolate. But other towns, large and small, are not far behind Tehran either in quantity or quality.

The three brands of Iranian bottled beer are *Medjidieh*, *Skol* and *Star*. They taste rather like lager and are always served ice cold.

Iranian wines are not the subject of ardent discussion, and although not consistent they are pleasant table wines. The best-known are *Pakdis*, white, red, rosé and a 16% alcoholic dessert wine, from Azerbaijan; and *Velvet*, a rosé fairly consistent in quality. Iranian vodka is good and mixes well with fresh lime juice. The local brandy is pleasant enough if drunk with soda or water and no illusions are harbored that it is a five-star (or even three) French brandy. There does not seem to be much of a market among the Iranians for their wines, so probably the good Omar Khayyam was singing to himself when he sang about that "jug of wine and thou". And why not?

THE FACE OF IRAN

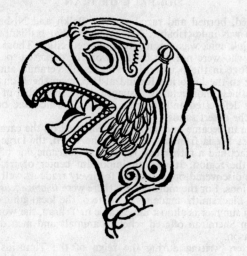

TEHRAN

The Capital and its Surroundings

Tehran, so young a capital for so ancient an empire! What was it during the fifth millennium when the artists of Tepe Sialk were creating their ceramics for posterity? What was it at the time that Darius was building Persepolis? Or more recently when Shah Abbas abandoned Kazvin to make his capital in Isfahan? The answer is perhaps found in the digs being made by Iranian archeologists who have uncovered at Tepe Gaytarieh in Shemiran a 3,000-year-old cemetery which seems to prove the existence of an Aryan or even pre-Aryan settlement on the same site. That is not all: pottery fragments discovered there would tend to prove—if their age is confirmed—the existence of a settlement contemporary with Susa.

A Bit of History

Around 1200, Genghis Khan emerged from Transoxiana and loosed his horsemen across northern Afghanistan and Iran. The devastation wrought by the Mongols was methodical. After the passage of his hordes, even the earth lay sterile. Entire cities were depopulated, burned and razed such as Balkh and Nishapur. The desolation was indescribable. Ray (Rhages) that brilliant landmark of the Seljuk epic, was among the martyred cities. Those of its inhabitants who were not put to the sword or deported to Mongolia sought refuge in the neighboring villages of Veramin and Tehran. According to the historian Rashid al-Din, even the Mongols, their bloodthirstiness momentarily assuaged, were incapable of restoring life to this deforested and ruined countryside which had been abandoned to the desert sands.

But Tehran became part of history. Situated on the caravan trails which cross Persia from the north to the south, the large village— which in fact had a rather bad reputation—became one of the most active in the region. It was an important center of traffic where merchants discovered opportunities for lively trade as well as plenty of distractions. For the more devout there were *imamzadehs* (pilgrimage sites). Blacksmiths made up the elite of the local guilds. Though the heat in summer is almost unbearable in Tehran, the wooded hills close by in Shemiran offered relief to animals and men during the hottest season.

Chroniclers writing during the reign of the Timurids and the Safavids rarely mentioned Tehran. Unnoticed, she played her role of large village, stopping place and bazaar. Shah Tahmasp I (1524–76) was the first Iranian sovereign to interest himself in the region, which was quite close to his capital Kazvin. Shah Tahmasp made frequent visits to Tehran, where he came to rest, hunt and pray. In order to assure his personal security, he had the settlement surrounded by a wall 5 km (3 miles) long with four gates: Tehran had become a city.

Modern Times

Shah Abbas, grandson of Tahmasp, moved his capital to Isfahan. Tehran was forgotten until the middle of the 18th century, when Karim Zand (1750–79) had a hunting lodge built there. But the Qajars were to decide the destiny of Tehran. In 1794 Aga Mohammed Shah attracted by its location, close to his tribal lands along the Caspian Sea, and to the northern frontiers constantly threatened by the Turkoman, made it his capital. This cruel eunuch had the skull of the last Zand placed under the sill of the fortress which he erected next to Karim's hunting lodge. Installed on his throne in 1796, Aga Mohammed was assassinated the following year. His nephew Fath Ali Shah (1797–1833) succeeded him. A poet and composer turned builder, he undertook to embellish the capital. The King's Mosque was built by him. In 1807 Tehran received the Gardane mission sent by Napoleon, an ambitious but fruitless anti-Russian project. The reign of Mohammed (1835–48) was too short and left few traces. This was not the case with Nasir-ud-Din Shah (1848–96) who ascended the throne at the age of 18. At the time the winter population of Tehran was about 100,000, two-thirds of whom spent the summer in the country to the north of the city. In 1861 the city had telegraphic communications with Turkey and Russia. A few years later the wall surrounding the city, already modified by Aga Mohammed, was again enlarged, and Tehran was beautified by the addition of the Sepahsalar Mosque and monumental portals decorated in faience. The last Qajars changed the appearance of the city very little.

Reza Khan Pahlavi (1926–41) endowed the capital with its present aspect. He cleaned up the hodge-podge of the old quarters, built large traffic arteries and razed the fortifications. Many public buildings were erected, if a bit hurriedly. They reflect a concern for building in the Persian or even Ancient Persian style. The Melli Bank and the Prefecture of Police are admirable examples of this. Today, now that international modern architecture has claimed its place along the avenues of the capital, these early monsters are looked upon with nostalgia: they are part of the urban scene and though no one would dare build them, no one wants to do without them.

In 1943, Tehran was the site of the first meeting between Stalin, Churchill and Roosevelt. Since the war the city has continued to spread out, engulfing the suburbs in a vast, Westernized conurbation, with skyscrapers, department stores, movie-houses, fashionable hotels and traffic jams. The Qajar monuments are lost in neighborhoods where you have to look hard to find a house over 50 years old, even though men have been living here for over 5,000 years.

Discovering Tehran

Tehran is a city which has a mean altitude of 3,750 feet above sea-level and is dominated by the snow-capped Elburz mountain chain. It has almost four million inhabitants and overlooks the desert. Is it the most sophisticated capital in the Middle East or is it still that enormous village of dried mud described by turn-of-the-century travelers? Seen through the shimmering summer dust, under pearly-grey or porcelain-blue skies, it takes on many guises and can fill you with amazement.

At first glance Tehran does not appear to be exotically Oriental and it must be remembered that the capital is a comparatively young, modern city. This impression is further enhanced by the sight of its traffic congested boulevards, its buildings with their pink ceramic or marble facings, its opulent window displays and its green parks. Tehran offers all the temptations of an up to date city and some of its

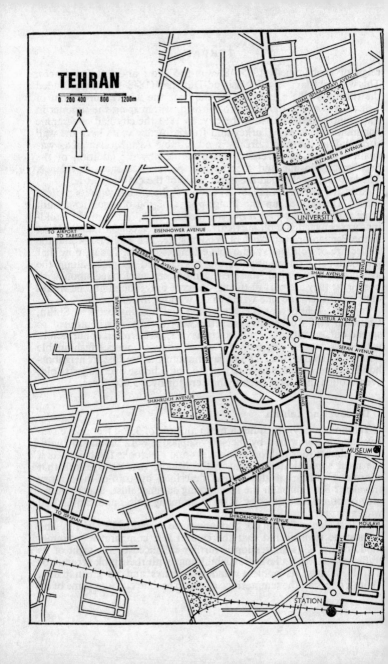

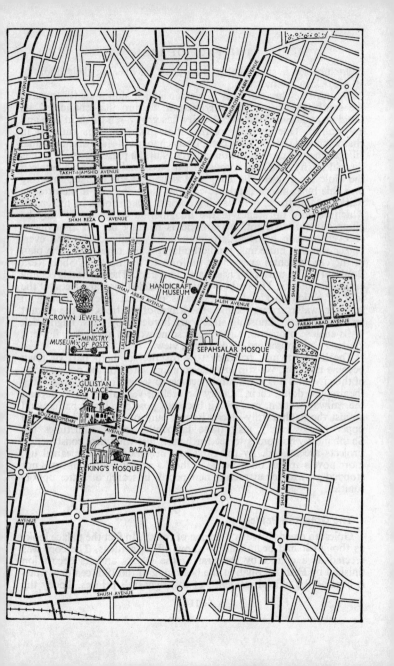

nightclubs go a step further than most by opening their doors at 10 o'clock in the morning.

Tehran stretches out over a plateau which slopes gently towards the south, this being the only natural feature that channeled its rapid growth. Since the war the city has grown ten times in size and importance. One quickly realizes that this growth is rational in character, and the Old King completely changed the face of the original village when he created the main arteries of the present city. Where is the old town? You may reconstruct it piecemeal in the area between the Golestan Palace, the King's Mosque and the Bazaar, inserting into this huge puzzle a faience-covered pavilion here, a picturesque market stand there, or by seeing colorful silken robes in the crowd which conjure up scenes in the imagination which could only be glimpsed in the Orient. All around is nothing but an anonymous checkerboard of boulevards punctuated by traffic circles and ever-bigger squares, museums, public buildings, and embassies. The plan of the city becomes even more uniform to the north of Shah Reza Boulevard. The university is situated in a park. The big hotels occupy entire city blocks. The main avenues are shaded by plane-trees, at the foot of which trickle *djoubs*, streams of water. Every morning in summer, watercarriers sprinkle the leaves of the trees. In the elegant residential areas almost all streets are bordered by trees. High brick walls enclose properties and, just as some women are veiled, flowers, gardens and houses are hidden from view.

The little streams, trickling towards the southern part of town become muddier, yet still provide running water for the poorer parts of the city, and it is not a rare spectacle to see entire families washing themselves, doing their laundry or peeling vegetables in it. Beyond the railway station, everything becomes possible. Little paths wind amidst the haphazardly placed houses built of corrugated iron. The upper classes rarely visit these labyrinths except sometimes the Shahbanou who comes to see for herself just what new construction projects are needed. By the time one neighborhood is cleaned up, more hovels appear on the edge of the desert, for Tehran has still not stopped growing or attracting new people in search of better opportunities.

The Golestan Palace

Golestan means literally "garden of roses". In fact the palace looks as though it had been built to show off its gardens. The core was erected as a citadel by the first of the Qajars and its decoration finished by Fath Ali Shah at the beginning of the 19th century, when it became the official residence of this dynasty's princes. Today the royal family uses it only on ceremonial occasions. It is here that the diplomatic corps expresses its good wishes to the sovereign on Norouz, the Iranian New Year's Day. On October 26th, 1967, the Shahanshah and the Shahbanou were crowned here in the Hall of Jewels, the most sumptuous of all the rooms in the palace.

The palace faces the citadel square, the *Maidan-e-Ark*. It is flanked by two huge pink and green square towers. Passing through the gardens reflected in ornamental pools, one reaches a hall completely covered with mirror mosaics; this is quite a shock. One either likes or dislikes gaudy Qajar and it is best to be forewarned that the best as well as the worst exist side by side behind these promising walls. The best is represented by the kachis, faience tiles which cover the landing and an adjoining hall. These are the work of a 19th century artist; all are different, and they represent the hunting themes so dear to the Persians.

On the walls of the vast throne room hang pictures by Iran's best-known painter, Kamal-Al-Molk, above the gifts offered to generations of sovereigns: Sèvres, Meissen, Chinese and Japanese porcelain vases, as well as two mechanical clocks which may once have struck the hour to the delight of the King of Kings. The present dynasty is repre-sented in portraits of the royal family on coronation day and by that of Reza Shah. In the place of honor stands the Sun Throne, a kind of monumental sofa which was ordered for Fath Ali Shah's coronation. Mounted on gold legs and decorated with flowering branches—emerald leaves, ruby and sapphire flowers, some 5,000 gems, it defies description. The top of the back is decorated with huge rubies and a diamond sun, formerly turned by a mechanism. Ceremonial seats for the Imperial family complete this holy of holies, which is strewn with silk carpets, and whose price in dollars the guide always quotes.

In the anteroom, show cases display collections, especially of foreign dinner sets. The most interesting is the display of ancient Persian lacquerware: pen-boxes and boxes decorated with flowers, figures and lively scenes. More rooms, more paintings and more crystal chandeliers. Only the most formal and least animated parts of the Golestan are open to the public. The library with its wealth of illuminated manuscripts, decorated with fabulously beautiful minia-tures, is not open to everyone. When leaving, let your eyes wander over the faience façades and don't miss the open-air Takht-e-Marmar (Marble Throne), decorated in the baroque iwan style.

The Ethnological Museum

To the right of the entrance to the Golestan Palace stands the Ethnological Museum, whose purpose is to recreate ancient Persia as it was prior to the upheaval wrought by Reza Shah and the two world wars. To regret the past is pointless but one cannot help being moved at the sight of so many objects relegated to showcases which less than 50 years ago were part of everyday life.

There is a collection of vehicles, or rather carrying chairs, each differing according to the rank of the person for whom it was designed. Fascinating for the uninitiated are the accessories used for the solemn processions on Ashura day during Muharram, the month of mourning; these include the banners of the different guilds, mirror lanterns, inscriptions, and catafalques in carved wood. There is something to please everyone in the vast array of household dishes, ancient tools, jewelry and amulets. However the outstanding display, on the lines of Madame Tussaud's wax museum, shows tableaux of village people and tribes of the 19th century in their costumes against a natural background. In spite of the changes in clothing and accessories one realizes how little the man in the street has altered. He drinks his tea and smokes his pipe with the same gestures; the public scribe still offers his services from his place next to the main Post Office; the barber shaves, the faithful prostrates himself, and the school boy rocks back and forth as he drones out his lesson.

The Bazaar and the King's Mosque

The Bazaar is the heart of every Oriental city. As you approach it, the crowds become denser. Your eye is first caught by an incredible jumble displayed along the avenues: junk, cotton goods and plastic ware. The human flow stagnates around these stands. You have to elbow your way with energy if you don't want to be stuck and prevented from reaching the main objective of any Occidental: the money-changers. Stocking up on the currencies of neighboring countries is perfectly legal here, so no need to lower your voice.

Exploring a bazaar defies description. You have to experience it, as you wander from noise to silence. Here the copper beaters ring out the tempo; there you find yourself in the hushed world of the textile merchants. A little further on, the odor of raw leather gives the noisy hubbub of the arcaded streets a new dimension. A minute ago you gazed on jewelry, now you see nothing but rugs. Every once in a while there is a respite: a patch of sky, a fountain, sometimes a few trees. Time seems endless.

The artisans of Tehran excel at making everything imaginable, especially suitcases out of empty and carefully flattened tin cans. From among this collection of masterpieces you can select a suitcase which will enable you to carry your belongings all over the world under the aegis of a brand of beer, peas or mineral water!

Don't miss the second-hand bazaar. According to the experienced, one can buy back at reasonable prices all the articles one has "lost" during the week: handbags, wallets, clothing, a variety of car accessories, etc.

In Tehran the bazaar is more than a commercial center. Public opinion is molded and developed all along its 10 km (6 miles) of covered streets. Trades are still organized into guilds which accept the authority of prominent persons, especially of religious leaders. A government cannot last, and a law has absolutely no chance of passing, unless it is approved in the bazaar. At least this was true until recently. Several mosques, the Masjid-i-Djomeh and especially the Masjid-i-Shah (King's Mosque) built during Fath Ali Shah's reign, situated in the heart of the quarter are tangible expressions of the spirit of the bazaar.

To reach the great courtyard, one must first go down a few steps which are lined with tinsmiths' stands. Is it your first Persian Mosque? Enameled faiences, iwans, stalactites, ablution basins . . . Crossing the courtyard, one feels the calm and serenity enclosed by the grilled arcades. The sight of the faithful busy with their ritual ablutions or lost in prayer gives profound meaning to the minarets, the golden bulb dome, and the kachis with their yellow backgrounds. Undoubtedly you will see more beautiful and older mosques but there is nothing more stimulating than seeing your first one.

While in the area, take a glance at the *Chamsol Emareh*, a large building dating from the Qajar epoch, with huge twin towers whose apertures are decorated with blue-green faience work.

The Parliament and the Sepahsalar Mosque

Baharestan Square, the political heart of the city, is reached via Sirous Avenue, always teeming with shoppers and sight-seers. The imprint of the Qajars is found in the dome of Masjid-i-Sepahsalar, in the façade of the Majles (Parliament), in the pavilion of the Handicraft Museum and in the old Senate building. In the middle of the little park a tall Reza Shah watches over the correct functioning of Iranian democracy.

The Masjid-i-Sepahsalar, which today is a Moslem theological school, dates from the last century. The library of this haven of peace shelters a magnificent collection of manuscripts. One is tempted to climb to the top of one of its eight minarets to enjoy the surrounding view. The guards' reticence may be overcome by a small gift. Though only built in 1878, the huge edifice is a fine example of the open-air mosque, relying for decoration mainly on the splendid tilework.

The Parliament is recognized by its Qajar style façade, anchored by two structures, something like towers, left over from the palace of an intimate of Nasir-ud-Din. Here, too, mirror-mosaics are the prevalent decoration. Visits only by special arrangement.

The Handicraft Museum (Museum of National Art)

The Fine Arts School faces the Parliament. Along with other university buildings, it is situated in the gardens of the palace of Nagarestan. Fath Ali Shah's architectural taste is emphasized by the one surviving pavilion, which has been taken over by the Persian Handicraft Museum. Before going in to admire the finished products, it is interesting to visit the adjoining workshops and watch the craftsmen at work. The kingdom's best craftsmen have been brought here, and they pass on their know-how to young people who wish to keep up the traditions.

The trades thus protected are those which modern industry threatens most: the creation of luxury items which no individual could afford if he had to pay the actual price for the time consumed in their making such as brocades woven with gold and silver threads. You can watch the work being done and you will recognize the Safavids' favorite motifs: birds and floral designs in exquisite hues. There is nothing extraordinary about this, for the original cartoons have been found and reconstituted. The study of these ancient models guides the tastes of the modern weavers. The court buys much of their production.

The same faithfulness to the past is true of miniaturists who work only in the styles of the 15th, 16th and 17th centuries. The concept and realization of these pictures follow extremely rigid rules and one marvels at the effects of transparence, the skin tones, and the rendering of fabrics and furs in each of these little masterpieces. There is much tradition too, in the work of enamelers and silversmiths.

On the other hand the faience workshop is the scene of a great variety of experiments. Clearly it is an attempt to get away from the kachi, the enamel tile the scope of which seems to be exhausted and surpassed by industrial techniques. Modern kilns and chemical enamels offer new inspiration. Who knows, tomorrow we may see a new blossoming?

For those who enjoy brain-teasers, there is the khatam workshop. The delicate intricacies of this miniaturization is a mystery to those who have never watched it in the making. You can also watch larger inlay-work being created for massive furniture of a more recent tradition. With a little bit of luck you may gain access to the rug workshop, where weaving is done to the curious singsong directives of the instructor.

Shahyad Tower

The Shahyad Tower (shah means king, yad remembrance) is a distinctively attractive, modern archway-type edifice located at the western entrance to the city. Designed by the Iranian architect Hossein Amanat in 1971, it draws its inspiration from the ancient Sassanid palace at Madaen. Inside and underground are located a museum, encompassing the broadest range of Persian art and artifacts (ideal for those visitors without the wherewithal to visit Tehran's specialized museums); and a fascinating arts center featuring a mobile multi-media show. The latter is created and coordinated by a Czechoslovak firm, pioneers in communicative art.

The Archeological Museum

The Archeological Museum is a large iwan in the neo-Sassanid style. Some may say that the contents are worth more than the container. Many Persian art treasures found their way into the Louvre and the British Museum upon discovery. However the past is rich enough to fill the Persian galleries also with a wealth of objects covering the centuries and dynasties which will fascinate any visitor. Everything is extremely well displayed and marked. The best thing is to decide what one wants to see, not get sidetracked, and take a cursory glance at the rest.

The principal examples of Iranian art from the beginning of time to the Sassanid period are displayed on the ground floor in chronological order. The most ancient articles date from the 5th millennium and consist of decorated pottery, a knife-handle in carved bone and various bronze and brass objects. After such a humble start one has the right to expect something better next. Unfortunately the years do not always save the most beautiful, but the most durable. The rows of arrow heads are not of enormous interest, but the seals and cylinder-seals show a continuity of inspiration. The most ancient date from 3500 B.C., the most recent are Sassanid. From Tepe Sialk, Hassanlu, Susa and Tepe Giyan come reconstituted fragments, along with beautiful specimens which escaped foreign museums and private collectors. There are arms, bone tools, jewelry, etc. which come from other sites.

Don't overlook the lion goblet in chiseled gold, and the gold dagger found in the tomb of Kalr-Dacht, along with a gold pectoral, griffin with lion claws and ivory plaques etc. which were discovered at Ziwiye.

Among all these proofs of a very ancient civilization, Luristan bronzes are objects well worth examining closely if only to compare the originals with the clever copies which antique dealers will surely show you. The most typical are pieces decorated with animal motifs, as well as pins, mirrors and belt plates.

The Achaemenids are already more familiar. They are remembered as the colorful enemies of the Greeks and greater attention is paid to them. Monumental sculpture makes its appearance, giving us a promising foretaste of the great sculptural ensembles of Persepolis: bas-reliefs, columns, stairs, and various architectural fragments. A few enamel panels from Susa are wrought in a technique which foreshadowed the exciting future development. There are the gold and silver plaques, with the royal message inscribed in old Persian, Akkadian and Elamite, which Darius I had inset in a stone matrix and buried in the foundations of Persepolis: "Here is the kingdom that is mine." As one contemplates this text, 25 centuries old, one is reminded of the film recounting the beginnings of the atomic era, which the Americans have deposited in a vault for future visitors in the millennia to come.

The few examples of statuary, created during the centuries of Parthian domination, show a marked Hellenistic influence. One almost has the impression that the head was created by Greeks quite independently of the rest of the figure, which is dressed in local costume. Though few in number, the Sassanid relics are rich in quality. The most remarkable are ceremonial silver and gold tableware, faithful copies of those in the Leningrad Museum. The originals were discovered in southern Russia. They probably landed there as the result of commercial exchanges and gift-making; possibly they were taken there by banished or fleeing artisans, or by members of religious sects which were persecuted at the time in Iran. Mention should be made of the Bishahpur mosaics, probably the work of Syrian or Roman artisans.

On the second floor we enter into the era of Islamic art. Here taste and techniques have been completely renewed. Faience bowls and porcelain vases inspire various interpretations. The most original are decorated with Kufic inscriptions in brown and red on an ocher background. Some seem inspired by Chinese celadon porcelain, or revert to Sassanid themes. There are several delicately made pieces of glass. Bronzes and brasses, enhanced with gold and silver, are mostly in the shape of perfume-burners and ewers. Illuminated copies of the Koran, rugs, precious fabrics and miniatures speak of the courts and ephemeral kingdoms of medieval Persia. Along with these luxurious articles there are a certain number of architectural fragments: alabaster flagstones, stucco or faience mihrabs, encrusted doors and lintels. A stylistic evolution is evident: from the elegance of its beginnings to the ornate Qajar period, through the glittering zenith of the Safavids. Don't leave this floor without admiring Shah Abbas' Ming porcelain. After receiving the splendid plate from the Emperor of China, the Iranian sovereign kept it at Ardabil, cradle of the Safavid dynasty.

The Crown Jewels

The Iranian crown jewels are not kept in some obscure medieval fortress, but in the ultra-modern basement of the Markazi Bank. This is not just by chance, for Iran's money is backed by these jewels. Their Imperial Majesties sometimes borrow this or that diadem or scepter for special ceremonies, but most of the time they content themselves with copies, which are lighter and less apt to tempt the would-be thief.

In our imagination, a treasure is a large coffer filled to overflowing with precious stones, pearl necklaces entangled with crowns, bracelets, ceremonial swords and tableware of precious metal. It is to capture something of this image that one descends as in a dream into the vaults of the Markazi Bank. Forgotten are the civilian guards, the security locks and the bullet-proof windows, as one succumbs to the magic spell. It is a veritable cavern, which brings to mind all the myths of the fabulous Orient. Riches, such as would make the peasants of fairy tales lose their heads, are all here, but untouchable.

Do you like turquoises? Here you can admire the most beautiful ones in the world, clear blue, without spots or marbling. They decorate ewers, goblets and a great number of pieces of personal jewelry, but there are still many which are unset, the precious raw material from which the court jeweler can draw when executing some imperial order. And yet these little opaque stones are the least valuable of all. Here there are garnets, rubies, topazes and emeralds, some in settings, others simply heaped in the show-cases in a profusion which takes one's breath away. Before these avalanches of diamonds, ladies hide their engagement rings, which seem ridiculous. For here is the *Darya-e-Noor*, the Sea of Light. It is an inch and a half long, one inch wide and three-eighths of an inch thick and weighs 182 carats. The value of this incredible gem has been reduced considerably by the name of Fath Ali Shah being carved on one side.

We have not yet mentioned the quartz, the beryl and the other coranda. There is a terrestial globe of pure gold weighing 75 pounds and thickly studded with over 51,000 precious gems. The total weight of these alone amounts to 18,200 carats. This fantastic work was finished in 1869, using emeralds for the seas and rubies for the continents, with diamonds reserved for Iran and the British empire.

Here, too, is the Peacock Throne, reputedly brought from Delhi by Nadir Shah, more likely a reproduction, in which the opulent taste of the Qajars has been given free rein, not least in the incredible number of stones used. The crowns of the Qajars and Pahlavis revert to Sassanian models, while the superb emeralds, diamonds, and pearls worn by the Shahbanou on state occasions were styled by Parisian jewelers.

Perhaps the most amazing of all the riches assembled here is the amount of work which went into the making of 66 tassels, each composed of some 3,000 fine pearls, no larger than a pinhead, which had to be pierced and strung one by one to serve as a fringe on a canopy.

The Streets of Tehran

With your eyes bedazzled by the sight of the fabulous treasure, it is time to take a look at the street, which has new revelations for you. Tehran is a stroller's paradise. There are many virtually unknown mosques which stand out among the brick façades only because of their faience porches.

Let us set off from Sepah Square at the edge of the former fortress-residence of the kings, the Ark. Nothing remains of this forbidden city except for the Golestan itself. An equestrian statue of Shah Reza stands in the center of this vast esplanade which is framed by the city hall, the Bazargani Bank and the Ministry of Posts and Telecommunications. Cupolas, galleries, neo-Safavid faience: the miscellany style of the 1930s.

Sepah Avenue itself has a few curiosities, for instance an ancient gate of the Qajar period, decorated with faience figures. It formerly led into a garden and it has kept the name of Dar-e-Bagh-e-Melli. From the gallery which encircles the upper part of it, the royal orchestra can serenade the crowd. There are other Qajar kachis at the Masjid-i-Madj several blocks farther on, but we will not describe them. It is up to you to discover, to compare, to distinguish originals from imitations.

Now we turn from faience to the shop windows. On Lalezar Avenue they remind us a little of the Markazi, full of jewels and antiques. Turquoise is much in evidence; it is a good chance to compare the nuances of these stones, to learn to appreciate their form, purity and polish. The stores which are not devoted to silver or to gems are crowded with antiques. You have to be very naive to expect to find anything more than a hundred years old for such articles are not authorized for export.

Carpets are another serious matter. They can be found mostly on

Firdowsi Avenue. The walk along this street is one of the most interesting in the city. The warm colors of the silk and wool lend a shimmering quality to the street; you are looking at the most beautiful carpets in the world.

Everything you can't find elsewhere is offered for sale on Shah Avenue: caviar, books, fabrics, vodka. The latter is sold by Armenians, and they may also proffer something which no good Moslem would ever dream of—sausages and pork chops.

Everywhere are the street noises, the strolling vendors, the little craftsmen which delight the visitor.

Parks and Gardens

If you have had your fill of archeological dust and you want to cool off, we suggest you take the air where the people of Tehran go.

There are over 19 parks and squares in Tehran where the crowds enjoy strolling. The Park-e-Shar, between Shahpur and Khayan Avenues, in the heart of the city, is the most visited. A lake, a pond and a hundred jets of water bring coolness to the torrid city. Refreshment stands and colorful lighting make it very popular with the public, while its nurseries and green-houses supply an attractive flower market.

Reza Shah's Marble Palace, a pink Italianate edifice with a striking coffee-colored dome, stands in a pretty garden on Pahlavi Avenue. Across Kakh Street is the interesting modern Senate building facing another park. Higher up on Pahlavi Avenue, gardens surround the City Theater. On upper Pahlavi Avenue are the Saadi Park and, near the Zoo, Park Shahanshahi. The largest is the Farah Park on Elizabeth II Boulevard.

The royal estate of Niavaran, at the end of Saltanabad Road in Shemiran, is open to the public. All over the city, walls are being removed so that views can be seen which were hidden before, as the Shah wishes all his subjects to enjoy the gardens and scenery.

Shemiran and Tajrish

Shemiran is really a privileged suburb of Tehran, echoing with running springs and rustling trees. Qajar pavilions and modern villas set the tone of this aristocratic neighborhood where the Hilton and Sheraton hotels are located. In short, should you be invited to Shemiran, accept, for the address is a good one.

Tajrish, capital of the "cool places", is 300 m (1,000 feet) higher than Tehran, and there is an appreciable difference in temperature. This is a summer residential area. Fath Ali Shah had a summer home at Niavaran, and the present royal family a home in Saadabad. The curious can see one or two imamzadehs and the ruins of a Qajar palace.

Tehran has found its ancestors here on the heights of Shemiran. So far mostly tombs have been unearthed. Earthen funeral ware, bronze jewelry and arms have made it possible to reconstruct the daily life of the capital's inhabitants during the first millennium B.C. It is interesting to go to the excavations which are being carried out on top of a small hill. The digs are surrounded by barbed wire, but an obliging guard allows the visitor to glance at the tombs by removing their nylon covers. The skeletons and pottery found in them have been left in place. You are also shown the most recent discoveries, fruit bowls, cosmetic pots and various utensils, most of which are without decoration or with only a few incisions. More cannot be expected of such an ancient site.

Be sure to look at the Elburz range of which there is a splendid view from here. On the other side of the road the Qeytarieh garden, surrounded by crumbling walls, is a shaded paradise: clumps of plane and locust trees provide a screen for the Qajar summer palace. The guard will allow you to stroll around for a bit. As you leave by the main entrance you will be confronted with a pile of fake ruins, topped by a turquoise cone. These are the Moulin Rouge studios where foreign films are dubbed.

Resorts near Tehran

North of Tehran, a little beyond Tajrish, Darband boasts a good hotel and agreeable shaded groves, which make it a popular picnic site at weekends. Ab-e-Ali is 60 km (37 miles) from the capital on the Mazanderan road. "Ali water", famous for years for its many qualities, is bottled for Tehran restaurants. Recently Ab-e-Ali's fame has been more for its snow than for its water, for it has become one of the most popular skiing resorts in Iran. During the winter, ski-lifts function without stopping. The king, who was at school in Switzerland, made this gift to prosperous Iranians.

The skiing season in Shemshak lasts until mid-April and is followed by the hiking season. At the end of May the mountain trails are edged with tulips and giant poppies. A new winter resort has been created at Dezin, near the village of Gadjéré, which some say will be the most modern skiing area in the world because of the large number of trails and ski-lifts.

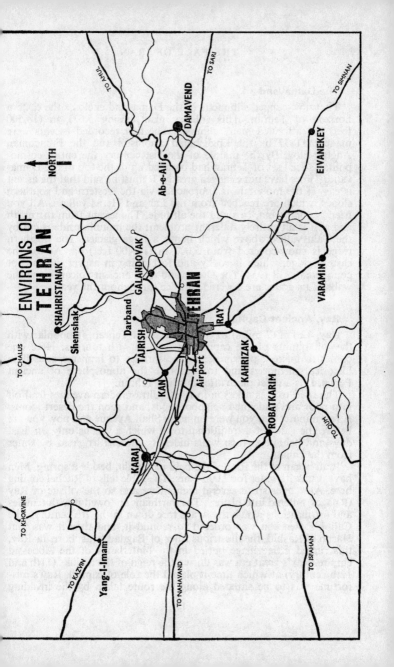

ENVIRONS OF
TEHRAN

NORTH

TO CHALUS

TO AHUL

DAMAVEND

TO SARI

TO SIMNAN

EIVANEKEY

Ab-e-Ali

SHAHRISTANAK

Shemshak

GALANDOVAK

Darband

TAJRISH

TEHRAN

RAY

VARAMIN

KAN

Airport

KAHRIZAK

TO KHORVINE

KARAJ

ROBATKARIM

TO QUM

TO KAZVIN

Yang-I-Imam

TO NAHAVAND

TO ISFAHAN

The Damavand

The snow-capped silhouette of the Damavand encloses the eastern horizon of Tehran. This solitary giant, rising 5,671 m (18,500 feet) has attracted many climbers. The first recorded ascents were made in 1837 by the Englishman Thomson and the Frenchman Aucher-Eloy. By the middle of the last century the entire cosmopolitan social set of Tehran had paraded up to the top of the Damavand. Times have not changed greatly. It must be said that the ascent is easy if the mountain is approached via the western and southern slopes, which are reached from the Lar and Heras valleys. All you need is good wind, to stand the altitude. The ascent from the north and east is an entirely different problem: the mountainside is cut by the Talu valley, above which hangs a large glacier. The northern ridge is snow-covered from 5,000 m (16,400 feet) on. As for the eastern ridge, which is rocky and forbidding in aspect, it was not conquered until 1954. The Damavand is an ancient volcano, and the walls of its crater are covered with ice throughout the year.

Ray, Ancient Capital

Ray, 12 km (7 miles) to the southeast of Tehran, is popular with the inhabitants of the capital, as well as with tourists. Here one comes to make a pilgrimage to the springs, to immerse oneself in historical memories and to recapture the atmosphere of ancient Persia. It is a quiet place after bustling Tehran.

The road to it is a lesson in itself. Ultra-modern avenues lead off into poor and undefined neighborhoods, and soon the desert looms. A few minutes ago you were on noisy Shah Avenue and now you are before the gates of a traditional town which awakens only on feast days and behind earthen walls hides its gardens irrigated by water from the kanats.

It all began at the foot of the bald mountain, beside a spring. Men have drunk its water for 7,000 years. The Bible tells of Rachel coming here. Alexander spent several nights here and so the village of Ray (Rhages) entered into history. The Parthians endowed it with temples and fortifications which the Arabs tore down in the 7th century. The Caliph's own son was ordered to rebuild it, and thus it was that Harun al-Rashid, the illustrious ruler of Bagdad, was born in Ray, this ruined little village buried in the hinterlands of the Abbassid empire. Ray's great era was during the reign of the Seljuks (11th and 12th century) at which time it played the role of capital. Ray's misfortune was to be situated along the route taken by the invading

Mongols, who sacked and razed the town in 1220. Attempts by Mongol rulers to restore it were unsuccessful; the city was doomed.

The triumphal avenue leads to the mausoleum of Shah Reza, founder of the dynasty. It is a modern marble and alabaster building and includes a small museum in which souvenirs of this energetic monarch are displayed. The Old King, who died in exile, wished to be buried here, and his ashes were transferred with great pomp on May 7th, 1950.

One should go on foot into the bazaar which begins to the left of the tomb. Crowds of pilgrims direct their steps toward the sanctuary of Shah 'Abdul 'Azim. The Shi'ites come here to pray over the tomb of Hussein, son of the Imam Reza. Though the cult is an ancient one the shrine dates only from the last century and it is best not to incur the mullahs' wrath by approaching too closely. On the other hand, the bazaar, whose alleys are a sort of labyrinth, is very exotic. An asphalt road encircles this picturesque section and after going around a traffic circle rejoins the road back to Tehran.

To the right, a few hundred yards away, rises a 12th century funerary tower, the only monument which survived the Mongols' fury. The Persians call it the *Nagareh Khaneh*, House of the Drum, probably because of its cylindrical form surrounded by buttresses. Not far from here the celebrated Chechmeh Ali spring is an attractive place. Its water is so clear and contains so few minerals that it is perfect for washing rugs. In the spring people in Tehran send their carpets to Ray. Persian rugs are washed once a year with water and soap, and are spread out to dry on the flat rocks in springtime, thus covering the mountainside with a multicolored cape. It is possibly because Nasir-ud-Din was so delighted by this sight that he wished to perpetuate his memory here with a bas-relief which shows him seated on his throne and surrounded by courtiers. In a recess, we again see this monarch holding a falcon on his wrist. At the top of a hill, a second bas-relief depicts another Qajar monarch fighting a lion.

This is Ray, a dead city. A practiced eye could probably distinguish mounds and embankments, the sole remnants of temples and fortifications. There is probably a lovely legend to tell about Bibi Shahr-i-Banu, daughter of the last Sassanid ruler, whose remains rest in a small mausoleum at the foot of the mountain. And on the other side of the ridge rises one of the Towers of Silence in which the Gabars exposed their dead.

Varamin

Varamin is another ancient capital. A large village, 30 km (18 miles) beyond Ray, it is distinguished by the cone of its tower, dating from the Mongol epoch. After the destruction of Ray in 1220, the town became one of the most prosperous of the province and for a time became its capital. Towards the end of the 14th century the town was gradually overshadowed by Tehran, then beginning to grow. Farming petered out. The village was depopulated. Earthquakes quickened the destruction of abandoned buildings and monuments. Such was the fate of the Friday Mosque (Masjid-i-Jami) built in 1326, partly restored a 100 years or so later. An exploration of the ruins reveals a few mosaics in enameled faience on the north portal and cut-brick decoration on the arcades. The prayer hall is in slightly better repair. An iwan decorated with stalactites leads to the mihrab, which is surrounded by a large stucco frieze. The whole is topped by a cupola decorated with calligraphic and floral motifs in enameled mosaic, alternating with the raw brick. The traveler departs lulled by dreams of Central Asia, which are confirmed by the Mongol tower he sees a little farther on. This is a 13th-century mausoleum decorated with faiences. What else is there to see in Varamin? A few imamzadehs, such as Abdullah's with its pear-shaped cupola and the Mongol funerary tower of Qechlaq—3 km (a mile or so) from the town over bad roads—which rises next to a curious little walled cemetery.

Practical Information for Tehran and Vicinity

WHEN TO GO. April to September. Preferably the autumn, which is warm and sunny. The effects of the altitude (1,100 m—3,600 feet) are felt in winter, as the temperature sometimes drops to −16° C (3° F) and streets are buried under the snow. July and August are often hot and dusty, so that air-conditioning is essential.

HOW TO GET THERE. More than 20 *airlines* connect Tehran with the capitals of the world. Planes land at the international airport at Mehrabad, 17 km (10 miles) west of the city. For a few rials a bus will take you into town; a taxi will cost you at least 100 Rs. *By road:* if you are coming from Iraq and Turkey the toll-way from Karaj leads close to the Shahyad monument, whence Eisenhower and Shaha Reza Aves. continue to the center of the city. An inter-city bus terminal capable of handling 750 buses and 18,000 passengers daily is scheduled to open adjacent to the Farahabad Park in the southern part of the city; not far from the *railway* station at the end of Pahlavi Ave. Trains and buses connect the capital with the country's other cities. See the section on general practical information, *Travel in Iran*, in the front of this book.

TEHRAN

WHAT TO SEE. Tehran is a modern city and has few ancient monuments. Most of the Qajar monuments were torn down at the time of Reza Khan's building program. But there is an extremely interesting modern monument, the distinctive Shahyad Tower, located at the western entrance to the city, housing a museum and a very worthwhile arts center. There are a few remarkable museums which contain pieces assembled from all over the country. The Archeological Museum (Iran Bastan), situated on Sepah Ave., traces an artistic evolution spanning a period of 6,000 years. The Museum of National Arts (Honarhaye Melli), on Kamal-ol-Molk, is more of a repository of arts and crafts. The collection of the Crown Jewels in the Central Bank (Markazi Bank) on Firdowsi Ave. is very impressive. The Golestan Palace, Maidan-e-Ark, residence of the Qajar dynasty, is still used for official functions. The Marble Palace of Reza Shah, Kakh St., is now open as the Pahlavi Museum. A look at the Bazaar, the Sabzeh Maidan, the King's Mosque and the Sepahsalar Mosque is a must for those unable to visit the rest of the country. The *Honarhaye Tazyini* (Museum of Decorative Arts), 227 Amir Kabir Ave. and the *Mardom Shenasi Museum* (Ethnological) on Bou Ali St. are only of secondary interest. The little city of Ray, 12 km (7 miles) from Tehran, has a picturesque bazaar, mausoleums and the spring of Chechmeh Ali.

HOTELS. There are about 100 hotels in Tehran, 3 of which are luxury class members of well-known American chains, offering the expected comforts (air-conditioning, pool, etc.).

Deluxe

Arya Sheraton, enlarged in 1975 to 500 rooms, and the equally large **Royal Hilton**, well-situated next to each other on Pahlavi Ave., near the autoroute which connects this area with the Exposition Park and the airport.

Intercontinental, located in the Park Farah, a few minutes from the city center. 416 rooms and expanding. From its award-winning *Rôtisserie Française* restaurant on the 13th floor there is a splendid view of the Elburz mountains (as well as an open charcoal fire).

First Class

In four-star hotels, air-conditioning and TV are general, but not pools; though otherwise comfort and prices in the large, modern buildings are fairly even.

Marmar, Fisherabad Ave.; *Commodore*, *Imperial* and *Sina*, only the last with a pool, are central on Takht-e-Jamshid Ave. The 150-room *Evin*, with pool, on the parkway, deserves our extra star equaling the officially deluxe *Park*, Hafez Ave., Tehran's oldest hotel; and *Tehran*

International, pool, somewhat out-of-the-way in Kourosh-e-Kabir Ave. but offering guests reduced rates at the popular Ice Palace recreation center; a favorite with airline crews; Hyatt managed; opposite the *Darband*, pool, *Kings*, Khosrow Khavar St. off Pahlavi Ave.; *Versailles* and *Victoria* on it; the latter has family service facilities for parents traveling with children.

New Naderi, Naderi St. off Goharshad St.; *Roudaki*, Arfa St. we raise one star; *Semiramis*, Roosevelt Ave.; *Tehran Palace*, Shah Reza Ave.;

Tehran Towers, Damghan St. off Villa Ave., open pool on third floor; disco; *Vanak*, Vanak Sq.

Ave.; *Maysun*, Fisherabad Ave.; *Nader Shah*, Shah Abbas Ave.; *Parisa*, Villa Ave.; *Pars*, Sepand St.; *Pasargad*, Jamshid Abad St.

Moderate

Accommodation is slightly simpler, though still mostly air-conditioned, in three-star hotels. *Atlantic*, *Caspian*, both small, Takht-e-Jamshid Ave.; *Bel Air*, Sepahbod Zahedih Ave.; only the *Continental*, Sepand St. and *Kian*, Zaetosh St. have pools; *Elizabeth*, very handy on Elizabeth II Blvd.; *Miami*, Pahlavi Ave.; *Naderi* (the old one), Naderi St.; *Napoleon*, Zahed St.

Inexpensive

In the two-star category, *America* and *Apadana*, Takht-e-Jamshid Ave.; *Armstrong* and *Asia*, Ekbatan Ave.; *Caravan*, Kooshk St.; *Diamond*, Shahrivar Sq.; *Excelsior*, 50 rooms, quite elegant; *Iran*, Ramatia, Pahlavi

Rock-bottom

In the category of very simple one-star hotels there are still rooms with showers: *Arya*, Kurosh Kabir Ave.; *Clarich*, Shah Abbas St.; *Crystal*, Lalezar Now; *Elroade*, Abbas Abad St.; *Empire*, Elizabeth Blvd.; *Lausanne*, Iranshahr Ave,; and without: *Ziba*, Sepah Ave.; *Khadem*, Naser Khosroes Ave.

There are a few pensions whose number and quality vary from year to year. *Kent*, Shah Reza and Firdowsi Sq.; *Sapin*, Villa Ave., 11 Koutche Fardis; *Suisse*, Forsat Ave.

Mountain hotels: these exist at Abe Ali, Dezin, Darband, and Shemshak, for skiers and mountain climbers.

 RESTAURANTS. There are innumerable restaurants in Tehran, their variety confirming the cosmopolitan character of the city. From the tiny stalls, where one can join the crowds in the bazaar to enjoy a kebab, to the luxurious dining rooms, where one eats caviar by the spoonful, the choice is very broad. Most of the restaurants, whose fame rests more on the social columns than on their gastronomic reputation, are located on Pahlavi Ave., going toward Shemiran.

The best known establishment in Tehran is the Russian restaurant, **Leon,** 306 Shah Reza Ave., near the Pan Am offices. The vodka and caviar served are authentic Iranian products and are excellent. Other specialties: blinis, borsht and Kiev dishes.

Also in the foreign category: **La Residence,** 118 Villa Ave., which attempts French cooking. Specialties: duck and smoked salmon.

The **Xanadu,** Mehbod St. (at the top of Baharmi Ave.), also offers French cooking and specializes in seafood.

The *Greek Restaurant*, Vozara Ave. corner of 11th St., features Greek and French cuisine to bouzouki music. The *Tehran Steak House* is on Pahlavi Ave. near the Saadi Park. The excellent *Gerbera* is at 295 Fisherabad Ave.

You can have onion soup at the *Pastis* on Pahlavi Ave.

Lovers of German food will appreciate the reasonable prices of the *German Hotel*, Arbab Jamshid Sq. and Kushk St.

Goulash and Viennese apfelstrudel are served at the *Paprika*, 99 Villa Ave.

Pizza—and its 16 variations—

at *Ray's Piccola Roma*, 212 Villa Ave.

The *Rasht 29*, 29 Rasht Ave., caters to artists.

Chicken roasted on a spit is the speciality of the *Hatam*, Pahlavi Ave.

The *Tashrifat*, Firdowsi Ave., which is open for lunch only, offers good simple cooking. The same is true for the *Chattanooga* on Pahlavi Ave.

Soft music and seafood at the *Tally-Ho*, Karimkhan Zand, at the beginning of Kheradmand Joonubi. *Chinois*, Pahlavi Ave. and Abdol St.

The *Ice Palace*, Pahlavi Ave., is unique. Besides an orchestra it provides two swimming pools (one covered), movies and skiing on artificial snow.

Iranian Cuisine

There are many typically Iranian restaurants. Tchelo-kebab can be eaten at the *Chayan*, 14 Ave. of the Bazaar, and by candlelight in a Spanish decor at the *Tehran Wine Cellar*, 109 Kaj Ave. The *Royal Tehran Tchelo-kebab* offers a typical Iranian setting and is located on Pahlavi Ave., at the beginning of Takht-e-Tavous. The *Firouz* is located on Manouchehri Ave. and the *Nayeb* on Pahlavi Ave.

If you prefer Indo-Pakistani food—more spiced—you will enjoy the hotel-restaurant *Angeles*, Naderi Ave. and Chahrouk St., or the *Atlantic Hotel*, Takht-e-Jamshid Ave., on the corner of Fisherabad.

The little Armenian stalls should not be overlooked. One of their sandwiches, accompanied by a glass of vodka, makes an agreeable meal. They are numerous and tempting.

Tearooms have become increasingly popular in the capital; they are elegant and expensive. The *Fiamma*, 339 Shah Reza Ave., is famed for its Italian coffee and its cakes. The *Hertha*, 164 Takht-e-Jamshid Ave., specializes in German pastries. There are many other cafés along North Pahlavi Ave.

NIGHTLIFE. Tehran's nightclubs are renowned throughout the Middle East, which doesn't mean that the visiting foreigner will find them to his taste. The most westernized of these are located in or around the large hotels: *Arya Sheraton, Intercontinental, Hilton* (Persian Room, dinner-dancing from 9 p.m. to 2 a.m.); *International* (tea dance on Fridays at 5 p.m.); *Park, Marmar Tavern*, etc. . . .

Le Château, on the Hilton autoroute, is a discothèque which provides an elegant atmosphere. The *Moulin Rouge* offers entertainment in the local style. Private boxes are available.

Tehran's best cabaret is the *Shoukoufeh Now*, Simetri Ave.; it has a first-class floor show. The *Cleopatra* presents a show at 11 p.m. The *Chattanooga*, Pahlavi Ave., and the intimate little cabaret of the *Hotel Darband*, where dancing goes on until dawn, should also be mentioned. Thursday nights are crowded. *Discothèque 007* is located in the hotel *Miami* on Pahlavi Ave.

Fashionable: The *Baccara*, Pahlavi Ave., in the Atlantic cinema building. The *Coffee Shop*, Naderi, Chaharrake Istanbul, offers dinner-dancing.

BARS. Between Shah Reza and Takht-e-Jamshid Aves. there are a dozen establishments of very special character where you can have a drink in the company of charming hostesses. A glass of iced tea sipped in such surroundings will cost you 200 Rs, which is not exactly a bargain.

There are also bars in the international clubs and large hotels. The bar in the *Hotel Marmar* is very fashionable (once a week, caviar is served on the house; the barman is a great character). Also fashionable are the *Xanadu* bar (beer on tap; attractive setting) and the *Tehran Club* bar (open fireplace). The airport bar offers an intimate atmosphere.

Added suggestions for touring grand-dukes: *Couchini*, Elizabeth Blvd.; *Miami*, 692 Pahlavi Ave.; *Rainbow*, Shah Reza Ave. and Forsat St. As a general rule, bars stay open very late.

 ENTERTAINMENT. There are lots of small theaters in Tehran where melodramas in the local style and even adaptations of French and English plays are presented. The Iranian *Petit* gives performances by amateur actors. The *Kasra Theater*, on Shah Reza Ave., puts on comedies. Foreign cultural centers produce plays regularly: for instance, Shakespeare is presented in the open-air theater of the British Embassy. There are movies every Saturday and conferences every Wednesday at the French Institute.

Concerts are performed in the *City Theater*, in Pahlavi Park on Pahlavi Ave. by the Symphony Orchestra of Tehran and by foreign groups during the season. Operas alternate with traditional musical and dance spectacles in Tehran's cultural center, the *Roudaki Hall* on Hafez Ave., which opened for the coronation. Foreign troupes also perform in this hall.

There are many movie houses, several of which present films in their original version: the *Astara*, Tajrish Sq.; the *Majestic*, Shah Ave.; the *Moulin Rouge*, Kurosh Kabir Ave. and the *Takht-e-Jamshid* on Takht-e-Jamshid Ave.

 MUSEUMS AND MOSQUES. The *Shahyad Museum* is open daily 9 to 12; 3 to 6. Cost: 30 Rs. The *Archeological Museum*, Sepah Ave. opens daily (except Monday) from 9 to 12 and from 3 to 6 in winter, 4 to 7 in summer. Friday mornings only. Entrance 20 Rs. The *Museum of National Arts*, Baharestan Sq. and Kamal-ol-Molk St., 8.30 to 12.30 and 3 to 6; closed Thursday afternoon and Friday. 5 Rs. The workshops are open in the morning only.

The *Crown Jewels*, in the basement of the Markazi Bank, Firdowsi Ave., are on display every afternoon (except Monday and Friday) from 3.30 to 6 winter, 4.30 to 7 summer. 100 Rs. The *Golestan Palace*, Maidan-e-Ark, is open every day (except Friday) from 9 to 12 and from 4 to 6. 30 Rs. The *Decorative Arts Museum* (*Honarhaye Tazyini*), Amir Kabir Ave., is open from 8 to 12 and from 4 to 7 except Tuesday and Friday afternoons.

The *Shahyad Monument*, Shahyad Sq., offers a panoramic view, museum and audo-visual hall with cineramic films of Iranian cultures. 9 to 12 and 3 to 6 in winter, 4 to 7 in summer; closed on Friday.

The *Sepahsalar Mosque*, Baharestan Sq., is open every day. The *King's Mosque*, Bouzarjomehri Ave., is open to the public every day except during religious festivals.

TEHRAN

 SHOPPING. The most beautiful handicrafts produced in the country are assembled in the capital, especially in government stores, which have their own workshops in the provinces. *Centre de l'Artisanat*, 381 Takht-e-Jamshid Ave. and *Markase Sanaye Dasti*, Shah Reza Ave. Articles sold here have a better finish and are much more elaborate—as well as more expensive than those found in the bazaars. These consist mostly of textiles—silk from Rasht and Yazd; scarves from Tabriz—embroidery and Baluchi woven goods and antique style glassware, etc.

Souvenir shops, such as the *Tehran Shop*, located on Takht-e-Jamshid Ave. across from the United States Embassy, will lure you with a whole gamut of brass articles, modern platters in every size, fretwork lamps, miniatures on enamel, papier-mâché articles, as well as ceramic tiles, and blue faiences from *Hamadan* and *Khatam*. You will be offered miniatures painted on ivory, on camel bone and even on plastic. The jeweler *Partieh*, right next door, sells very beautiful turquoise, as does *Atosa*, 2/132 Soraya Ave.

Recently a few *pousfines* (embroidered leather coats in the Afghan style) have made their appearance in shops. Iranian clothes and arts and crafts are available at *Bostou's*, Television Ave. in the Abbasabad section.

Look at the turquoise on sale in the *Turquoise Shop* on Lalezar Ave.

A variety of extraordinary carpets are to be found in Tehran. You can get an idea of prices by visiting the government shop, *Iran Carpet Company*, 160 Firdowsi Ave. In fact, the entire avenue is like a vast rug exhibition. A useful address: *Azizi's Persian House*, 114 Firdowsi Ave. One should bargain even (and especially) in the most exclusive shops, or risk paying higher prices than in Europe. For ordinary rugs go to the bazaar.

The Iranian antiquities market is very prosperous: you will find alongside the Luristan bronzes, which are expensive and rarely genuine, engraved Sassanid seals and more or less prehistoric potteries; you will be offered miniatures, papier-mâché objects (pen boxes decorated with roses), wooden doors and windows as well as Turkoman and Baluchi jewelry, arms, coins and manuscripts. The headquarters for antique dealers is on Firdowsi and Lalezar Aves. An address to remember: *Hadj Baba Rabbi*, Takht-e-Jamshid Ave, across from the *Sina* hotel.

Perse Express in the Namazi building on Saadi Ave., will handle your shipping problems very efficiently.

 MOTORING. The roads around Tehran are asphalted and well kept. Traffic is heavy and extremely disorganized in the Iranian capital. Taxis, which are very numerous, are the kings of the road and their casual driving style has spread like an epidemic. Don't expect direction signals. Cars stop suddenly, passengers get out of cars without looking, in short, everyone behaves as though he were alone in the world. At intersections it is usual to start up again the instant the red light blinks on in the other direction. As for cars damaged in accidents, it is customary to leave them in the middle of the street.

A few peculiarities: U-turns on main roads, which are quite customary, are hindered by movable barriers. During rush hours, portable traffic signs forbidding left turns appear at the principal intersections. Traffic on Kakh Ave., is one-way toward the center of town until noon and one-way out of town in the afternoon. Avoid taking it at the hour when the tide is turning. There are numerous traffic circles; the streets between main thoroughfares are almost all one-way (alternating directions). Motorcyclists show a marked preference for the sidewalk on which they drive in both directions.

A few addresses: *Automobile Club*, 37 Varzesh Ave. Car rentals without chauffeur: *Iran Taxi*, 267 Fisherabad Ave.; *Hertz*, 245 Shiraz Ave., *Avis*, same address. Garages and service-stations: *Peykan*, on the old Shemiran road, and 619 Amir Kabir Ave.; *Auto-Central*, Shah Ave. and Firouz St.; *Auto-Service*, Roosevelt Ave.

HOW TO GET AROUND. The main thoroughfares of the city are served by municipal **buses.** Tickets are sold at the kiosks near the stops; 2 Rs on the regular blue or red/yellow buses, 5 Rs on the green and mini buses.

Different types of **taxis** share the rest of the passenger load. Collective (*Keraye*) taxis, which are blue, follow fixed itineraries and take up to five passengers for 7 Rs each. Orange taxis, which theoretically take only one passenger at a time, charge 80 to 120 Rs for the trip to Shemiran or to the airport. In town they charge 30 to 40 Rs per ride. Luxury taxis, huge American cars, charge a minimum of 150 Rs. (Taxi-telephone: 72111 or 74211.)

The *Tourist Information Office*, 174 Elizabeth II Blvd., organizes half-day and full-day excursions in Tehran and vicinity for 250 Rs and 400 Rs respectively.

SPORTS. Pools: those of the principal hotels are open to non-guests of the hotel and an entrance fee is charged. The French Club on Fisherabad Ave. has excellent equipment. The Amjadieh Sports Center has an Olympic pool with diving boards. There is an indoor heated pool on top of the Vanak Hotel on Vanak Sq. (sauna, massages).

Tennis: at the Vanak and Hilton hotels; instructors available at the Amjadieh Sports Center.

Golf: the Club Sportif Imperial's (country club) 18-hole golf course located south of the Hilton on Pahlavi Ave.

Polo: the polo grounds are on the Karadj road; spectators are welcomed. **Racing:** at Park-e-Shahanshahi. Turkoman riders. **Horseback riding:** at the Club Sportif Imperial, Pahlavi Ave. The Club Hippique of Tehran, near the American Officers' Club (Darrous) and the Moghddam Club at Shemiran also take in temporary members.

Flying and Gliding: apply to the civil aviation club on Shah Ave. Instructors for beginners are available.

Water skiing: at the Karadj dam.

Zourkhane: for invitations to the Melli Bank's gymnasium, ask at the *Tourist Information Office* or go to the Zourkhane Jafari on Varzesh St.; every day except Friday between 6 and 7 a.m.

TEHRAN

Skiing: you can ski from January to mid-March in the Elburz mountain resorts, one hour's drive from Tehran (snow chains on cars are obligatory and their use is enforced by the police). *Abe Ali* (62 km, 38 miles, to the east) is equipped with a dozen T-bar lifts, one cable-car system and 6 trails. It is very crowded on Fridays. The *Noor* slope (71 km, 45 miles, from Tehran) on the Tehran–Amol road is equipped with ski-lifts and is recommended for seasoned skiers.

Shemshak: (59 km, 37 miles) at an altitude of 2,600 m (8,500 feet). Good hotel; 2 trails. A long chair-lift system and two T-bar lifts. *Gadjéré:* the new ski station of *Dizine* was opened near this village in 1969. A 17 km (10 miles) dirt road connects the village with Gachsar, which is reached by asphalt road from Tehran. A cable-car takes skiers up to an altitude of 3,200 m (10,500 feet), and a T-bar and a chair lift to over 3,500 m (11,500 feet). The trails are longer than those at Shemshak but are less difficult. There is a three-star hotel with heated pool. Though skis are cheap in Tehran, boots are very expensive.

Mountain Climbing and Hiking. The Kakh-e-Versesh (Mountain Climbing Federation), north of Park-e-Chahr, welcomes foreign climbers and gives them advice and information. It maintains refuge huts. *The ascent of Damavand* (5,671 m or 18,500 feet): via Tehran–Amol road to the village of Polour. Then by mule track (15 km, 9 miles) to the village of Reïneh. Federation hostel, mules and guides. Three days are necessary for making the classic ascent along the south face. *Ascent of Towchal* (3,975 m or 13,000 feet): the summit of the Towchal which rises above Tehran is reached either by the Jajeh Rud valley or the Shirpala cascade.

For the hiker: a series of narrow valleys at the foot of the Elburz mountains, north of Tehran. Superb walks and agreeable picnic sites. Take Pahlavi Ave. and continue north to the village of Evin and to the valley of the *Haft Hose* (Seven Lakes). Excursions to Pascale (departure behind the Darband Hotel) are also extremely popular; mules can be hired.

HUNTING AND FISHING. *Iran Safari*, P.O. Box 492, Tehran, has the exclusive right to organize big game hunting excursions in the area (ibex, moufflon, stag). Hunting licenses must be obtained from the Fish and Game Dept., 21 Shah Abbas Ave. There are many streams around Tehran which are well stocked with trout: the Jajeh Rud, the Karaj and the Lar. The dammed lakes of the Karaj and the Sefid Rud are also filled with fish. Observe regulations.

CAMPING. There are two camping grounds in the vicinity of Tehran. The first, the Gol-e-Sahra, about 10 km (6 miles) on the Saveh road, is quite well equipped; pool, shops and service-station. The second, for which there is a sign on the Karaj road 14 km (8 miles) before reaching the airport, offers only rudimentary comforts.

THE FACE OF IRAN

USEFUL ADDRESSES. Tourist information: 174 Elizabeth II Blvd., tel. 621291–8; branches at the railway station and airport. *Travel Agencies:* Arya Express, 232 Shiraz Ave.; Mondial Travel, 15 Villa Ave.; Near East Tours (correspondent of Wagons Lits/Cook), 130 Takht-e-Jamshid Ave.; Orient Tours, near the Armenian church, Villa Ave.; Pars Voyages (Intourist), Soraya Ave.

Bus Companies: till the opening of the inter-city terminal: Adel, Bab Homayoun Ave.; Levan Tour, Firdowsi Sq.; Mihan Tour, Firdowsi Ave.; T.B.T., Fisherabad Ave.; Iran Peyma, Amir Kabir Ave.

Airlines: Air France, 307 Shah Reza Ave.; Air India, Hafiz Ave.; Ariana-Lignes Afghanes, 34 Iranshahr Ave.; British Airways, 323 Shah Reza Ave.; Iran Air, 44 Villa Ave.; Pakistan International Airlines, 52 Villa Ave.; Sabena, 48 Villa Ave.; Swissair, 152 Shah Reza Ave.

Embassies: Afghanistan, Pahlavi Ave, 16 Ebne Sina St.; India, 166 Sabay-e Shomali St.; Iraq, Pahlavi Ave.; Pakistan, 199 Iranshahr Ave.; Turkey, 314 Firdowsi Ave.; U.K., 145 Firdowsi Ave.; U.S.A., 260 Takht-e-Jamshid Ave.; U.S.S.R., Churchill Ave.

International Clubs and Cultural Centers. Several foreign communities have established their own clubs with sports facilities in Tehran. Your hall porter or tourist agent will be able to supply the latest details about forthcoming events. Every Thursday, hotels are supplied with little booklets called "This Week in Tehran", in English, which they will give to you if you ask for them. They are full of useful information.

Main Post Office: Sepah Ave., next to the gate of Cannons. *International Telegram Office:* Naser Khosroe Ave. *Passport Office:* Aban-e-Shomali Ave.

Churches: Roman Catholic: "Consolata" Cathedral, France Ave; Anglican (Episcopalian): Saint Paul's Church, Roosevelt Ave.

Hospitals: Shahram Hospital, Arya Mehr Sq.; Melli Bank Hospital, Firdowsi Ave; Pahlavi Hospital, Eisenhower Ave.; Institut Pasteur (vaccinations), Pasteur Ave. *Pharmacies:* American Pharmacy, Pahlavi Sq., Takht Tavous Drug Store (open 24 hours), Tehran Ave.

Ladies' Hairdressers: Karl's, Kouche Goharchad (between Churchill Ave. and Naderi); Soheila, Roosevelt Ave., near the Diamond movie theater; Goli, Pahlavi Ave. (across from Borzomehr Ave.).

Useful telephone numbers: ambulance: 68304; first-aid: 21726; police: 02; Tehran Clinic: 311218; general information: 29029; telegraph: 03; taxis: 72111 and 74211.

KAZVIN AND REGION

Land of Assassins and Hidden Treasure

Kazvin (also Qazvin or Ghazvin), 125 km (77 miles) northwest of Tehran, is on the traveler's road whether going to Tabriz, Kermanshah or toward the Caspian Sea. Often one merely drives through on the inevitable Pahlavi Ave. bordered with uninteresting shops and punctuated by traffic circles. A closer glance reveals a garden full of beautiful trees and a two-storied arcaded pavilion, the Governor's offices.

Kazvin, in days of old a capital, is now a provincial city with 80,000 inhabitants. Originally called Shad Shahpur, it was probably founded by Shahpur I, the conqueror of Valerian. The sacrificial altar stood on the site where the mihrab of the Friday Mosque rises today. Nothing much remained of the place when the Abbassids left a garrison behind. Harun al-Rashid had the entire settlement surrounded by strong fortifications for this commercial crossroads became an important strategic position. The first centuries under Islam were calm and uneventful until the arrival of the Mongols. Like so many other towns, Kazvin was sacked. Then came the iron age of the invasions, followed by sporadic reconstruction.

At the beginning of the 16th century when the Safavid left his native Azerbaijan to unite the small kingdoms of Persia under his banner, he chose Kazvin as his capital, judging Tabriz to be much too close to the Ottoman domain. It was a wise decision. Three sovereigns had their court in Kazvin which they endowed royally. Later, when Nadir Shah, conqueror of the Afghans, was offered the throne by his soldiers, he assumed the crown in Kazvin before returning to Meshed, which reproached him for his Indian dreams.

But Kazvin was not born to a high destiny. Today she contents herself in her role as a commercial center and large agricultural market. Her winding streets have not suffered from urban development. One wonders at the treasures waiting to be discovered in those dusty neighborhoods far from prying eyes.

Discovering Kazvin

The Ark, the royal residence of the Safavids, has been dismantled, and today very little remains. Arriving from Tehran, a large park on the left, the Sabz-e-Maidan (Green Square) attracts the attention. In the middle rises an arcaded pavilion, reminiscent of the palaces of Shah Ismail, but restored in the taste of the day by a succession of the city's rulers. Today it is the regional museum.

Following a small street around the square, one reaches the Ali Qapu (High Gate), the official entrance to the castle which rises at the end of an alley bordered with plane trees. This is where the splendid royal processions took place on victory days: the young Abbas prancing on his horse, accompanied by the cup-bearers and dancing girls, followed by the soldiers brandishing their loot and the heads of the vanquished chiefs on the end of poles and dragging prisoners. The building has been disfigured by clumsy restoration. A pediment was added, and the stalactites which give Oriental architecture its special character have been removed. The Safavid calligraphy is intact.

At the end of Sepah Ave., a little to the right, is the Friday Mosque, whose antiquity has fascinated the archeologists. Though the building contains many beautiful things dating from different epochs, the most arresting feature is the mihrab built at the beginning of the 12th century by Khumartash, vassal of Malik Shah. The galleries, the iwans and the kachis in the Isfahan style were completed five centuries later by Shah Abbas II. Bands of writing in Kufic characters carved in the plaster are the showpiece of the sanctuary's main room. They are very simply decorated with stylized flowers.

A walk along the roofs of the Friday Mosque affords a general view of Kazvin.

Further to the south, past empty and sad neighborhoods, one reaches the Imamzadeh Hosein, located in the middle of a vast cemetery. The saintly patron, next to whom all of Kazvin wants to be buried, was but a babe, his only merit being that he was the son of Imam Reza. Two gleaming minarets flank the portal, and the mausoleum has a small cupola. Nothing remains of the Safavid

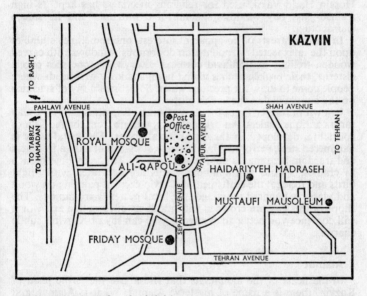

monument except for the inlaid cenotaph and a sculptured wooden door; everything else is enamel and mirror in the pure Qajar style.

The Haidarieh rises a few streets to the east of the Ali Qapu. The room of the mihrab, which is Seljuk (12th century) with a few Mongol touches, is reminiscent of the Friday Mosque. Beneath the cupola, lovely plaster sculptures frame Kufic writings originally painted in blue. The main buildings of the theological school are of the Qajar epoch, but dilapidation has fused these two unusual styles into a gracefully outdated whole. Still further to the east, on the edge of a deserted area, the eye is caught by a conical cupola of a vivid bright blue. It is the tomb of the sage Mostofi, who in the 14th century was renowned even in the West as the "Persian Geographer" and Minister of Sultan Oljaitu.

You will not be able to visit the old Persian houses with their crumbling paintings. None can say how long the *dervazes* will be preserved; these city gates have triple arcades and are flanked by slender minarets. In the southwestern part of town, there is an ancient hammam (public bathhouse) into which the light of day filters through transparent limestone. Across the street an old house, the Hosein Hadji Vakil, used for religious meetings, has kept its high stained-glass bay windows, its mirrored moldings and its stucco wainscoting.

In narrow streets of no apparent interest, one sometimes stumbles upon the unexpected: wrought-iron doorknobs, windows with carved wooden trellises and Safavid cornices. Everywhere one sees public cisterns, their broken arches giving upon shadowy well-heads where people come to draw the precious water. Sometimes a ray of sunshine on the cupola makes the kachis glitter.

Known in former times for its craftsmen, Kazvin is famous today for its antique dealers. An original style, remote from the faddism of court life, developed in these provincial shops. The metal-work is hammered steel, perforated by elaborate designs that have a freshness and freedom here that is not found elsewhere. Everyday objects such as cradles, spoons and spinning-wheels are decorated with bright birds and foliage; the craftsmen of Kazvin excel at painting on wood and glass. A hundred years ago, the local potters were famous. The shops of this city are crowded with products of forgotten arts which will convince you better than anything we can say of Kazvin's subtle charm.

Alamut

In the heart of the mountains that rise above the fertile plain of Kazvin, there is a name of mystery: Alamut. What is Alamut, and who are the Ismailians, known in the West since the time of the Crusades by the terrifying name, Assassins? The members of this cult inspire horror in us as we recall their exploits. It is easier to excuse Genghis Khan for his barbarism than to condone crime supposedly imbued with mystic virtues.

In fact, the only thing that is known with any certainty about them is that their society was powerful between the 10th and 13th centuries. A hierarchy in which rank depended on successive degrees of initiation was the framework of the social structure. The initiated gave their complete obedience to a freely elected master. The Ismailians, or the Sect of Seven, claimed to be an offshoot of Shi'ism, the Sect of

Twelve, but the metaphysical bases of their actions remain obscure.

Hassam Sabba, the contemporary and friend of Omar Khayyam, organized the Ismailians in Iran at the time of Malik Shah (11th century). He founded the citadel of Alamut as a place of meditation, educational center and military base. Marco Polo picked up quite a few tales about it. It is thought that inside the double-walled Oriental fortress, there were fragrant gardens in which adepts of the first degree were introduced to the joys of paradise. Among the intoxicating pleasures, hashish doubtless figured; Hashishans became assassins in the vocabulary of the Middle Age. In a state of drugged exaltation, the disciples of the "Old Man of the Mountain" went forth to murder without mercy as commanded—their victims usually princes or others in power.

The ruins of the citadel of Alamut, slight traces of the vast constructions of Hassan Sabba, stretch across 500 m (1,650 feet) of mountainside above the village of Kasr Khan, a huge rubble-heap in which almost nothing can be identified. From this height one can see to the east the forts of Ilan and Nevi Sarchah, which also belonged to the sect. Of all these eagles' nests, the most impressive is Maymoun Diz, above Chans Kilaya, an impregnable labyrinth dug into the rock, 600 m (1,950 feet) above the valley floor. If you go eastward, upstream along the Chahrud to a point 4 km (2½ miles) north of Charistan Bala, you will come to the fortress of Lamassar, which is both better preserved and of a more classical aspect.

In 1264, the Mongol Houlagou decided to get rid of these messengers of death, attacked the fortified points of the Valley of the Assassins, took them one by one, razed their defenses, and burned—unfortunately—all the precious books from which the Assassins drew their inspiration.

Khorvine

For many centuries the villagers of Khorvine (Hurvin, 75 km, 46 miles as the crow flies, northwest of Tehran) knew of the Gaug Tepe, the hill of treasure, in which, according to legend, an immense fortune had been buried. As a matter of fact, from time to time some lucky person would dig up gold or silver jewelry there. The archeologists, treasure hunters in their own way, came to have a look at Khorvine—first the Iranians in 1949, then the Belgians in 1954. They dug up the hill of treasure and the black mountain and discovered that the area was a vast necropolis established by the Aryans, still a nomadic people, when they began to live in Iran toward the end of the second millennium B.C. They found incised ceramics in beige or black; vases with graceful spouts and handles in the shape of rams' heads, decorated with birds, oxen or horses in relief in an extra-ordinary variety of shapes, and sizes; arms and bronze tools; gold 'ewelry and precious stones, agate, cornelian and lapis-lazuli; pendants and amulets, mirrors and cosmetic jars. The inventory of objects found in the tombs seems endless. Since the scholars left, the peasants of the area have practiced a little amateur archeology, and needless to say, their finds do not end up in the archeological museum of Tehran. From time to time the authorities become annoyed, police occupy the two sites, and nobody can touch anything. Then when vigilance is relaxed, trade again takes over.

Practical Information for Kazvin and Region

 WHAT TO SEE. The *Regional Museum*, especially, and a few monuments such as the *Ali Qapu* and the *Friday Mosque*.

Excursion to Khorvine. On the Tehran–Kazvin road, about halfway between the two, is the prehistoric site of Khorvine. A small mausoleum with a pyramid roof is the landmark near which you turn off into the Elburz mountains to reach Khorvine, about 30 km (18 miles) into the mountains.

HOTELS. *Mehmansara (Inn)* ***, on the outskirts; *Grand, Karoon, Rahmani* *.

SHOPPING. Kazvin is famous for its antique shops; prices here unfortunately are scarcely less exaggerated than in Tehran. It is renowned for delicately painted woodwork, and wrought-iron.

THE CASPIAN SEA

For Rice-Paddies and Caviar Catching

There is another world at the gates of the landlocked interior of Iran, a world of greenery and water at the foot of a majestic backdrop of mountains. The scenery is magnificent, not least in the swamps, but the Caspian itself—sea only by courtesy of the ancient geographers who considered it part of the earth-encircling ocean—is usually a muddy brown. Fifty m (164 feet) below the proper sea-level one might well expect stifling heat, were it not for the sea breeze and the rain. Enthusiastic Iranians who flock here in great numbers have to be restrained by coastguards in boats from venturing beyond shoulder-height into the water to prevent drownings.

The beach resorts of Guilan and Mazanderan are of no particular interest to Western tourists, but a drive along the coast is highly recommended. There are tea and rice plantations just inland and wooded hills. Ramsar is the top resort in what is known as Iran's "caviar coast". Today it is the most heavily populated region of Iran.

Discovering Guilan

Of all the Caspian provinces, Guilan was for a long time the most isolated. This explains the great originality of the local costumes. Between the sea and the nearly impenetrable forests of the hinterland, the Guilakis created a balanced economy. On the narrow coastal strip, tea plants march in parallel rows toward the hills and the cracked mirror of the rice-paddies reflects curious images such as scenes reminiscent of the Far East like water buffalo at work and the peasants carrying two baskets at the ends of a pole balanced across their shoulders. There are fragile huts made of branches which stand on spindly legs in the blue waters of the marshes.

From Astara to Sefid Rud

Rasht (pop. 150,000) is the capital of this little China. It is an industrial city (silk spinning mills) whose avant-garde spirit made itself felt in the 1908 insurrection. Teeming avenues, bazaars which stay open after nightfall, Armenian shops—all these make for a lively atmosphere. The sea awaits you 40 km (24 miles) to the north at Bandar Pahlavi. The latter place often appears under its former name of Enzeli, in the accounts of 19th-century travelers. The port, founded in 1815 by Fath Ali Shah, was not very attractive and this first contact with Persia left the traveler a bit disappointed. The new port facilities are no more pleasing but the lagoon has been decontaminated, and has become an agreeable place for summer visitors to enjoy the coolness of the beaches. In May, the innumerable streams along the coast celebrate the rites of spring and, for as far as the eye can see, water lilies are in flower, wet and gleaming against the dark green pads. From Bandar Pahlavi to Astara, the ancient province of Talech stretches along the narrow coastal plain, with its wheat fields and rice-paddies. The traveler will probably remember only the splendid *kilms* (woven rugs) of the bazaar at Hashtpar.

East of Rasht Guilan proper begins in the labyrinth delta of the Sefid Rud. Among the rice-paddies are large wooden houses capped by thatched roofs which reach almost to the ground, their verandahs facing the rising sun. This unpretentious local architecture is wholly admirable for the substructures, with their great wooden beams, serve also as the poultry-house and as a home workshop where women come to weave rice-fiber mats. Above this a large platform supports the family rooms and a circular gallery. Among these thatched houses one sometimes sees hideous structures of concrete and corrugated iron—the summer houses of city people.

Lahijan and the Tea Country

Onwards from Lahijan, the hills, now closer to the sea, are striped with the regular furrows of the tea plantations. A scrawny tree, a tiny edifice, another glimpse of the Far East—the wooden roof of Astaneh's mausoleum. The little imamzadeh of Sheikh Ambar is perched among the tea-plants above the road, one and a half miles east of Lahijan. Its complicated roof of green and yellow tile, its wooden galleries, its rice-fiber matting remind us of some Buddhist sanctuary. But in reality it is the resting-place of Sheikh Zaid, the spiritual master of Safi, ancestor of the Safavids, to whom he gave his name.

Tea, which is now the wealth of Guilan and gives the countryside its character, was introduced there early in this century by a Persian diplomat, Kachef-o-Saltaneh, who had served in India. He became prime minister and for many years enjoyed his enormous fortune, which was based on his tea plantations which seemed to grow overnight. He also built factories and today 60 of these process more than 12,000 tons of tea a year. Only women's hands can harvest the fragile tea-leaves without crushing them and, from April on, the dresses of these women are bright spots of color in the hills.

Roudsar (pop. 60,000) is known for its oval felt carpets with colorful designs. Also on this coast is Qasemabad celebrated for its songs and dances and for its silk brocade made in family workshops, which are unfortunately fast disappearing.

Mazanderan

The Mazanderan region begins at Ramsar. The hot springs brought travelers here; the beauty of the countryside made them stay. Royal favor also had something to do with it (Reza Shah came from this region) and this is why the hillside boasts the showy complex that includes the royal villa, the Grand Hotel, and the recently built Nouveau Ramsar. The legendary "Wagnerian" statues of the Grand Hotel have now been relegated to the beach.

After Shahsavar, the lemon capital, comes Chalus. Its satelite resort at Now Shahr is a lively spot, as are all the coastal towns from here to Babolsar. These places are not, like Ramsar, to be compared with the pre-war Monte Carlo but rather with the North Sea coast of France and Belgium: dance-halls, popular restaurants, family boarding-houses, cottages and dunes.

Now the coastal plain widens and the hills recede toward the horizon. Amol (pop. 30,000), former capital of Tabaristan, is a small town with tiled roofs and balconied façades. It has kept certain relics of its past: the Meshed Mir Bozorg, a 16th-century mausoleum, the Se-Sayad Imamzadeh from the 13th century, and two other funerary towers. Babol also has a 15th-century mausoleum, the Quasem Imamzadeh. We must not forget Sari, the provincial capital, which supposedly gave its name to the traditional garment of Indian women because the silks from here were so renowned in the Middle Ages. Finally there is Beshahr, at the foot of a cliff, and the nearby White Palace of the king, from which there is a magnificent view over the bay of Gorgan.

Excursion to the Alam Kuh (Alamkouh)

At Marzanabad, 30 km (18½ miles) from Chalus on the Karaj road, one cuts to the west toward the Alam Kuh massif. The roads do not lead very far into this narrow but extremely rugged range, which includes many peaks of over 4,500 m (14,800 feet). We approach it by crossing gently rolling countryside which brings us to the plain of Kalar-Dasht where the famous pre-Achaemenid treasure, now at the Tehran museum, was found.

Hassankif is simply a long bazaar on either side of the muddy highway. Far more typical and attractive, perched on its bluff, is the little village of Tchalajour, whose pretty white houses with their wooden shingles look out over the jade-green waters of Lake Sama. At Roudbarak a mountain stream runs through a village of small wooden and earthen houses. Up toward the head of the valley is the ever-changing foliage of the nearby forest and above gleams the peak of Takht-e-Soleiman. Roudbarak is the meeting-place of Iranian climbers; the Alam Kuh massif is an inexhaustible mine of hikes and climbs. Takht-e-Soleiman (4,700 m, 15,500 feet) and the narrow ridge leading to the north face of Alam Kuh (4,850 m, 16,000 feet) were not conquered until 1936. Every summer since then, many groups of climbers have repeated this feat. First comes a long approach march through the forest, along the Sardab-rud. After Akapoul the way leads through enormous boulders. At the Vander-aboun teahouse (2,000 m, 6,550 feet), one leaves the main valley to follow the bed of the Barir into the heart of the massif. A refuge has been carved out in the glacier of Alam Kuh and higher up, there is a more adequate shelter.

Gorgan and Gonbad-e-Qabus

Although Gorgan is a part of Mazanderan province, it has kept a character of its own. This is a frontier zone, formerly the path of the

Turkoman invasions. These plundering nomads at last settled down when the Russians pushed into their lands (1865–85) and ever since the borders were drawn they have become equally sedentary on the Iranian side. You will see Turkoman horsemen, their black caps made of a single lambskin, and whose faces are remarkable for prominent cheekbones and slanting eyes. Yes, Central Asia reaches down into Gorgan, whose capital city of the same name now boasts 25,000 inhabitants. Twenty km (12½ miles) to the north, the town of Pahlavi Dej lies at a road junction. Every Thursday the Turkoman peasants converge on its market; trading begins at sunrise and ends at 9 a.m. You can get some good bargains there if you haggle— jewelry of gold-plated silver, woven goods and carpets. You can stroll along the pretty brick bridge, or follow the trail north for about 10 km (6 miles) until you come to a row of earthworks, the remains of the famous "Alexander Wall". This is a fortified line of Sassanid construction, stretching 70 km (43½ miles) from Gonbad-e-Qabus to the sea and was built in the hope of barring passage to invaders from the steppes.

About 100 km (62 miles) northeast of Gorgan, Gonbad-e-Qabus, a town of 15,000, former capital of the Gorgan region, can be seen from afar, with the mausoleum of Qabus, a Ziyarid king who died in 1012, rising above it. This brick tower, 54 m, (177 feet) high, is unique in Iran for its antiquity, the beauty of its proportions and the simplicity of its decoration. All the research that has been done to determine the location of the funerary chamber in the tower has proved fruitless.

Five km (3 miles) to the east, peasants tilling the Dasht-e-Halqeh (Plain of Rings) discovered in 1974 double ramparts 7 km (4 miles) in circumference, separated by a double moat, enclosing a mound believed by archeologists to be the citadel of famed Parthian Hecatompylos, the lost City of Hundred Gates.

Caviar

Leased to the Russians from 1895 to 1927 and an Iranian state monopoly since 1927, the sturgeon fisheries are at the mouths of the many rivers which flow into the Caspian. To say sturgeon is to think caviar. Each year 150 to 200 tons of this gift of the gods are processed in canneries at Bandar Pahlavi, Babolsar and Bandar Shah. More than half is exported to the Soviet Union. The beluga, a giant sturgeon, provides the large-grained caviar that is appreciated by gourmets throughout the world. The caviar factory at Bandar Pahlavi as well as the caviar museum at Babolsar are worth a visit.

THE FACE OF IRAN

Practical Information for the Caspian Sea

WHEN TO GO. The Caspian coast enjoys a temperate climate, as is evidenced by the cultivation of such delicate plants as tea and citrus fruits, which flourish here. The season begins at Norouz, March 21, and reaches its climax in the months of July and August. Autumn (end of October) colors the leaves of the forests of the hinterland, making a magnificent setting for long walks. Hunters continue roaming the countryside all winter, but it is better to avoid this season, which is rainy and dreary. In November–December and in May–June, one can watch the caviar "harvest". The tea harvest begins in April.

HOW TO GET THERE. By air: Regular Iran Air flights four times a week from Tehran to Ramsar, twice a week to Rasht and back. A new airport is being completed at Now Shahr. **By train:** on the Tehran–Sari–Gorgan line, four times a week. The train makes the run at night; on the three other days, these stations are served by a daytime local. **By bus:** the towns of the Caspian coast are linked to each other and to Tehran by various bus companies. We recommend T.B.T., Adel, Iran Peyma for Rasht and Guilan; Iran Peyma again and P.M.T. for Sari and the Mazanderan and Gorgan areas.

WHAT TO SEE. The mausoleum of Gonbad-e-Qabus (11th century) is astounding in its simplicity and majesty. You will be charmed by the scenery, which is entirely different from everything else you have seen in Iran. From Astara to Lahijan there are swamps and rice-paddies and handsome wooden houses with thatched roofs. From Lahijan to Chalus there are hills shrouded in mist, tea plantations and the sea. Then comes Central Asia with its wide-open spaces, its horsemen in fur hats and shepherds in felt cloaks. Don't miss the Turkoman market in Pahlavi Dej.

HOTELS. Prices during the summer season are much above the Iranian average for similar categories. Several nameless and deservedly unclassified motels on the beach of Bandar Pahlavi charge 1,000 Rs for one bed in a tiny room. Large families squeeze into accommodation that appears to Western visitors as little short of squalid.

Abbas Abad. *Motel Diana***, 30 km (18½ miles) west of Chalus.

Amol. *Grand***; *Masoud**.

Astara. *Mehmansara***.

Babol. *Miami**.

Babolsar. *Casino****; *Metropol***; *Khazar, Villa 12**.

Bandar Pahlavi. *Bandar Pahlavi****, on the beach; as also the *Grand, Parandeh***; in the port, *Iran***; *Amirian, Marmar, Tehran**.

Behshahr. *Ashraf, Razzaghi**.

Chalus. *Chalus, Chalus-e Jadid****; *Meymoza, Orkhide, Shekoufeh Now***. Opened in 1976, the *Hyatt Regency*

148

Caspian is a deluxe 200-room hotel located in the ambitious resort area Namakab-Rud, 8 miles west of Chalus. Facilities include golf, tennis, beach, casino; cable-car service to nearby mountain top.

Gachsar. *Gachsar****, halfway between Tehran and Chalus.

Gorgan. *Miami***; *Anahid, Haghighat, Saadi, Taslimi, Villa Zhilla**.

Klarabad. *Camping Motel Ghoo**, 23 km (14 miles) west of Chalus.

Lahijan. *Abchar, Iran**; 20-room lakeside *Mehmansara*.

Lashtaneshah, 3 miles east of Bandar Pahlavi, *Zibake-nar****, on the beach.

Now Shahr. *Motels Now Shahr* and *Sahra*** on the road to Sisangan;

Gol-e Sorkeh**, at Sisangan; *Motel Pouchini**, toward Chalus.

Ramsar. *Grand***** traditional but refurbished in 1976, casino; *Ramsar Motel****, on the beach, pool.

Rasht. *Iran, Ordibihesht Now****; *Pamchal***; *Asia, Caravan, Fars, Firdowsi, Iran Janan, Keyvan, Park, Rezvan, Savoy**, no showers, very primitive.

Roudsar. *Tourist,* simple.

Saghi Kalayeh. *Motel Ghoo****, largest and best on the coast; *Caspian, Mehmansara***; *Nader, Sari**.

Shahi. *Shahi***.

Shah Pasand. *Kourosh***.

Shahsavar. *Marjan***; *Jahan-e Now**.

ENTERTAINMENT (May–October). Since the coast is a magnet for Tehranis in search of a little entertainment, the nightlife here is far more animated than elsewhere in Iran. Apart from the *Ramsar Casino*, a masterpiece of the 30's, you can squander your fortune at *Babolsar Casino* and at the *Shoukoufeh Now Casino*, 5 km (3 miles) west of Chalus. Then you can recover at the *Rotonde Hawaiienne* restaurant at Klarabad; at the *Star Club* (discothèque, dancing), 4 km (2½ miles) east of Chalus, or in any of the similar establishments along this part of the road.

MOTORING. From Astara on the western border with the U.S.S.R. to Asalom about 30 km (18½ miles) northwest of Bandar Pahlavi, the graded dirt road is quite good in dry weather, but is pitted with pot holes when it rains heavily—and this often happens. A good asphalt road more or less follows the coast to Gomishan near the eastern border with the U.S.S.R. The main northern artery branches east at Kordkuy via Gorgan, Shah Pasand and Meshed into Afghanistan. Between Shah Pasand and Shahrud (120 km, 74 miles) the dirt road crosses a pass which may be blocked in winter. From Shahi to Damavand (and Tehran), the graded road is dangerous in bad weather.

From Chalus to Tehran, via Karaj, there is a good asphalt road, crossing a pass by means of a tunnel at an altitude of almost 2,700 m (8,850 feet). Amol–Tehran via Abe Ali, also asphalt; pass at 2,100 m (6,900 feet). You must have chains in winter, and you should inquire as to whether the passes are open before starting out on any of these routes. From Rasht to Tehran via Kazvin, there are no problems.

THE FACE OF IRAN

Excursions. From Tehran, there are several ways to reach the Caspian coast. The shortest and most picturesque is via Karaj to Chalus (202 km, 125 miles). From there you can follow the shoreline west, via Ramsar and Rasht (198 km, 124 miles) and return to Tehran via Kazvin (323 m, 200 miles). Allow 3 days. At Chalus, you might prefer to cut eastward, to Gorgan (306 km, 190 miles) and from there go to Gonbad-e-Qabus (85 km, 52 miles) or Pahlavi Dej (20 km, 12 miles). Afterwards you will have to retrace your steps to Amol in order to take the road back to Tehran, or else, if you have a good sturdy car, you can take the dirt road from Shahi to Firouzkouh and Damavand, which is most picturesque. (3 days.)

SHOPPING. Caspian craftsmanship is in sharp contrast with that of the rest of Iran. In the shops you'll find wooden plates with designs burnt on them, alpen-stocks, chests of burred wood and olivewood salad bowls which are always well made. More original are the carved calabashes and the brightly-colored embroidery on felt. The government store on Shah Ave. in Rasht has the best goods. In the village markets are flat baskets, mats woven out of rice fiber, brooms and other basketwork wares. At Roudsar you'll find oval felt rugs, decorated with vivid colors.

SPORTS. Every town on the coast has its sandy beach, perhaps even a few cabins. **Bathing:** facilities are no more elaborate than this except at Bandar Pahlavi, Ramsar, Now Shahr and Babolsar. **Shooting:** inquire at the Chik-arbani in Sari, Farah Ave. The best shooting country is north of Gorgan for birds, and in the wooded hills south of Ramsar for animals, including bear and panther. We recommend that you take a guide.

Fishing: remember that sea fishing is a state monopoly. For rivers and streams, ask at the Chikarbani in Sari.

Mountain-climbing: The Alamkouh region is of particular interest to climbers, hunters and those who enjoy hiking in the forest but can do without comforts at overnight stops. Take the Tehran–Chalus road to Marzanabad. From there, take the left fork to the village of Roudbarak (30 km, 18½ miles), cross the bridge and ask for the Saffar house at the edge of town. This is a refuge hut established by the Tehran mountaineering club. From Roudbarak, several excursions are possible: trips in the high mountains of the Alamkouh massif and the ascent of this peak and of Takht-e-Soleiman. This takes three days from Roudbarak, and can be done from June through September. From Roudbarak you can hike to the fortress of Alamut in 6 days, camping in the mountains. A less ambitious hike is to the shores of Lake Sama. Fifteen km (9 miles) before Roudbarak, at the hamlet of Kord-e-Chal, a dirt trail on your right leads to the village of Tchalajour (4 km, 2½ miles). You should allow three hours to reach this.

CAMPING. Park-Jangali in Amol; in Babol, Yazda-Hectar, on the Shahi road; a beach-front site near Bandar Pahlavi; well-equipped ground at Chalus; in Gorgan, Park Naharkoran, pool, restaurant. Now Shahr has a

THE CASPIAN SEA

campsite and there is one in Sisangan National Park. Permission can be obtained to camp on some of the beaches which have restaurants. Such beaches are to be found, for instance, on the way out of Now Shahr going towards Babolsar.

 USEFUL ADDRESSES. In Sari: *Tourist Information Office:* Reza Shah Kabir; *Melli Bank*, Chardari Place; *Car Rentals:* Pir Zadeh Garage, Nader Ave.; *Spare Parts:* Auto Rebit, Shah Abbas Ave.; *Bus:* Iran Peyma, Nader Ave.; P.M.T., Shah Abbas Ave.; *Hospital:* Chir-o-Khorchid, Shah Abbas Ave. In Rasht: *Melli Bank*, Pahlavi Ave.; *Bus:* T.B.T., Shah Ave.; *Adel*, Saadi Ave.; *Hospital:* Chir-o-Khorchid, Pahlavi Ave. and Namjou Ave.

Useful telephone numbers: in Sari: police, 4020; road police, 4058; ambulance 4047.

AZERBAIJAN

Iran's Own "Northwest Frontier"

Azerbaijan is an immense mountain massif carved by river basins isolated one from the other. The tortuous and steep road winds over rocky passes from one basin to the next, following stream beds, going through tunnels at the bottom of deep valleys, finally emerging on the high plains where the foothills end. In the bottom of the basins villages nestle under the protective foliage of poplar groves. The cultivated land around them is irregularly checkered with the brown and ocher tints of the earth. It was here that the successive waves of Turks, part of that slow migration from the central Asian steppes, settled down on the Iranian and Anatolian plateau.

In Azerbaijan, the Turkomans of the Seljuk period defended the boundaries of the empire against Christian Georgia and Armenia. When the Mongol invasion came, they were eventually able to exploit it to their advantage. "White Sheep" and "Black Sheep" continued to dominate their ethnic group throughout western Iran and Anatolia, but with frequent squabbles among themselves (with the same deadly rivalry which existed in the "Wars of the Roses" in England) until the day when the tribe of "Redheads" (Quizilbach) "by devouring one another brought the plaintiffs to agreement". With the arrival of the Safavids, the expansion of the Shi'ite sect organized by Shah Ismail appealed to the Turkomans of Anatolia and caused them to return en masse to the land of Iran.

The turbulence of this independent and unruly province was to be a bone in the throat of successive rulers of Persia. What could be more effective in promoting the drive toward independence than linguistic uniqueness? Even today there are many examples of political situations caused by a minority's stubborn attachment to its own speech: in India for example, and even in Britain. The Azerbaijan problem is much less acute today, and the time of the Tabriz Revolts is past, but despite its submission to the crown, the province has kept its language and idiosyncrasies. The language, which is called Azeri, is also spoken on the other side of the Arax in Soviet territory, where it has acquired its nobility in literature and the sciences. This idiom is also understood in Turkey, for it became distinct from Osmanli only in the 13th century.

Although they have mostly become sedentary farmers, the Azerbaijan Turkomans still practice semi-nomadism; in summer they follow their flocks to the high pastures of the Sahand and the Salavan ranges. In winter they return to the valleys or the Mughan steppes. Thanks to government irrigation projects, their life becomes more settled from year to year as new villages are founded and as the cultivated land moves higher and higher up the slopes of the foothills.

To visit Azerbaijan is to explore all that is non-conformist in Iran and all that the classic landscape of the Iranian plateau is not. Lake Rezaiyeh, sunk in its ring of volcanic mountains, seems an anomaly when compared with other basins where the water seeps away into the sand. Nothing similar to the vineyards round the lake and the orchards of the province are to be found, except in certain scattered oases on the edge of the desert. In the north is the extreme fringe of the monasteries and churches built by the vanished state of Armenia. In the south one begins to encounter the first Kurdish tribes in the region of Mahabad. To the east, Azerbaijan has a window on the Caspian, between Astara and Assalem. Here, after a spectacular descent through a moist and tepid forest, one finds oneself in a subtropical atmosphere. Coming from Tabriz, it is only after Miyaneh, or even after Zenjan, as one emerges from a long river valley where the last poplars sway, that the parched earth of the Iranian plateau is seen.

Discovering Azerbaijan

Bazargan is the Turko-Iranian frontier post. The length of time required for the passport and customs check depends on the number of cars and trucks. As you leave the border enclave, there is a simple hotel where you can be served a tchelo-kebab or even spend the night. If it doesn't suit you, Maku is only a 20-km (12½ miles) drive down a gentle grade through mountain scenery pierced, as in a last farewell from Turkey, by the snow-capped peaks of the little and big Ararats.

Maku is situated in a natural rock amphitheater which lends a certain majesty to the site. The old city's earthen façades and narrow streets are hidden behind the brightly lit triumphal way bordered by modern buildings. Seen at night, it is a striking spectacle. Beyond the town, the road skirts a river which has dug a curious cliff-walled ditch into the narrow valley. This strange natural phenomenon, set in its decor of crumbling rocks, might almost be the lair of some divinity. It is best to travel through this countryside at dawn when morning mists make the first rays of light iridescent as they strike the barren rocks and stony fields. 86 km (53 miles) after Maku, the village of Khoy is entered through a Safavid gate in the crumbling walls; the main sights are the 13th-century Djameh Mosque, the 19th-century Khan Mosque, and the Minaret Shams-el-Moluk, constructed from gazelle heads. The road south leads to Lake Rezaiyeh.

If you bypass Khoy you will soon reach Marand the fruit city whose orchards, enclosed by earthen walls, stretch for 20 km (12 miles) around. The city suffered greatly from repeated attacks by the Kurds. Nonetheless the Friday Mosque, rebuilt in the 15th century by Abu Said, has a lovely and elaborately worked stucco mihrab. The mosque is located to the southwest of town—ask directions at the service station. You'll also have a chance to buy amusing wickerwork on Pahlavi Ave., before continuing on your way.

From Marand, Tabriz is only 61 km (38 miles) away. After crossing a small pass, the road follows a sort of steppe, over which caravans travel on the old trail. Soon the provincial capital appears through the smoke coming from the brick kilns on its outskirts.

Tabriz

The capital of Azerbaijan (500,000 inhabitants, including a very active minority of Armenians and Chaldean Christians) is situated in the long valley of the Aji Chai ("bitter water") at an altitude of 1,400 m (4,600 feet), only 270 km (170 miles) from the Turko-Iranian frontier. Its horizon is bounded by high mountain ranges, notably the Kuh-e-Sahand to the south and the Kuh-e-Salavan to the east and the city has changed greatly in the last few decades. The modern buildings housing administrative offices and the station—much too large for today's train service—are the result of this desire for renewal, but fortunately do not mar the rather old-fashioned character of Tabriz, so dear to its inhabitants.

According to historians it was originally called Gazaca and was the capital of ancient Atropatene (after Atropates, one of Alexander's lieutenants). In any case Tabriz (Tauris) was already an important city in the 10th century and was described by numerous chroniclers. Ghazan (1295–1304), a member of the Mongol dynasty of the Il-Khans, made it the capital of his kingdom. Except for a brief period during the Timurid epoch, it held this position until the end of the 15th century. Then the Safavids came upon the scene. Shah Ismail I also reigned in Tabriz, but in the face of the Turkish menance, the city was abandoned first for Kazvin, and then for Isfahan. Until 1918, Tabriz, the western bulwark of the Persian Empire, was to know the frequent presence of Turkish troops, against whom the Russians retaliated with some success as early as the beginning of the 18th century. The Russians occupied Tabriz in 1826. The Bab, founder of the Babi religion, was executed here on July 9th, 1850 in Tabriz.

At the beginning of the 20th century, the city was the stage of perpetual political agitation, always cruelly repressed—sometimes with the help of the Russian army—and in 1908 was the point of departure of a genuine revolution. During the First World War, Turks and Russians took turns occupying Tabriz. Finally, from 1941 to 1945 a new Russian intervention took place with political consequences that one can easily guess. In December 1946, the Iranian army took forceful action and wiped out the Tabriz headquarters of the Popular Azerbaijan Republic, which enjoyed Soviet backing. Today Tabriz, taking advantage of its ideal location as a center of communications, is attempting to become the great commercial center it used to be.

You will probably not have enough time to explore Tabriz properly for the rare monuments it has to offer are not many, yet the city itself has charm. To be sure, light-blue taxis have replaced the carriages, neon has invaded the façades, and a big city atmosphere has begun to encroach little by little on the slightly old-fashioned ambience which until recently contributed so greatly to Tabriz's charm. Yet one can still find a provincial cheeriness in the more subtle picturesqueness of the city's outskirts—Victorian-style buildings, with clock towers— and in the Golestan garden, where the Shahanshah stands in a pose reminiscent of El Cid Campeador. The evenings at the Hotel Dajahan-nam also have a rustic charm behind a thin veneer of modernism.

On market days Tabriz reverts to her role of large rural village where peasants come to trade the fruits of their labor for Western manufactured products. This is the true character of the province, whose every community is represented in this colorful crowd.

Ancient Quarters of Tabriz

The Chambab Ghazan, to the west of the city, was the meeting place for caravans arriving from Europe and China. Caravanserais, mosques, madares (schools), libraries, public baths and khaneghahs testify to the activity of this prosperous and animated quarter, of which nothing remains today but a maze of picturesque alleys. One can wander around it tirelessly, discovering it little by little. The same is true for Rab'e Rashidi, the eastern suburb founded by Vizier Rashid al-Din Fazlollah during the reign of Sultan Oljaitu. But in order to pierce the mysteries which hide behind Tabriz's high walls, it is best to rely on the Tourist Office, whose organized tours include

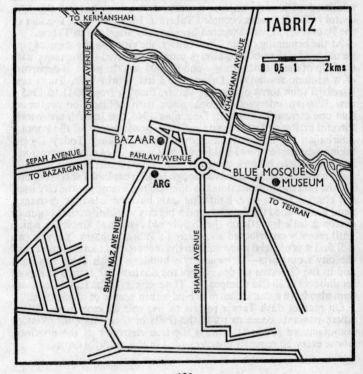

several typical Iranian dwellings which sometimes nestle in small parks, invisible from the street.

The Khiaban (Avenue) Pahlavi also boasts its pleasures, starting with the silver merchants, whose shops, full of marvels, line the street. You will be unable to resist the desire to touch the thousand different products of this delicate craft. The tapestry workshops will fascinate you just as much, and you will admire the workers' labor as they tie each separate strand of wool. The street draws you onward, its pastries, dried fruits and nougats all vying for your attention. To the north, Firdowsi Ave. is the popular quarter, where men crowd inside the tchaikhanes to smoke immense hookahs. Skewers of meat are cooked in the open air; street vendors are numerous; finally one reaches the bazaar.

Recently restored, in fact practically rebuilt according to the traditional layout, the bazaar has a roof with cupolas through which the slanting rays of sunlight brighten the shadows of the alleys inside. In the center there is a long gallery, a treasure house of popular handicrafts, and on the sides are rooms, each covered with a dome. Manufactured products are gradually gaining on the local articles, but the shops selling foods and fabrics, where the country people come to stock up, are still colorful and full of Oriental charm. According to custom, each trade has its own section. From the leather-workers' corner comes the pungent fragrance of saddles and harnesses, halters and holsters which stand side by side with an astonishing variety of boots. Farther on, mountains of rugs are piled against the walls. These are of rural manufacture, but among them you can sometimes find an interesting carpet. But what you should look for here is one of those charming natural silk scarfs with a dark-printed design, or else caps of lamb's wool or blankets of goat's wool. In the course of your walk you will perhaps run across the Friday Mosque with its elegantly columned hall. It is said that it goes back to the Seljuk period, but the buildings you see here date from the 16th century.

The Blue Mosque

Even if you have only one hour during which to visit Tabriz, you must see the Blue Mosque, on whose recently rebuilt walls the superb faience sections stand out all the more because of the bareness of the whole.

The Blue Mosque (Masjid-i-Kabud) is on Pahlavi Ave., going east on the left, but its entrance is on a small parallel street, the Khiaban-e-Khoneh. Attributed to Shah Jahan (1436–67), it is an admirable example of the Timurid art which emanated from Samarkand, capital of the empire of the steppes.

The minute you enter you stop to admire the rather well-preserved decoration of the great portal, which is in the center of the façade and is shaped like an iwan: an immense rectangle opening into a vaulted bay, accentuated by a very beautiful rope molding in turquoise faience. The two minarets which stood on each side have disappeared. The portal is entirely covered with mosaic panels, which should be closely examined one by one if you wish to capture their extraordinary finesse.

The Tabriz mosque is a landmark in the use of color in architecture. It is more. For does it not represent the self-revelation of Persian genius brought about through the artistic influences of a world which stretched into the far reaches of the Mongol steppes and into China itself? Here technique has reached such perfection that the artist is no longer restrained but free to use every artifice, every color which enamel pastes make available to him. To the ceramist's basic palette of turquoise, dark blue, white and black have been added reds, greens and yellows. These subtle hues enhance the floral decorative motifs and the graceful Arab writing which has replaced the more angular Kufic characters.

Sometimes floral and animal motifs are the principal decorative elements of certain panels: peacocks and phoenixes, Buddha trees, cypresses and many flowers—China's contribution to her ephemeral Mongol masters.

A look at the architecture will reveal the originality of this building, which is a variation of the typical Iranian mosque. The principal room, under the restored cupola, has taken the place of the usual central square court, onto which open the four traditional rooms, of which one has the mihrab.

The huge building next to the Blue Mosque (on Khiaban Pahlavi) houses the Archeological, Historical and Ethnographical Museum of Tabriz, well worth a quick visit.

The Citadel and Surroundings

Though a huge ruin it is hard to locate, for it is hidden in a garden behind the façades on Pahlavi Ave., in the neighborhood of Firdowsi Ave. The citadel (Ark) was built by Ali Shah, Vizier of Khan Ghazan (1295–1304) and his brother and successor Khan Uljaytu (1304–16) as a mosque, one of the world's largest, with a staggering brick vault 33 yards in diameter (which soon collapsed); by the middle of the 14th century, the lavish decorations as well as the ornamental lake had been replaced by massive fortifications, 26 yards high and 10 yards thick. Though nothing remains except a sort of redoubt flanked by towers on either side of its south face, these vestiges are proof of the important role played by Tabriz at the time, for it was the Mongol empire's advance position. From the top of the fortifications you will discover a beautiful panorama of the city, as well as openings into dungeons which will make your blood run cold. As you leave, pause at the memorial to the patriots who fell in the struggle against the pro-Soviet separatist movement of Azerbaijan in 1946. Then take a rest in the Garden of Roses (Golestan), under the protective eyes of Reza Shah and his predecessors, Shah Abbas the Great and Nadir Shah, to mention the most illustrious.

Of the numerous excursions from Tabriz, the most popular is only 9 km (6 miles) east to the vast pool of Shahgoli surrounding an island with a restaurant. Another is to Osku via a comfortable asphalt road. Leave Tabriz on the Maragheh road near the station. Beyond the garage-caravanserais the road goes through orchards and olive groves almost the entire way. Don't forget to turn left at Khos-rowchah. Osku's principal attraction is its cottage industry in silk. Here you can watch the lovely silk scarfs sold in the Tabriz bazaar being woven in obscure workshops. Their decoration with dark spots is done by the ancient wax method (*bakhti* in Persian). The areas which are to be untouched by the dye are covered with soft wax. Once the fabric has been dyed, it is washed and rinsed. The wax is thus removed, and the original color comes through—usually orange.

Excursion to St. Thaddeus

This excursion, which is one of the most interesting in Azerbaijan, can be done in one day from Tabriz, following the Maku road to the village of Qaraziaeddin. Nearby are the ruins of the 7th-century B.C. Urartian fortress of Bastam) ramparts, gates, a temple and columned hall, from which a track leads to the Armenian sanctuary of St. Thaddeus, known locally as Kara Kélisa, in the heart of the mountains. The site is arid but colorful; in the distance you can distinguish the massif of Ararat, which crowns the landscape. According to the Armenian legend, Thaddeus (said by tradition to be Jude, the brother of James) reached this corner of Armenia in 66 A.D. and built the first Christian sanctuary. Subsequently he was martyred and buried in his own church.

The present cruciform building, supposedly built on the foundations of the original church, stands on a hill within fortified walls. It is composed of two distinct parts: a domed apse built for the most part out of black stone and probably dating from the 10th or 11th centuries, and adjacent to it, the main part of the basilica, built out of grey stone and itself covered by a bigger cupola whose 12-sided drum is pierced with 12 windows. According to an inscription dated 1329, this latter part was built after the earthquake of 1319. Considerable work was done on it during the 19th century. There seems to have been some question of moving the seat of the Armenian Catholics here from Echmiadzin in the U.S.S.R., where it is now established.

The exterior walls, as in other primitive Armenian churches, are decorated with the effigies of saints, with friezes of vine leaves and with animals in attitudes reminiscent of naive Romanesque art. Be sure to notice the alternating rows of dark and light stones around the typically Armenian dome, and the bas-beliefs in white stone on the eastern wall.

A yearly ceremony takes place in July to commemorate the death of St. Thaddeus. Hundreds of Armenians from Tabriz and the surrounding area come on pilgrimage, attesting to the fact that the 190,000 Armenians of Iran make up the oldest Christian community in the country (along with the Chaldeans). The ruins of buildings inside the surrounding wall prove that at one time a large monastery existed here. The unpaved road (better avoided) continues to the border at Bazargan.

Excursion to Maragheh

Maragheh is reached by a paved road of about 150 km (93 miles). Leave Tabriz on the west, bearing south. The road which winds up and down through arid country leads to Bonab. At the traffic circle of this town, take a left turn. A few kilometers farther, the road coincides with a landing strip, where you can abandon yourself to the joys of speed. Then from the top of the ridge, you behold a magnificent panorama of the Maragheh Oasis.

The city (50,000 inhabitants) first knew glory during the reign of Harun al-Rashid, later under the Kurdish dynasty of Ahmalidi, and finally during the Mongol era when it became the capital of Azerbaijan. The 11-Khans—especially Hulagu—built many monuments including an observatory which today is but a pile of ruins. Maragheh declined when the Mongol capital was moved to Soltanieh.

The principal reason for visiting Maragheh is to see five tombs, in various states of preservation, which exemplify important stages in the development of the art of brick and faience mosaics. You will probably not find these easily, for as we go to press no accurate directions are available to assist you in finding your way.

On reaching Maragheh, don't cross the river until the second bridge. Immediately after a traffic circle, take a left turn which will lead you into an undeveloped area on the banks of the river. Here you will come upon the Gonbad-e-Ghafarieh, surrounded by a brick wall.

Two memories of a magnificent past.
Above, the Apadana, the King's Audience Hall, at Persepolis.
Below, a rock carving at Bishahpur

The Picnic, a Persian miniature which
shows the influence of Chinese art,
imported by the Mongols

Ask the caretaker who lives across the way from the mausoleum for the keys. The Gonbad-e-Ghafarieh is square with angles softened by four matching lozenge-shaped columns. The tomb was built on a stone substructure which contains a crypt dating from the beginning of the 14th century. The principal (north) façade, decorated with handsome faience mosaics in blue, white and black, bears the following inscription above its door: "This blessed edifice was ordered built by the Great Sultan, God's shadow on earth, Sultan of Sultans, of Arabs and of Adjemi, Abu Said Bahadur Khan. May his reign last!" The personage whose remains repose here apparently was a freed Mameluke slave who had a rather eventful life. We are told by a chronicler that after becoming viceroy of Egypt and then viceroy of Syria, he was forced to seek refuge in Tartary and ended up as governor of the province of Maragheh under Sultan Oljaitu.

In order to continue the visit, it is best to retrace your steps back to the traffic circle, then go left until you reach the next traffic circle. You'll find two other tombs behind the Melli Bank. To reach them you go past a school. You'll discover side by side the Gonbad-e-Kaboud and a circular tower of which the only interesting feature is the door. Dating from 1168, the tower's enameled decoration is vastly superior to that of the Gonbad-e-Sorkh, described below. The inscription at the top of the arcade is full of wisdom and inspires meditation: "Everything which lives must taste death." The Gonbad-e-Kaboud (1196) (Blue Dome) is worthy of greater attention. Tradition has it that it is the tomb of Hulagu's mother, even though it was built long before the arrival of the Mongols. No matter, for it is its beauty rather than its history which interests us. Though only one color, turquoise blue, is used, its elaborate decoration is extremely graceful, covering each panel of the polygon with a faience knotwork which makes the monument seem caught in a huge net. Verses from the Koran and brick stalactites complete this original ornamentation. A look at the crypt reveals a beautiful composite vault.

From the traffic circle on which the Melli Bank is located, you now head directly south on Nasir Ave. Cross the Pahlavi traffic circle, continue past the Arya Hotel, and immediately after, turn right. You'll run into extremely rough terrain, strewn with the stones of a Moslem cemetery. Cross it; inside a wall, the Gonbad-e-Sorkh or Gonbad-e-Kirmiz (the Red Dome) awaits you. Despite restoration which gives it a brand-new look, it is the oldest of Maragheh's mausoleums. Built in 1147, this tomb has a square plan with columns at its angles, and is entirely decorated with bricks in geometric motifs. On the main façade is a beautiful inscription in Kufic characters, running around the curve of the arcade. Notice also the originality of the motifs on the angle towers which frame the façade. Apparently this is the tomb of a prince of the Kurdish dynasty of the Ahmaladi, at that time rulers of Maragheh.

The other monuments of this ancient Mongol capital are all in ruins. Among these are a fifth tomb, the Koy-Bordj, dating from the post-Mongol period, the Friday Mosque and the astronomical observatory. So as to leave out nothing, we mention the Mausoleum of Imam Hassan, located in town on Pahlavi Ave. and entirely decorated with bathroom tiles!

Excursion to Takht-e-Suleiman

This excursion, which takes two or three days, will lead you to a site of Iranian antiquity which spans an epoch, running from prehistoric times to the Mongol period. It should be mentioned that this important archeological site will only interest specialists. The trip, however, may tempt those who enjoy discomfort. Though the road as far as Miyandoab presents no problems, a Land-Rover is needed for the rest of the way. At Miyandoab, take the road to Bijar, via Tekab. Takht-e-Suleiman is near the village of Nostratabad, 49 km (30 miles) north-east of Tekab. A visit to the Tourist Office in Tabriz is useful for getting details of the itinerary (550 km, 340 miles, round trip) half of which is over "jeepable" road. On the site of Takht-e-Suleiman a fire temple was built called Ganjak in Pahlavi texts, Gazaea by classical authors and Chiz according to Arab writers. It consists of a lake in a volcanic crater, whose level remains constant thanks to subterranean drainage, surrounded by a wall trimmed with 37 stone turrets of the Arsacid epoch. Not far from here, the remains of a prehistoric temple called the "Throne of Solomon" were found. Near the lake fragments of raw brick walls, probably the work of Medes, can be seen, as well as the remains of a stone fire temple. A pile of ruins is all that is left of the castle, rebuilt by the Mongol Abaka Khan after the destruction of Chiz by the Byzantine Emperor Heraclius in 628. It was above all under the Sassanids that Takht-e-Suleiman knew its hour of greatest glory. The site known as the place where Ganjak's celebrated "Fire of Warriors" or "Royal Fire" burned, was therefore a sort of acropolis for the kings of Ctesiphon. The Sassanid monarchs went there on foot after coronation, in order to deposit offerings and consult the oracles. The gifts with which Bahram de Gour, Khosroés I and Khosroés II endowed the temple have been described by historians. These consisted of gold, silver and precious stones.

Takht-e-Suleiman differs from other known fire temples only in dimension and antiquity. Fire ceremonies took place in the open, as everywhere else, and even though there were several altars, only one fire chamber fed the other hearths. Probably the original temple was built during the Arsacid period on the shores of the miraculous lake. Its fame drew crowds, resulting in the building of more sanctuaries and the addition of annexes, including a caravanserai, all of which were needed to assure the proper functioning of this holy site. A. Godard points out: "Isn't the same thing true of many of today's shrines?"

Around Lake Rezaiyeh

The two previous excursions took us as far as Miyandoab and thus around part of Lake Rezaiyeh. This body of water, at an altitude of 1,300 m (4,250 feet), 140 km (86 miles) long and covering an area of 500 square kilometers (190 square miles), is the favorite vacation spot of the inhabitants of Tabriz during the hot season. Its salt water—so salty that fish cannot live in it—is as famous for the delight it offers to tourists as for its curative powers. Those suffering from rheumatism and skin ailments come to bathe in these waters and to be massaged with mud from its shores. Not very deep—14 m (45 feet) maximum—its size increases when the snows melt and the Soufitchaï and Moronitchaï coming from the top of the Sahand pour their icy flows into the lake.

Halfway between the two Kurdish towns of Miyandoab and Mahabad is the Achaemenian rock tomb of Faqarqa, a mile off the road. About 20,000 Kurds live in Mahabad and their picturesque costumes brighten the sunny streets. The road turns north to the village of Haidarabad, close to the lake. 13 km (8 miles) west, along the branch to Naqadeh, is the high mound of Hassanlu where a team from the University of Philadelphia excavated gold objects, supposedly the work of Manneans, who are said to be the oldest Azerbaijani (ninth century B.C.). The site has produced interesting evidence about the life which was led in this region in ancient days. In times of war the people sought refuge inside a citadel. Its plan is still distinguishable along with that of two rooms whose roofs were upheld by columns. There are warehouses and a dwelling known as the "House of Pearls". Yet the tremendously thick walls did not prevent the city from falling under the attacks of the Urartians in about 800 B.C. Several other early Iron Age sites have been uncovered in the Solduz and Ushun valleys.

The new road hugs the lake for some 60 km (40 miles) to Rezaiyeh, pleasantly situated among orchards, tobacco fields and vineyards, which produce an excellent wine. On the wide avenues Christians, Chaldeans, Armenians, Turks, Kurds and even a few Persians walk side by side. The Friday Mosque, situated in the bazaar near the Reza Shah Kabir Sq., was built in the Seljuk epoch over a Sassanian fire temple in this reputed birthplace of the prophet Zoroaster. The splendid Mongol stucco mihrab dates from 1277.

Not far away, another monument, reminiscent of Maragheh's funerary towers, deserves to be mentioned: the Seh-Gonbad (Three Domes) built on a stone crypt, and though it is devoid of faience decoration, its porch, entirely trimmed with carved brick, is a beautiful example of Seljuk art. One of the Three Wise Men is supposedly buried below the modern church of St. Mary. The best chance for a swim is at Golmankhaneh 21 km (13 miles) away, which is moderately equipped but agreeable.

The final lap round the lake leads through Shahpur, Khoy and Marand. Rebuilt after the earthquake of 1931, Shahpur—a short distance from ancient Selmas—has nothing much to offer except a 13th-century funerary monument. From Shahpur to Khoy, the road, which goes over a mountain pass, is uncomfortable and can be difficult in bad weather. The wild countryside is fascinating. This is also true of the road between Jamalabad and Shahpur.

Soltanieh

You will probably visit Soltanieh and its famous dome when leaving Azerbaijan on your way back to Tehran. From the capital, the trip to Soltanieh, which is midway between Tabriz and Tehran, can be made in one day.

Leaving Tabriz, the road climbs over the top of the mountain, the landscape widens out and is brightened by a small lake before narrowing again inside a green and picturesque valley. The road goes around Miyaneh, where Imam Ismail is buried, then follows the sometimes ominous and sometimes pleasant course of Zanjanrud to Zenjan, the gateway to the Iranian plateau. The countryside becomes drier, the earth cracked and nothing is lacking but a sand wind to complete the picture. 40 km (25 miles) after Zenjan (or Zanjan), a dirt road to the right leads to Soltanieh, whose mausoleum can be distinguished in the distance (6 km or 3 miles).

Soltanieh means "Imperial". The capital of the Mongols as early as the 13th century, the city reached its peak during the reign of Sultan Oljaitu Khodabendeh (1304–16) and remained the metropolis of the Persian Mongol sovereigns until 1384, the year it was destroyed by Timur. Only the mausoleum was spared. A clever politician, Oljaitu attempted to make Soltanieh the holy city of the Shi'ite sect to which he had just been converted and ordered that the mausoleum he was then building be transformed into a mosque, to receive the precious remains of the martyred Imams. Unable to get custody of them, the Sultan decided to use the edifice for its original purpose. Modified during the 16th century the interior of the monument was decorated with the carved and painted plaster so typical of the Safavid period.

The decoration of the exterior, which combines turquoise, ultramarine and white, is masterful. You will need a telephoto lens in order to capture the well-executed details. Be sure to ask for permission to go up to the gallery which runs around the interior of the cupola. From there you can admire a whole collection of small arches covered with polychrome carved plaster. One never tires of counting the different geometric and floral motifs which constitute this refined decoration. But it is above all the sweep of its vaulted dome resting on angle squinches and soaring to a height of 52 m (170 feet) which gives the whole its majesty. It is one of the most perfect examples of Mongol architecture and served as the model for many mausoleums built through the centuries in Iran. Notice the charming view over the roofs of the village seen through the arcades.

The Northern Route

If you have the time and if you are not worried about wear and tear on your car, you may prefer to return to Tehran via Ardabil. From there you can go down to the Caspian coast, a more pleasant drive in the summer. The direct road to Ardabil is from Bostanabad, 50 km (31 miles) or so from Tabriz, and passes through Sarab.

But the northern route through Ahar and Meshkinshahr is far richer in natural beauty and human interest. Be sure weather conditions are favorable. We should also warn you that, even though special permission is no longer necessary in order to follow this road, you may be subject to police control along the way—this is a simple formality and takes little time.

Leave Tabriz from the north and as soon as you reach the earth-walled suburbs, bear left where the road forks. Very quickly thereafter the road starts tortuously winding up the mountain in dizzying horseshoe turns, and you'll have a fantastic view of the town. At the bottom of the ravine, the river and villages along its bank wait for the sun to reach its zenith, in the hope of a few rays. Other villages reach more boldly for the sun from their perches on the steep slopes of the mountain. Here life seems to cling obstinately to the arid rocks, ignoring the comparative comfort available at the bottom of the valleys. A little farther on, the track improves and turns into a good dirt road (as far as Ahar), skirting mountains resplendent with a wide variety of mineral colors.

In the crook of a turn at the 30 km (18 miles) marker, a village, bathed in morning light (for naturally you left at dawn), appears by the river banks. After passing through it, notice a small cemetery on your left guarded by three pink stone rams. These strange funerary statues honor brave warriors, a custom apparently practiced during the domination of the "Black Sheep" (15th century).

After a drive of 110 km (68 miles), Ahar welcomes you. (Tomb of Sheik Sahab-ed-Din—large brick iwan, in town.) The road skirts 4,800 m-high Mount Sabalan, associated with Zoroaster's vision of the Avesta (Holy Scriptures), passing through the summer pastures of the Shah-Sanan tribe to Meshkinshahr, distinguished by a Mongol tomb tower of red brick with faience mosaics. To the south is a Sassanian inscription by Shahpur II.

Pastoral life continues along the remaining 63 km (39 miles); over another pass, and finally Ardabil appears at the edge of a vast plain. Buses take about 7 hours for the 270 km (170 miles) journey.

Ardabil and the Astara Road

Probably founded in the fifth century, Ardabil (90,000 inhabitants) prides itself on being the native city of Sheik Safi-ed-Din (1252–1334), founder of the Shi'ite Military Confraternity, the Qizilbach, and the ancestor of the Safavid. Divided by deep religious differences from their Turkish Sunnite brothers—who were just as fanatic—the Qizil-bachs became more Iranian than the Iranians themselves. This led to the birth of the dynasty founded by Shah Ismail (1502–24), whose mortal remains repose in the mausoleum of Ardabil.

Two beautifully tiled courtyards precede the glazed brick, drum-shaped tomb tower whose geometric decorations are interlaced with ornamental elements inherited from Timurid art. Gold-plated doors open into the painted shrine; behind a silver grill an ivory casket covered with precious rugs contains the remains of Safi next to those of two of his sons. In a smaller, blue-tiled, side chamber, beneath a second tiled tower, the coffin of Shah Ismail is enclosed in a carved sandalwood case, presented by the Indian Grand Mogul Humayun. Pieces of precious khatam are inlaid in the wooden sides, which are further embellished with chiseled ivory inscriptions. From here comes the famous Ardabil carpet now in the Victoria and Albert Museum in London, while in the octagonal room with recesses shaped like bottles, Shah Abbas the Great kept the magnificent collections of porcelains and jades presented by the emperor of China, now in the museum of Tehran. The restoration, under the aegis of U.N.E.S.C.O., has recreated an overall effect worthy of the *Thousand and One Nights*.

The bazaar is amusing. Animated and colorful, it seems to go on forever and is littered with a variety of household objects which will enchant you. There are also a few vestiges of the fortifications which were designed by French officers and proved quite useless against the onslaught of Nicholas I's Cossacks in 1826. They are reminders of one of the pet projects of Napoleon, who was only too happy to oblige Fath Ali Shah (1807—Treaty of Finkenstein).

Now you leave Ardabil for Astara. The road, straight at first, soon begins meandering acrobatically around curves and leads you from the brow of Kuh-e-Salavan, at an altitude of several thousand feet, down to sea level. Cottages with thatched or tiled roofs gradually replace the traditional earthen houses of the high plateau. Then the forest engulfs you, allowing a glimpse here and there through an opening, of the Russian and Iranian lookout posts which face each other along the frontier—a reminder of man's folly in the middle of such a marvelous and peaceful scene. Shortly before Astara, the Caspian suddenly appears on the edge of this grandiose panorama.

Practical Information for Azerbaijan

 WHEN TO GO. Late spring, summer, and early autumn are the most favorable times to go to Azerbaijan, say from April 15th to October 15th. If summer is a bit hot there, the severity of the winter could spoil your trip by making certain sites inaccessible to you. Snow and rain make some of the roads absolutely impassable. And beware of the spring thaw. Nights are always cool, if not cold, in Azerbaijan, except in July and August. Because of the continental climate of this province, the temperature ranges from −25° C (−13° F) to 40° C (104° F).

An annual event is the great Armenian religious assembly in July at the Monastery of St. Thaddeus.

HOW TO GET THERE. The jumping-off place for a visit to Azerbaijan is the provincial capital, Tabriz, which is linked to Tehran by daily Iran Air flights. There is also *air* service from Rezaiyeh. The *buses* of Mihan Tour and of T.B.T. on their international runs stop at the brand-new bus terminal in Tabriz from which buses also operate to Tehran and Maragheh, as well as locally.

The *railroad* station is 5 km (3 miles) west of the city at the end of Reza Pahlavi Ave. There are daily rail connections with Tehran, three times weekly through Turkey with Europe, and once weekly through Jolfa with Baku (U.S.S.R.).

Coming from Turkey, the city starts just beyond the railroad station. Take Reza Pahlavi Ave., which goes across town from west to east, and ends on the road leading to Tehran.

 WHAT TO SEE. Azerbaijan is a varied region whose many facets, from the Caspian to the Ararat range, will detain you along the way if you are driving to Tehran. Tabriz deserves a day (Blue Mosque, bazaar, rug workshops etc.).

The *Tourist Information Office* organizes tours of the city. For a good view of Tabriz, go to the top of the Ain Ali hill, east of the city (*imamzadeh* at the top). It is a walk of about an hour. Make the excursion to Maragheh, where you will see five funerary towers dating from the 12th to the 14th centuries. To the north, near Maku, you can visit the Monastery of St. Thaddeus and the Azerbaijani village next to it. To the south, Takht-e-Suleiman will reveal the secrets of distant antiquity to budding archeologists. Ardabil, to the east, has an interesting faience monument, the tomb of Sheik Safi. Don't miss the Mongol mausoleum of Soltanieh, beyond Zenjan on the road to Tehran.

 MOTORING. Coming from Turkey, one crosses the entire province as far as Tehran on a narrow but well-paved road. The trip from the frontier to Tabriz (270 km, 165 miles) and from Tabriz to Tehran (650 km, 400 miles) can be made in one day in a fast car. The road from Tabriz to Maragheh is also paved, and the continuation from Bonab to Khoy around Lake Rezaiyeh should be finished by 1977. Likewise the section from Bostanabad to Sarab on the otherwise paved Tabriz to Ardabil road. The alternative route via Ahar is by far more picturesque, but it is also more difficult. The same thing is true of the section between Ardabil and Astara (73 km, 45 miles).

Excursions: to visit Azerbaijan, take the following route: Bazargan (frontier post)—Maku—Monastery of St. Thaddeus—return to Tabriz—excursion to Maragheh and Osku (typical village); return to Tabriz. Tabriz, Ardabil, Astara, Rasht, Tehran. You should count on five or six days for this trip. It will take two more days to drive around Lake Rezaiyeh and for the excursion to Takht-e-Suleiman.

In all of Iran, Tabriz is the city where traffic regulations are the most respected. A profusion of precise directions channel traffic toward other provincial towns (blue panels) or toward the various municipal administrative offices (yellow panels). Your parking problems are taken care of by several private parking lots in the center of town. In case of car trouble or accidents, there are garages located on Pahlavi and Firdowsi Aves., or on the Maragheh road. A project to regroup repair shops and garages on the Tehran road, east of town, is under consideration. Gas pumps are found along the road as you enter or leave town.

HOTELS

Ardabil. *Ardabil Inn***; *Arya**; *Sepid* and *Pak*, one beside the other on Pahlavi Ave.

Khoy. *Khoy-Inn***, on the road to Tabriz. Two small hotels in town.

Mahabad. *Mahabad Inn***, outside of town and the *Kyan**.

Maku. *Maku Inn***, on the Bazargan–Tabriz road.

Marand. *Marand Inn***.

Maragheh. *Maragheh Inn***; *Arya* and *Kourosh*, both simple.

Miyandoab. *Berenjan**.

Miyaneh. *Mehmansara* (Inn)**; *Khayyam**.

Rezaiyeh. *Mehmansara* (Inn)***; Zangueneh Ave., *Niagara*, *Park***, Pahlavi Ave.; *Baradaram***, Sowlati Passage; *Iran Park*, Dariouch Ave.;

Karoun, Memari Passage; *Jam*, *Ramsar*, Pahlavi Ave.

Shahpur. *Noor*, very simple.

Tabriz. *International*****, Pahlavi Blvd.; *Asia****, Shahnaz Ave.; *Tabriz Inn***, Maidan-Rah-Ahan, near the station; *Metropol**, Pahlavi Ave.; *Keyhan**, Ark St.; *Moravid**, *Karoun*, *Djahannama*, *Ramsar*, *Park* and *Sepia*,

all on Pahlavi Ave.

Zenjan. *Bimeh***, overcrowded with transit traffic.

Beyond the provincial border, on the road to Tehran, **Takestan.** *Takestan Motel***, small but air-conditioned, excellent restaurant, at filling station. It is also possible to spend the night at the frontier post of Bazargan.

RESTAURANTS. Nothing special in Tabriz. A few Armenian establishments serve pork meat and sausages. If you want to taste Azerbaijani specialties, the *Inn* and the *Asia* serve them, as well as the usual kebabs. Tchelo-kebab restaurants: *Ahmadpoor* and *Canary*, both located on Pahlavi Ave.; *Hadj-Ali Agha* in the Koladouzan Bazaar.

ENTERTAINMENT. The Djahannama Hotel has a dance hall. Besides a few movie houses located on Pahlavi Ave., which show foreign films from time to time, there are two theaters which present Persian plays: the *Aramia* and the *Chir-o-Korchid*.

MUSEUMS. Tabriz: the *Archeological, Ethnographical and Historical Museum* on Pahlavi Ave. (8.30 to 12; 3 to 5) consists of two floors. In the Archeological Room are several beautiful faience mosaic fragments. Also worth looking at are some samples of prehistoric pottery from Takht-e Suleiman and Hassanlu, "blue" Safavid porcelains and a few vases from far away Cipango (Japan). Be sure to notice the beautiful Gorgan platters in faience with a metallic finish, grimacing bronzes dating from the second millennium, and objects from the first millennium representing animal themes of a much more amiable character. Most amusing is a sample of archaic pottery in the form of a double jar with a horse's head, on which a lion is represented drinking, a seven-branched oil lamp and bronze chandeliers with animal-shaped bases.

On the second floor you'll find a few ink-wells and penholders, souvenirs of this or that famous treaty, as well as arms and interesting documents pertaining to the Tabriz Revolt (1908). A collection of photographs shows faraway archeological sites. The basement houses the ethnographical section, with jewelry, modern ceramics and above all a complete collection of traditional costumes of the region.

GETTING AROUND IN TABRIZ. The different urban *bus* lines ply up and down Pahlavi Ave. and the principal streets crossing it. *Taxis* are worth using, for the rates are extremely reasonable.

Excursions: excursions into Azerbaijan start from Tabriz, if one prefers to operate from a fixed base. The *Tourist Information Office* organizes tours of 1 or 2 days to Maragheh and Rezaiyeh, with optional return by air and a boat ride across the lake. For the lake crossing, there are daily boats from Golmankhaneh (port of Rezaiyeh) to Danalou (50 km or 31 miles from Maragheh) and boats twice a week between Golmankhaneh and Charafkhaneh to the north of the lake. Schedules vary according to the seasons. Buses await passengers at the boat landings.

SHOPPING IN TABRIZ. Tabriz is famous for its silver. The silver shops are crowded along the northern sidewalk of Pahlavi Ave. Many are owned by Armenians. In the bazaar, you can buy multi-colored silk scarfs, bright-colored woolen socks and gloves, raw wool caps, natural goat's wool blankets, turned wooden hookahs and a few antiques.

CAMPING. In Tabriz, at Shahgoli—southeast of the city—small, but well equipped.

USEFUL ADDRESSES. *Iran-Air:* the office is at the airport. *Tourist Bureau:* Pahlavi Ave. (5011). *Travel Agencies:* Tourist Guide Center, Shams Tabrizi Ave., Levantour and T.B.T., Pahlavi Ave. Mihan Tour and Press Express, Firdowsi Ave.

American Consulate, south Shahnaz Jonubi Ave. (52101).

Main Post Office: Shah Bakhte Ave.

Churches: Roman Catholic, Pahlavi Ave., near the Metropol; Armenian Rite, north Shahnaz Ave., south Shahnaz Ave, and Baron Awak Ave.

Hospitals: American Hospital, south Shahnaz Ave. (4411); Chir-o-Korchid Hospital, Hafez Ave. (3738).

Useful Telephone Numbers: Police: 02 and 2191; road police: 3416. Airport Information: 2166. Ambulance: 3738; telephone operator: 00.

ISFAHAN AND SURROUNDINGS

Brilliant and Legendary Capital

The old Persian saying that "Isfahan is half the world" was not so exaggerated as it sounds today when it is remembered that at the close of the 16th and throughout the 17th centuries everyone who visited the city was enraptured with its beauty. Longer ago, in 1005, Nasir-i-Kosroe, a celebrated traveler of the day, described it thus: "I have never seen, in any place where Persian is spoken, a finer, larger and more prosperous city than Isfahan." Even in 1937 Robert Byron in his book *The Road to Oxiana* writes of the smaller dome chamber of the Friday Mosque as having attained the perfection of architecture. Or again he says: "The beauty of Isfahan steals on the mind unawares. You drive about, under avenues of white tree trunks and canopies of shining twigs; past domes of turquoise and spring yellow in a sky of liquid violet-blue . . . across bridges of pale toffee brick, tier on tier of arches breaking into piled pavilions; overlooked by violet mountains . . ."

Isfahan, the legendary city, will either enchant you or, since you have heard so much about it, be a bitter disappointment. It is situated some 4,600 feet above sea level, and thus assured of a pleasant temperature throughout the year, in a plain irrigated by the Zayandeh Rud ("the life-giving river"). Isfahan is first of all a beautiful oasis. It is essential that you climb to the top of a minaret to discover the vast green belt which surrounds the city. Irrigation has always been the major concern of Isfahan's rulers, and even Timur's (Tamerlane's) ravages could never wipe out the region's agricultural prosperity.

It was to become one of the most brilliant capitals in the world. Contrary to what is commonly believed, the city became famous long before Shah Abbas I (1587–1628). The Seljuks were the first to make it their capital in the 11th century and remains from this epoch are a proof of artistic activity just as vigorous as that which was later displayed during the reign of the great Safavid. Yet it is the memory of this glorious dynasty which you can appreciate in the shade of minarets and cupolas of sparkling faience. In this air which shimmers with heat and endows most solid objects with the unreality of a mirage, you half expect to see the fabulous feasts described by Sir John Chardin come to life again. Arriving from Tehran, whether by air or by the road which follows the Zagros, the magic city of an Oriental tale stretches before you.

Once Upon a Time . . .

The city we are about to describe is a gift from the gods. Tahmuresse-e-Dirbande, "the conqueror of demons" in the beginning of time built on this site—3,000 years ago—twin villages, Sarouyé and Méhrine. Achaemenid Persia occupied the area, then known as Gabae. This is told by Strabon and from then on, legend gives way to history. Except for one brief moment, for the name of the city is a mystery. Karé, a humble blacksmith from Feriden, put an end to Zahhak's tyranny and offered the throne to the gentle Fereydoune. The latter exclaimed, pointing to the city: "Here is the city of the Espahans"— that is to say of the brave, of the warriors. Or is the origin Ptolemy's Aspadana which is thought to derive from Sipahan or Aspahan (army)? The envious amused themselves by claiming its root to be the local word "asbahan", which means "dog", and added: "All this city needs is decent people." Be this as it may the Sassanid sovereigns assembled their armies destined for new conquests here and left their wives behind in the palace. One of these queens founded the Jewish quarter, the Yahudiyeh, at the beginning of the fifth century.

The warrior bows only to warriors. New conquerors arrived, brandishing the banners of Islam, and Isfahan fell to them in 643 A.D. From the Ommayads to the Abbasids, the Arab domination lasted until 931. The city was ruled by a series of minor princes from Fars and Iraq, among whom was Mardawidj-ben Ziyar, a sort of nocturnal pyromaniac. This potentate's pleasure consisted in setting fire to gigantic wood-piles erected on the heights surrounding Isfahan.

In 935 his lieutenants—the Buyids—succeeded him. Then Mohammed ibn Makan, commander of the Khorassan army, took it over (956). A short time later the Seljuks appeared on the scene. Togrul Beg, "the Hawk Prince", having conquered Isfahan and made it his capital, embellished it, as did his successors, Alp Arslan and Malik Shah.

During the invasions of Genghis Khan, Isfahan escaped destruction, but had to bow to Mongol suzerainty (1228). The eleven Khans took no interest in the city, which passed under Muzaffarid rule, until it fell under Tamerlane's blows in 1388. Here is the description given by Ibn Arabehah, Tamerlane's biographer, of the revolt of the reckless people of Isfahan: "But when dawn had drawn its sword and thrown off the mantle of night, Tamerlane discovered this heinous crime. His nostrils widened with the wrath of Satan. He awakened the camp at once, bared the sword of his rage, seized arrows from the quiver of his tyranny and went forth howling and overturning everything which stood in his way, like a dog, a lion or a leopard. When he arrived in sight of the city, he ordered the massacre and pillage, the devastation and burning of the crops."

The Timurid interlude was followed by the duel between the "Black Sheep" and the "White Sheep", which lasted from 1453 to 1502, when the Safavids, who were to carry Isfahan to glorious heights, took over. Originally from Ardabil, this dynasty established itself first in Tabriz, then in Kazvin, before making Isfahan the capital. When the governor of the city revolted against his suzerain (1589)— one is tempted to believe that the air in Isfahan inspired indiscipline —Shah Abbas came in person to put down the revolt.

Isfahan's Golden Years

In 1598, he established his court in Isfahan thus inaugurating a lavish era. He endowed the city with sumptuous monuments, received foreign ambassadors from all over the world, patronized arts and letters and encouraged handicrafts. His generosity knew no bounds. But every coin has a reverse side, which is borne out by hearing tales of life in this far-off court, told by those who lived there at the time. It seems that although he had several hundred wives in his harem, Shah Abbas also enjoyed the company of young boys. Examples of his cruelty have come down to us: he succeeded his father by having his brothers assassinated and mutilated three of his sons. On a moment's suspicion, in a fit of ill humor or simply as a joke, he ordered the execution of this or that court personality. However, we

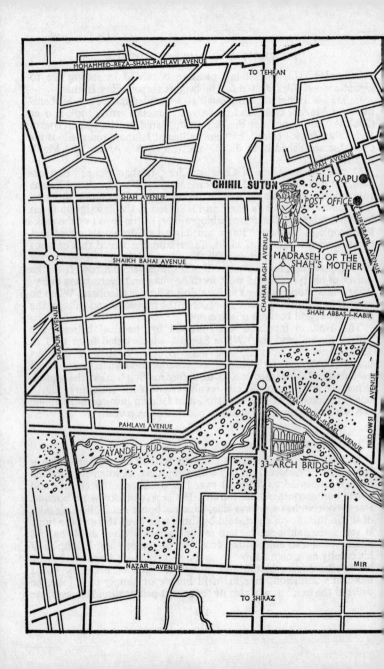

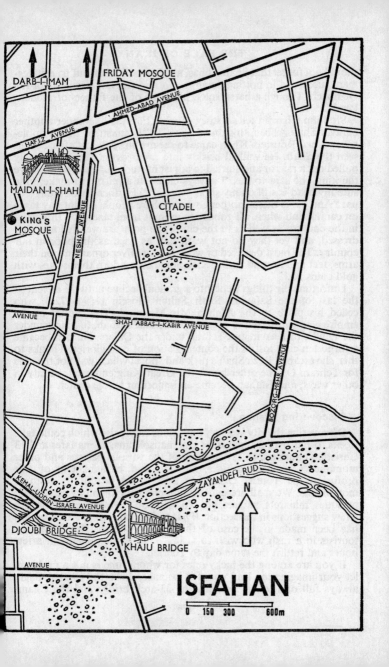

ISFAHAN

0   150   300   600m

should not forget that Shah Abbas, a clever politician and true states-
man, succeeded in putting down the formidable military caste of the
Qizilbach. Though a harsh ruler, he is one of the fathers of modern
Persia.

Sir John Chardin tells a story of what life was like under another
Safavid Shah Abbas, this one Abbas II: "I remember that a noble-
man named Roustem Khan came to see me one day just after he had
seen the Shah. He walked briskly into my apartments, immediately
pulled out a mirror and started to adjust his turban. 'Each time I leave
the king,' he said to me, 'I always check in a mirror to make quite
sure my head is still on my shoulders . . .' " Further on Chardin tells
us: "And yet is there another country where people do not pay taxes
on capital and where all goods are exempt from taxation? In Persia,
in the country as well as in the cities, the poor are well fed and well
dressed, and yet they do not work half as hard as the poor in our
country. The most deprived of women wear silver ornaments on their
arms, feet and around their necks. Some even adorn themselves with
gold coins . . ."

Unfortunately things went into a gradual decline until the advent of
the last of the Safavids, Shah Sultan Hosein (1694–1722), who
ceded his place to the Afghan Mir Mahmud. The capital of the
empire was transferred to Meshed under Nadir Shah, to Shiraz under
the Zands, to Kazvin and Tehran under the Qajars. Isfahan became
a forgotten city, lost in the contemplation of past glories. Thanks to
this, she escaped Reza Shah's pick and shovel which was not the case
for Tehran. On the other hand, the Great King endowed the city in
other ways, and Isfahan became an important textile center.

Discovering Isfahan

Discovering the city is a very ambitious enterprise which could take
weeks. It has over 200 mosques and mausoleums, 28 madares and 13
Christian churches, to say nothing of the various palaces and other
monuments, such as bridges, minarets and bazaars. Out of this
profusion the Tourist Office has selected 84 beautifully restored
monuments. We shall present these monuments to you by categories:
mosques, minarets, palaces, etc. To help you in your choice there are
a few suggestions in the section *What to See*, following. An exception
has been made in the case of the Maidan-i-Shah (Royal Sq.) for
tourists in a rush who wish to visit it and its monuments in a few
hours and return the same day to Tehran.

If you are among the lucky ones for whom time is not a problem,
let your imagination lead you, for instance, down the Chahar Bagh,
always full of strollers between the 33-arch bridge and the Chams

Abbad quarter. Back in the days of Shah Abbas it was already the favorite promenade of the city dwellers who came here hoping to find coolness and a chance to display their wealth. A central canal divided the avenue of the "Four Gardens" (the meaning of Chahar Bagh) and fed onyx basins, into which cut roses were thrown. Today nothing remains, except for the magnificent rows of plane trees which the Shah had planted, burying 2 coins of gold and silver under each tree.

Farther to the east, Hatef Ave. leads you from mosque to mausoleum, some of which are hidden in narrow streets. Towards evening you might go down on the banks of the Zayandeh Rud and stroll through the arches of the brick bridges and watch the last rays of the sun reflected in the waters. One does not visit Isfahan just to sightsee but also to dream.

The Royal Square (Maidan-i-Shah)

"Let me take you to the Maidan ... it is surely as spacious, as agreeable, as fragrant a place as any in the world." Thus spoke Sir Thomas Herbert, one among the numerous 17th-century visitors. Though its aroma has disappeared, its spaciousness and charm still exist against a backdrop of cupolas and minarets, columns and arcades, which have been part of the Maidan-i-Shah's iridescent horizon for over four centuries. In order to give a coherence to this whole complex, Shah Abbas built the monumental portals of the King's Mosque and of the Bazaar, as well as the surrounding double arcade in whose recesses he placed shops, smoking dens and pleasure houses. There used to be a canal which flowed around the entire place under a row of plane trees. The Maidan was used for many different events, some not so enjoyable. For it was here that executions took place, and later a gallows was permanently installed. More often, though, it was the site of gaiety. Covered over with fine sand, the Maidan served as a polo ground; the boundary stones which marked the goals at each end still exist. On the other two sides and facing each other, the Masjid-i-Shaikh Lutfullah and the Ali Qapu complete the Maidan. The reflecting pool and gardens in the middle of the Maidan were created some 35 years ago by Reza Shah. To this day it is reputed to be the largest square in the world.

The King's Mosque (Masjid-i-Shah)

The King's Mosque was the first monument commissioned by Shah Abbas. The building was started in 1612 but was not quite finished at his death in 1628. The monarch must have had a presentiment that he would not live to see his masterpiece completed for he

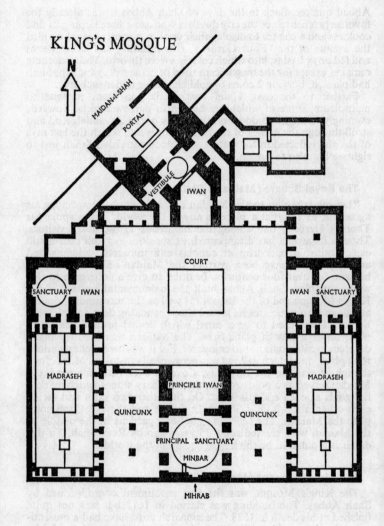

KING'S MOSQUE

N

MAIDAN-I-SHAH

PORTAL

VESTIBULE

IWAN

COURT

SANCTUARY   IWAN

IWAN   SANCTUARY

MADRASEH

MADRASEH

PRINCIPLE IWAN

QUINCUNX

QUINCUNX

PRINCIPAL   SANCTUARY

MINBAR

MIHRAB

badgered the architects, urging them to finish the work quickly and forcing them to use a thousand stratagems in order to hurry on the work. The haste with which it was built has resulted in great fragility, which poses many problems to those charged with its preservation. The King's Mosque is not alone in this, for most of the monuments built under Shah Abbas have suffered from the sovereign's impatience.

Haste was also the reason for the use of a new technique in preparing part of the faience decoration. Polychrome tiles—hence the name *haft rangi,* seven colors—with part of the whole design on each were substituted for mosaic (cut and individually colored pieces).

This monument in spite of its faults is one of the most imposing examples of Safavid art: not only because of its gigantic size but also because of its proportions and the harmony between its various decorative elements. Its beautiful dome, covered with blue tiles, is a striking feature of Isfahan. The entrance portal has an arcade emphasized by a triple turquoise rope-molding rising from two marble basins, while the door itself is framed with two beautiful "faience tapestries". A band of script isolates the upper part, where three niches create three shadow areas in the semi-dome covering the portal. The whole is flanked by two minarets, whose wooden balconies rest on a double row of stalactites at a height of 33 m (108 feet).

In the interior one finds the traditional plan of the Iranian mosque, in spite of the fact that the entrance is at a 45° angle to the rest of the construction, which is oriented towards Mecca. The four iwans surrounding the interior court are reflected in the central pool, giving the clever photographer a chance to take a picture of the reversed faience archways. The south iwan, also flanked by two minarets, leads into the prayer hall. This room is a true marvel, giving a feeling of elegance and lightness quite unexpected beneath so large a cupola. Its ceiling is decorated with a remarkable medallion of tapestry motifs. The minbar and the principal mihrabs are in marble, while the secondary mihrabs are in enameled faience. Don't forget to complete your visit by climbing to the top of one of the minarets of the south iwan, or, if you don't have the stamina, go into the east madresseh; you will have the best view of the dome over the main sanctuary.

The number of bricks in this building is estimated to be about 18 million and some half a million faience tiles were used.

The Masjid-i-Shaikh-Lutfullah

With its small cupola, its unusual color, its low proportions and its exquisite mosaic work, the Shaikh-Lutfullah Mosque counterpoints its glorious rival and is in no way overshadowed by it. Like so many travelers before him, Lord Byron fell under its spell. The Shaikh

Mosque is made to enchant. The placing of the entrance slightly off-center to the dome, is an invitation to examine it more closely. The faiences of the portal, sparkling in the sun, give an effect similar to that of stained glass, for the colors merge in the eye of the onlooker into a symphony of elusive violets.

The obscurity within is in sharp contrast to the dazzling exterior. There is no courtyard. At the end of a crooked passageway one enters a square room, sparsely lit by the light filtering through a series of windows pierced in the drum which supports the cupola. Gradually the shadows brighten, revealing the magnificence of the decor. The effect is similar to that of the exterior decoration. On an unglazed earth-color background, blue and yellow faience motifs spread their tentacles over wall and ceiling surfaces alike. Trying to follow their arabesques makes your head spin. Byron declared: "... Versailles, the porcelain drawing rooms of Schönbrunn, the Doge's Palace, Saint Peter's are all sumptuous, but this mosque surpasses them all with the exuberance of its decoration." The Shaikh-Lutfullah Mosque remains unique to the end: the Arab calligraphy—developed by the great Safavid craftsman Ali Reza Abbasi—on the bands along the top and lower edges of the drum, has here reached a zenith in delicacy and refinement.

The Lofty Gate (Ali Qapu)

Ali Qapu, the glorious gate, a name originally applying only to the portal of the Shah's palace, now encompasses the entire six-story edifice rising above it. It is the third monument of the Maidan, located on its west side and facing the Masjid-i-Shaikh-Lutfullah. The *talar* (balcony) endows the structure with its characteristic silhouette. It was built to serve as a royal loge, from which vantage-point the Shah and his guests watched the spectacles which took place on the Maidan.

The Ali Qapu was considered sacred and as a sign of respect the king himself never crossed its threshold on horseback. Those who had received the sovereigns's kindness came to kiss the gate and pray before it, singing the praises of their monarch. Just like Christian churches in the Middle Ages, the building was an inviolable *bast* (asylum) for fugitives, whether guilty or innocent, and it is said that the Shah himself was forbidden to remove anyone from within its protective walls. Unfounded legend has it that the doors of the Ali Qapu are those of the sanctuary of Ali in Kerbela, which were removed by Shah Abbas. This would explain the aura of sanctity given the site under the Safavids.

Behind the Ali Qapu's double porch is a large hall with two galleries from which a watch undoubtedly was kept on the comings and goings of visitors. Justice used to be dispensed in a huge room on the ground floor by the President of the Diwan. The kachis, coloring, paintings and miniatures used in the decoration of the upper floors, make them a fascinating place to visit. On the first floor go out on the talar, where graceful columns frame a little basin; from there you will have an extraordinary view, especially in the afternoon, of the shimmering dome of the Shaikh-Lutfullah Mosque and the mountains behind. Next you should visit the throne room, where the ceiling is a masterpiece of decoration. On the second floor are two small rooms, their walls enchantingly frescoed. The music room is on the third floor. Its walls and vault are covered with an extraordinary decoration. Silhouettes of scent bottles and musical instruments carved into the woodwork—undoubtedly in an effort to improve the acoustics—remind us that the art of making stringed instruments was born in the Orient.

The Qaisariyeh Bazaar

The Qaisariyeh or Royal Bazaar has lost a great deal of its past animation but still offers tourists a spectacle of tortuous alleys and openwork vaulting, through which filters the diffused light that is one of the main charms of an Oriental bazaar. This structure was built by Shah Abbas ten years after the erection of the monumental gate. The decoration of the latter is done in faience mosaic and not with haft rangi tiles; one can see the superiority of the old technique to the new. The principal decorative motif is an Oriental interpretation of Sagittarius, the city's astrological sign. The paintings recessed into the façade date from the second part of the 17th century. These scenes are rather crudely executed and are in very poor condition. One of these represents Shah Abbas in a battle against the Uzbeks; others show Occidentals [sic] glasses in hand seated at a table, in more or less sloppy attitudes.

Inside the bazaar the artisans' section is much more interesting than that of the merchants. You can watch silver being engraved, copper being hammered, babouches (Turkish slippers) being sewn, qalamqaris being printed and rugs being woven. In this amusing bustle of late afternoon activity you'll discover the delights of craftsmanship so long forgotten in the West.

The Mosques

Even the splendors of Abbas the Great's reign cannot dim the fascination of monuments built in earlier centuries. Less spectacular and more difficult to understand, these date mostly from the Seljuk, Mongol and Timurid epochs.

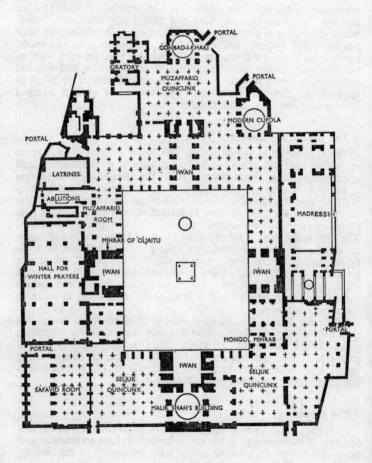

FRIDAY MOSQUE

0   10   20   30m

PORTAL

GONBAD-I-KHAKI

ORATORY

MUZAFFARID
QUINCUNX

PORTAL

MODERN CUPOLA

PORTAL

IWAN

LATRINES

ABLUTIONS

MUZAFFARID
ROOM

MIHRAB OF 'OLJAITU

HALL FOR
WINTER PRAYERS

IWAN

MADRESSEH

IWAN

MONGOL MIHRAB

PORTAL

PORTAL

IWAN

SAFAVID ROOM

SELJUK
QUINCUNX

SELJUK
QUINCUNX

MALIK SHAH'S BUILDING

The Friday Mosque (Masjid-i-Jami)

Three periods are represented with a few Safavid touches added in the labyrinth of its alleys, quincunxes (arrangement of five objects set so that four are at corners of a square and the other at the center) and sanctuaries, often well concealed. It is the most venerable of Isfahan's monuments.

The most ancient part, the principal mihrab room, situated on the southern end of the building, goes back to the reign of the 11th century Seljuk Sultan Malik Shah. It was apparently built on the site where the Abbasid Friday Mosque of Yahudiyeh once stood. Shortly after its completion, religious conflcts broke out between Malik Shah and his Grand Vizier Nizam al-Mulk. The mosque was destroyed. Mizam promptly rebuilt it. The struggle between Nizam and Taj al-Mulk, advisor to the Sultan's mother, fortunately turned out to be beneficial for the building. Having abandoned the use of arms, but not wishing to be outdone, Taj al-Mulk ordered the construction of another sanctuary to the north of the mosque. This is the Gonbad-i-Khaki, "brown cupola", which though of more modest proportions than the principal sanctuary, is a prodigious piece of architecture. Its dome rests on a series of smaller and smaller arches. At the top the square floor plan is transformed into a circle made up of 16 small arches which receive the final cap. It is a masterpiece of technique and daring, typical of Seljuk art. "Not that they possessed infinite mathematical knowledge," as Eric Schroeder says, "for theirs was an empirical knowledge. Because they made courageous experiments and had the intelligence to learn from past mistakes, the Seljuks, as early as the 12th century, built the ideal cupola not to be equaled again until the 18th century, thanks to progress in the science of mathematics."

Now to go back to Malik Shah's sanctuary. The south iwan alone tells the story of the mosque. The main work was most certainly accomplished during the Seljuk period, but is subsequent to the fire of 1121 (the two buildings just mentioned were the only ones to survive). According to an inscription dated 1476, its honeycombed vault, its minarets and the panels which decorate the sides, are the work of Ouzoun Hassan (1453–78), a "White Sheep" tribal chief. As for the bands of writing which frame the iwan's arch and pediment, they are of the Safavid epoch. All that is missing here is the Mongol influence. The latter is found in the Muzaffarid room, to the west, in the form of a magnificently carved stucco mihrab, the gift of Oljaitu Khoda-bendeh, the builder of Soltanieh.

Visit the mosque by entering through the southeastern portal, of the Seljuk period. Immediately to the right of the entrance is the door leading to the madresseh; it dates from the 14th century and bears an inscription to the Muzaffarid Qutb-ed-Din Shah Mahmud. A little farther to the left is a small 14th-century Mongol mihrab. Then you enter the courtyard, where you can admire successively, the south iwan (on the left) and Malik Shah's mihrab room, already described. Next, the east iwan which is of the Seljuk period and still has a few traces of the original decoration (niches above the marble sub-structure). Then the soberly decorated north iwan and the Gonbad-i-Khaki, already mentioned (reached by going through the quincunx on the right). Lastly the west iwan with its Safavid faiences created under Shah Sultan Hosein in the 17th century. Ask to see Oljaitu's mihrab, in the room to the right of the west iwan—you go through the quincunx. If you are short of time you can skip the madresseh, the ablution chamber etc.

N.B.: the Friday Mosque is located at the end of a narrow street on the left of the Khaiban Hatef, coming from the Royal Maidan.

The Ali Mosque (Masjid-i-Ali)

The Ali Mosque is also situated on the left of the Khiaban Hatef, at the end of several narrow streets, about 500 m (550 yards) from the Friday Mosque. Two other monuments should be visited at the same time: the minaret of Ali (12th century) and the mausoleum of Harun Velayat (16th century).

The Ali Mosque, attributed to Sultan Sandjar by popular tradition, seems more of the Safavid epoch. The neighboring minaret, built in or about the time of the Sultan's reign, probably was part of a large complex which may have included a much earlier building than the present-day mosque. In any case it is a very handsome building combining skilful architecture, harmonious proportions and elegant decoration. Particularly outstanding is the decoration of the portal on the main façade. The interior is formed by the traditional court surrounded by its four iwans. The harmonious lines of the mihrab room are not marred by overdecoration. Along the base of the large cupola, which rests on splendid arches, 13 verses of the Koran and the date of construction (1521) are inscribed. In the court there is a stele (slab with inscription), on which is engraved a poem which was sent by the Great Mogul to honor Shah Abbas.

The Zoleimat Mosque or Maghsoud Beg

The Maghsoud Beg is located near the Khiaban Hafiz, to the left, a little beyond the Royal Place, in a little street at the corner of an intersection.

Though the Safavids lavished sumptuous monuments on Isfahan, they enjoyed being copied by their more affluent subjects. Such was the case of Maghsoud Beg, Chamberlain of the Royal Household, who readily complied with his monarch's wishes. Although the architect did an honest job, the building is remarkable for its refined decorative elements. The plan of the mosque is very simple: a rectangular portal covered with remarkable kachis opens onto a large domed hall which contains a mihrab decorated with faience mosaics. The inscriptions are the work of the celebrated Ali Reza. Ironically enough, this mosque houses the remains of another famous calligraphist, a rival of Ali Reza, Mir Imad.

The Red Mosque (Masjid-i-Sorkhi)

The Masjid-i-Sorkhi is located near the northeast corner formed by the Chahar Bagh and the Khiaban-e-Mochir. Near the Public Health building, follow the Khiaban-e-Mochir and you'll find the mosque just beyond, on the left.

This monument is extremely interesting because of the beautiful inscription in white characters on blue over the portal; it sings the praises of the Shah in unabashed terms. The inscription is signed by Khalif-el-Sofredji (Sofredji means "in charge of the tablecloth", meaning master of ceremonies). Asked by the Shah to endow the city with a monument, he decided to build a mosque, which was called the Sofredji Mosque. Gradually local speech transformed Sofredji into Sorkhi (red), which is why we look in vain today for traces of that color on the monument.

Hakim Mosque (Masjid-i-Hakim)

The Masjid-i-Hakim is one of the best-hidden mosques in Isfahan. It is located in the same area as the Red Mosque, but a little farther on in the labyrinth of the bazaar streets to the north of Khiaban-e-Mochir. At the same time you can visit the Madraseh Sadr. It is in the same street, which can also be reached from the main entrance of the bazaar on the Maidan, by continuing straight on for about 200 m (220 yards).

A strange figure was Hakim Daoud, doctor to the king, obliged to flee Shah Abbas's court after some shady dealings. Having found just as lucrative a post at the court of the Great Mogul, he tried in vain to put an end to his exile by building the monument which bears his name. Erected in the 17th century over the remains of a 12th-century building, the Masjid-i-Hakim is remarkable for its triple iwan on the north and south façades of its interior court.

185

The Jorgir portal, situated near one of the entrances to the mosque, probably a vestige of an earlier monument, is a marvelous example of cut brick decoration.

Masjid-i-Sarutaghi

Situated in the bazaar area, the Masjid-i-Sarutaghi was built by a commoner who became the second most important figure of the empire. Sarutaghi, son of a Tabriz baker, rose to the position of Prime Minister under Shah Safi and Shah Abbas II. History relates that he was assassinated in 1645 at the age of 80. The mosque is the only part which remains standing of the magnificent palace buildings owned by him but is not a masterpiece. However, the interior decoration of the cupola is, according to Godard, "one of the most beautiful examples of Iranian decoration from the Safavid epoch".

The Madares

The Madares were traditional schools where not only theology, philosophy and literature were taught, but mathematics and science as well. There were about 300 in Isfahan, most of which were attached to mosques. The traditional floor plan of a madresseh consisted of a central court, often with a basin with running water, surrounded by individual cells, each of which was occupied by a student who lived alone devoting himself to meditation and study. At the beginning of this century, religious as well as secular education was still the monopoly of these establishments. Usually founded by the royal family, such as those built by Shah Abbas's great grandmother in the bazaar (the Djadde-ye-Borzorg and the Djadde-ye-Kouchik), some of the madares still operate today.

Madresseh-e-Chahar Bagh

The rectangle Madresseh complex is framed by the carefully restored Bazaar-e Boland, the Shah Abbas Hotel, Chahar Bagh and Shah Abbas-e-Kabir Aves., across from the Tourist Office.

Built in 1710 by the Safavid, Sultan Hosein, this residential college for theological students has been described by Sir Julian Huxley in his book *From an Antique Land* as: "a triumph of delicacy, surprisingly combining lightness with classical form".

You will notice the extraordinary fragility of the faiences on the portal and the gold and silver medallions which adorn the doors. From the octagonal vestibule with its traditional stone basin for ablutions, one enters a delightful garden, an oasis of peace in rude contrast with the tumult of the street. The shady branches of aged, gnarled trees are reflected in a pool.

The madresseh's sanctuary is on the south side of the court, behind an iwan flanked by two minarets, which frame the superb turquoise cupola in the background. On a smaller scale, the overall effect is that of the King's Mosque, with perhaps more grace and certainly more intimacy. Even though of the late Safavid period, there is nothing in the decoration which betrays decadence; one may search the faiences in vain for the least trace of the false elegance so typical of some Qajar ceramics.

The last sovereign of a dying dynasty, Sultan Hosein spent the night before his execution here in one of the cells. He was killed by the Afghans. Such criminal memories are difficult to contemplate in this peaceful atmosphere. Take a last look at the regular alignment of arcades, the bewitching arabesques decorating the cupola, the marble basin and the pleasant foliage carvings before tearing yourself away from the peaceful serenity of this privileged place.

Next door extends the most lavishly reconstructed caravanserai, the Kkan-i-Madar-i-Shah, named after the mother of Sultan Hosein; its profits were used to support the students and professors of the madresseh. Gradually the money was used for other things, and in 1905 when Lord Curzon, Viceroy of India and amateur archeologist, visited the school, only 50 of the 160 rooms were occupied by students. The caravanserai eventually was taken over by the state. It has been restored to its original purpose, but upgraded into a luxury hotel which until recently was reserved for distinguished guests of His Majesty.

The Shah Abbas hotel quickly became so popular, however, that it was greatly enlarged in 1975. Even if you do not stay there you must sip tea in the lovely flower-filled garden or dine in its magnificent dining room with green tiled ceiling and pillars mosaicked with tiny pieces of mirror. A shopping center in the same style was opened at the same time across Shah Abbas Ave.

The Imamieh Madresseh

Located near an important intersection of Hatef Ave., north of the Friday Mosque on the left, this madresseh is near the mausoleum Baba Qasem whose dome can be seen from the avenue. Originally these two monuments were probably part of the same complex. In fact the Imamieh Madresseh is known as the Madresseh of Baba Qasem by the local inhabitants. Built in 1325 by Suleiman Abdul Hassan Talut el Damghani in honor of his teacher the theologian Baba Qasem, this is one of the most ancient madares in Isfahan. It is composed of the traditional central court, each façade of which is pierced by an iwan, but the decoration has not yet attained the opulence of the Safavid epoch. Brick predominates, bringing out the painted elements of the decor and the sober inscriptions traced in white on two shades of blue. This college, along with the neighboring mausoleum of Imamzadeh Djaffar, is among the few remaining structures of the Mongol period.

The Mullah Abdullah Madresseh

Built inside the bazaar, this school was "this college of Abdullah, the largest and richest college of Isfahan . . . where Mohammed Baker taught . . . the wisest man of his century, especially in theology . . ." Although the kachis which decorate the entrance giving onto the bazaar date from 1803, it is likely that the rest of the building goes back to the 17th century. From the south iwan, which dates from the reign of Shah Suleiman, archeologists have learned that a certain Mirza Mohammed left all his worldly goods to the students of the Mullah Abdullah Madresseh.

The Minarets

With minarets we come to a new type of monument which should be explained. Before the Safavids, many mosques were built with minarets independent of the main building, just as the Byzantines built basilicas with independent baptisteries and campaniles which are seen in Ravenna and elsewhere in Italy.

The minaret has the same role in Islam as bell-towers in Christendom: to call the faithful to prayer. The muezzin climbed to the top of the minaret or to one of its balconies and chanted his call in all four directions. However, there was one inconvenience in this custom: there was always a chance that the pious man's eyes might stray towards the neighboring harems. In the days of the Safavids, only blind men were chosen for the task! Today this sort of problem no longer exists, not only because of women's emancipation but because amplifiers and loud speakers are used instead. For those interested in its origins, the minaret comes from Syria and goes back to the Omayyads.

The Ali Minaret (Manar-i-Ali)

This minaret is situated next to the mosque of the same name and the mausoleum of Harum Velayat. According to some, it is the oldest of Isfahan's 43 minarets, since it was built during the 12th century. Recent restoration has increased its former height of 48 m (157 feet) to the present 50 m (164 feet).

The Ali minaret is divided into three sections by two collar-like rings supporting the balconies of the muezzin. There are ornamental cruciform and star motifs and you should examine closely its checkered red patterns and on a band in stylized writing, the name of the venerated Ali, son-in-law of Mohammed. There is no trace of enamel in the lines etched into the masonry.

The Sareban Minaret (Manari-i-Sareban)

The Sareban Minaret, also known as the Cameleer Minaret, is part of a group which seem to be holding a convention about 600 m (650 yards) east of Hatef Ave. to the north of Saadi Ave., in the area facing the Friday Mosque. The Sareban minaret is the most inaccessible, for it is hidden in the maze of streets which crisscross this quarter.

It is certainly Isfahan's most beautiful minaret. Dating from the Seljuk epoch (11th–13th centuries) its slender needle, 44 m (144 feet) high, speaks eloquently for its builders. This minaret was part of a mosque, of which no trace remains. It is composed of three parts divided by two stalactite galleries. The first section, from the base to the lower cornice, is decorated with crisscross and star motifs. There is no faience and only the relief of the brickwork enlivens this huge surface. Ceramic is used only on the rings of the stalactites and to accentuate the beautiful inscriptions. The second part is also adorned with geometric non-enameled brick, of which not much is left.

The Minaret of the 40 Daughters

This minaret (Manari-i-Chihil Docktaran) is north of the Sareban minaret. Who were the 40 daughters for whom one of the oldest (11th century) minarets in Iran is named? Perhaps, as the number 40 is considered lucky in Iran, it is just a name. More thickset and squat than the Sareban minaret and the Ali minaret, it is less than 30 m (98 feet) high. Octagonal at the base and cylindrical in its upper part, it is decorated with elegant geometric patterns in brick and with an inscription etched in the terra-cotta. An unusual detail is that, two-thirds of the way up the shaft and facing south toward Mecca, there is a large window, surmounted with a wooden lintel and framed by pilasters.

The Two Dar-ol-Ziafeh Minarets

South of the Sareban minaret, the two Dar-ol-Ziafeh minarets rise on either side of a portal (the Dar-el-Battikh) which spans the street.

Originally they flanked the entrance to a madresseh of the Mongol epoch which has long since disappeared. Octagonal in shape up to the probable height of the building they framed, they are cylindrical in the upper part. Their tops are adorned with a stalactite whorl of leaves, which suggests that there once was a balcony.

The Dardacht Minarets

Situated not far from the Friday Mosque, near the remains of the Mausoleum of Bakht-i-Aqa, they are disposed in the same way as the two Dar-ol-Ziafeh minarets and are also the surviving element of a Mongol structure of which there are no traces. Chardin in his day mentioned "a college, situated in the Deredechte area, whose large portal was flanked by two high needles or turrets . . ." This formula was adopted in many Mongol and Seljuk edifices, and it may be that this rather primitive idea of a portal flanked by two minarets was the inspiration for the more successful architectural composition of the Friday Mosque and later found its culmination in the King's Mosque.

Dark blue spiral faience decoration, brickwork and the use of clay are typical features of the Mongol period. Not long ago the Dardacht minarets, minus their tops, served as a refuge to a family of storks. They are undated. The only clue to their age comes from a building surmounted by an adobe cupola which stands next to the abandoned porch. A tombstone found there is dated 1159. The minarets are probably more recent, by about 150 years.

The Falconry Minaret (Manar-i-bagh-i-Quch)

This minaret, which rises north of Sorouch Ave., in the north-eastern suburbs of the city, is the sole vestige of the Masjid-i-Baba Sokhteh, built in open country on the northern fringes of Isfahan. The delicate faiences in the form of long dark blue and turquoise ribbons, twisting upwards against a natural brick background, epitomize the refined classicism of Timurid art of the beginning of the 15th century. Serving to emphasize the balcony, a band of stalactites overhangs the traditional inscriptions and the delicate mosaic panels.

The Palaces of Isfahan

The citadel (Kal-i-Tabarak) rises at the end of the Khiaban-e-Ali which branches off the east of Shah Ave., about 300 m (330 yards) north of Shah Abbas Ave. Nothing survives but earth walls, crumbling bastions and the ruins of ditches and fortifications. In the walls barley grows! The foundations of these fortifications are attributed to the Seljuks. Between the 10th and 18th centuries they were constantly kept up by those in power. During the reign of Shah Abbas they consisted only of a crude wall, but 50 years later Chardin saw towers, ditches and battlements. In 1722 the citadel was besieged and fell, which explains why so little survives.

Chihil Sutun

The Khiaban Sepah, which joins Chahar Bagh Ave. at the Maidan, is bordered on the right by the Royal Park surrounding the Chihil Sutun palace.

CHIHIL SUTUN

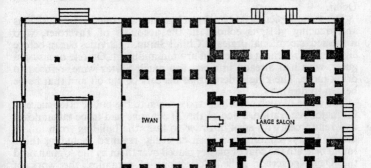

The Chihil Sutun, "Pavilion of Forty Columns", finished during the reign of Abbas II, was destined for official ceremonies, especially the reception of ambassadors. Why 40 columns, when the portico consists of only twenty? There are in fact twenty columns but these are perfectly reflected in a pool which turns them into forty. It has been mentioned before that the number 40 is considered lucky and when an Islamic Asian is asked for a number he usually says 40; 40 days and 40 nights of the Flood, Ali Baba and the 40 thieves, etc.

The high portico gives the Chihil Sutun its elegance. Its slender wooden pillars support a sumptuous ceiling. Originally it was completely covered with mosaic work consisting of thousands of minute pieces of mirror which fired the imagination of all who saw it. Some of this decoration still exists on the façade and the recess which was used as the throne room. Several small drawing rooms, decorated with portraits of personalities of the time, open onto the gallery.

You enter the audience chamber through low doors which open into the iwan of the throne. Here again the ceiling is a marvel: bas-reliefs in blue, red, emerald and gold plaster make up the richly decorative motifs. The paintings in this room have suffered greatly from time and clumsy restoration. It has taken all the skill of contemporary experts to save them. Among the subjects represented Shah Tahmasp can be seen receiving one of the Great Mogul's ambassadors, Abbas the Great attacking the Uzbeks and Nadir Shah entering Delhi.

The scene depicting Abbas II at a banquet, surrounded by musicians and dancing girls, is echoed in the accounts of Tavernier, who witnessed exceptional orgies at Chihil Sutun. Festivities began before eight in the morning and ended around midnight. On one occasion a guest, who had already imbibed too much Shiraz wine, refused to drink more. The king ordered that his ears be cut off and that he be beaten to death.

The scene of such exploits is today open to the public after successful major renovation. Each of the 20 columns had to be taken down and reinforced with steel in order to keep the building from falling down. Every painting has been carefully restored including those found beneath the coat of plaster placed over them by the Afghans and the Qajar governor Zelle. Collections of ceramics, the work of Chinese artists invited by Abbas I, are displayed in showcases.

Several imperilled monuments have been moved into the park such as the portals of the Qothiyeh Mosque (1543) and those of an ancient oratory (1496) as well as arcades from the Djavbareh Mosque (1548).

The Hasht Behesht

On Chahar Bagh, a little beyond the Madresseh-e-Chahar Bagh, a blue door gives access to the Bagh-i-Bolbol, the Garden of the Nightingale. Hidden here is the palace of the Eight Paradises (Hasht Behesht), recently restored and opened to the public.

In 1669 Shah Suleiman commissioned this octagonal building; eight small drawing rooms radiate off the main room. It was here that the Shah installed his eight favorites of the moment which explains the name Eight Paradises. In the 17th century the entire pavilion was faced with marble. The ceiling of the main room was of massive gold

Ancient peace and modern noise in Iran. The Mihrab of Oljaitu in the Friday Mosque, Isfahan, and the crowded entrance to the University of Tehran

Women wearing the *chador*, outside the entrance
to the Friday Mosque, Isfahan

and inlaid work supported by mirrored pillars, while the walls were adorned with paintings depicting historical or legendary scenes. In the gardens, miniature warships floated on the canals, simulating naval battles amidst the swans and pelicans!

Around 1880 a change in the decor took place: Fath Ali Shah had himself portrayed, first standing surrounded by his 600 sons, and then slaying a ferocious beast. Also added was a portrait of Strachey, the youthful Englishman, whose elegant figure the Shah so admired that he plastered the young man's likeness all over most of his residences.

The restoration of Hasht Behesht came just in time to save it from the fate of other gracious palaces of the last Safavids described to us by travelers, whose very location is now unknown to us. Among the vanished are: the charming *Ayimeh Khane* (Mirror Kiosk) in the gardens of Chihil Sutun; the *Imarat Behesht*, of which Chardin exclaimed: "One always leaves it with regret"; the *Haft Dast* (Seven Perfections) built by Tahmasp II as well as others. The *Talar Ashraf* with its three iwans still stands in the old royal gardens. Russian soldiers were billeted there during the First World War. Fortunately its boldly conceived paintings suffered no damage beneath their thick coating of whitewash.

The Mausoleums

Ibn Sina Ave., at the end of Chahar Bagh, leads to Sombolestan Park. Northeast of this garden, at the end of a little street in the middle of an ancient neighborhood, rises the Darb-i-Imam. Originally this mausoleum was erected over the tomb of the two "sons of Imam". Later, the vestibule (iwan), which had been encroached upon by tombs of the faithful, was covered with a cupola and its entrance closed off by a lattice-work window. The main cupola, which dates from the 15th century, is faced with exceptionally beautiful faience mosaics comparable in style and inspiration to those of the Blue Mosque in Tabriz.

At the time it was built, the sanctuary's vault provoked great admiration, as is attested by the inscription: "Next to its golden dome, the high tent (the sky) is nothing but a blue rag." The mausoleum, erected in 1453 during the reign of Shah Jahan, chief of the Black Sheep tribes, was modified in 1670 by Shah Suleiman. The work was completed by his successor, Shah Hosein, who built a new portal and a gallery leading to the vestibule behind the tomb.

The mausoleum's east wall, which is adjacent to an ancient convent, is adorned with white calligraphy bordered in black, around which is woven another smaller inscription in blue faience, repeating the names of the 14 "pure ones". In the courtyard in front of the mausoleum a lion stands guard over the tomb of a hero, probably an officer in the service of a Safavid king. The beast has a human face with a mustache —a strange symbol found on the other side of the world in pre-Colombian statuary.

The Mausoleum of Harun Velayat

To reach it, follow the same directions as for the Ali Mosque; the mausoleum of Harun Velayat is right next to it. Harun, whom Chardin called "the saint of the country", is a personage about whom we know nothing. This mystery naturally has caused much conjecture. Sir John had his own version: "Under Shah Ismail, a mason became Vizier, after promising to build the most beautiful mausoleum in all the country if the Shah would rescue him from his poverty." A couplet inscribed on the façade confirms this romantic story: "Thanks to Dourmich Khan, for whom all things are possible, let this monument stand in memory of Hosein the mason's gratitude." Whatever its story, this magnificent mausoleum, built during the reign of Shah Ismail (1513), is on a very ancient site of worship, for Moslems, Jews and Christians all venerate it.

From an artistic point of view, the mausoleum of Harun Velayat is an admirable example of early Safavid art. The enamel decoration of the portal giving onto the courtyard is extremely beautiful. "These transparent, vivid and vibrant kachis are certainly among the masterpieces of Iran's favorite art. Perhaps less original in their composition than those of the Darb-i-Imam portal, they surpass them in execution . . ." (Godard).

Past the threshold, one enters a small courtyard with a basin. The mausoleum itself is covered with a lovely cupola, while the mihrab sparkles with the whiteness of its stalactites and the glow of its enamels. The variety of the calligraphy is proof of the great fervor which has surrounded this mysterious sanctuary for centuries.

The Mausoleum of Baba Qasem

To reach the mausoleum of Baba Qasem, refer to the directions given for the Madresseh Imamieh. The monument is topped by a pyramid roof. Built in 1340 and dedicated to the memory of the theologian Baba Qasem Isfahani by one of his disciples, it was restored in 1634. Despite its perfection, it does not seem to have attracted attention in the past. Chardin related that God's judgement manifested itself in a very strange way on this site: "The Persians insist that if a false witness is brought here and he swears falsely in the presence of a magistrate, he will fall dead and his entrails will ooze out of his body." One is led to believe that by 1928 there were no false witnesses in Isfahan, for the monument was at that time occupied by a donkey. The Sunnite Baba Qasem was ejected from his last resting place, and the present occupant of this little jewel is the deceased *pehlevan* (gymnast) Mirza, a weaver by profession.

Steps lead down to the entrance. Over the portal, adorned with large stalactites, an inscription in white mosaic on a dark blue background gives the names of the donor and of the saint. Six little stars embellish the calligraphy. On one the word Allah can be deciphered, on the second Mohammed and on the third Ali. The names on the other three stars have been scratched out, for they were the names of Caliphs damned by the Shi'ites, Abu Bahr, Omar and Osman. This modest face-lift on a Sunnite tomb was undoubtedly part of the restoration effected during the 17th century. The roofing was repaired and the drum of the dome decorated with Kufic writing: "My Prophet is Mohammed, my Imam is Ali." With the Sunnite "heresy" thus eradicated, the sanctuary could be used by Shi'ites.

The Imamzadeh Ismail and the Chaïa Mosque

This mosque is situated at the end of a little covered street which runs east starting from Halef Ave., just about where the Djaffar Mausoleum stands, and should be visited at the same time.

A *chahar-sou*, an intersection covered with a cupola, gives access to the courtyard of a madresseh. This is flanked by a small mosque and by the Imamzadeh Ismail, originally presumed to be the tomb of the prophet Elias, venerated by the Moslems as Chaïa. The cenotaph, behind the Imamzadeh, consists of a masonry kiosk inside a wooden cage. The accompanying texts relate that the Chaïa Mosque, the first in Isfahan, was built by Abu Abbas in the time of Ali. Very little has been found of what probably was an Abbasid building, or, for that matter, of the sanctuary dedicated by the Seljuk Alp Arslan, except for a truncated minaret and a few arches.

Construction of the Imamzadeh Ismail was begun by Shah Abbas and finished in 1634. The madresseh was built later. The mausoleum's portal decorates the south side of its court. To the left of the portal, a stone slab is inscribed with an edict of the Shah specifying that property owners in the mausoleum's immediate vicinity are excused wearing the special clothes necessary during the Achoura, as well as the custom of the palm, etc. This alludes to the custom, much encouraged by the Safavids, of keeping a large wooden structure, featuring Hosein's coffin, for use in the Muharram processions. During the month of mourning, this *nakhl*, decorated with palms, feathers and gold paper, was carried from neighborhood to neighborhood by the faithful dressed in new clothes. It was adorned with candles; and close to it, honey cakes were cooked. These monuments, weighing 300 to 1,500 kilos (660 to 3,300 lbs.), inspired great rivalries between neighborhoods, and processions often ended up in rioting.

The essential decorative element of the mausoleum lies in its inscriptions. Around the drum supporting the dome, square turquoise Kufic lettering stands out against the brick background. The present-day Chaïa Mosque shelters its simple mihrab beneath a projecting arch, dated 1689.

The Djaffar Mausoleum

This mausoleum is on Halef Avenue, on the left just beyond Mochir Ave. The Imamzadeh Djaffar is a small octagonal court-yard built in 1325, at the height of the Mongol epoch. Its brick walls are decorated by blind arches with mosaic tympanums. It is probable that its cupola was capped with a pointed roof similar to those of the funerary towers of the epoch. Restoration undertaken in 1950 seriously marred the charm of its style. Inside, an engraved tombstone protected by a wooden grill symbolizes the presence of Djaffar. The prophet's companion has innumerable mausoleums throughout the country, but none can boast of having even one bone.

The Mausoleum of Baba Rokn-ed-Din

To reach the famous mausoleum of Barbaroux (as Chardin called it), cross the Zayandeh Rud on the Khaju bridge and continue straight ahead until you see on your right the conical roof of tihs monument in the middle of a vast cemetery.

The mausoleum (1629) was Shah Abbas's gift to the people of Isfahan, "who have always felt great affection for this saint". To judge by the number of graves which surround the tomb of the holy man, their devotion has not waned. The sanctuary's peaked roof can be seen from afar. Unfortunately the blue and black faiences, with which it was faced inside as well as out, have almost completely disappeared except for a few panels on the roofing and on the portal. Its originality lies in its pentagonal shape, surmounted by a ten-sided drum and roof. The saint, whose tomb is protected by a wooden grille, rests in one of the niches of the principal room.

The Bridges

Isfahan's river, the Zayandeh Rud, separates the city from its suburbs, Julfa and Jiber, which are inhabited by minorities and by the ancient Zoroastrian colony. It gives life to the oasis surrounding the city, only to die amidst brackish desert swamps. The bridges of Isfahan, those graceful monuments reflected in the water, are cool places where the crowds come to stroll and relax. One never thinks of them as mere means of crossing the river. They stand for luxury and refinement, further proof of the originality of Persian architecture.

The ancestor of all these works of art is the Sharestan bridge, which straddled the Zayandeh Rud as early as the 3rd century A.D. Later centuries sought to outdo the ancient builders.

The Bridge of 33 Arches

This bridge with its 33 arches (Seeyo-se-pol) is also called the Allahverdi Khan bridge. It is not surprising that it was included in Shah Abbas the Great's first city plan. Connecting the Chahar Bagh, the city's main artery, with the suburb of Julfa where the Armenians had just settled, the bridge was to have many other uses. The sovereign asked that rooms for travelers be included in its plan. Besides being an excellent place to celebrate marriages, a mullah could have his residence there. Jugglers and tumblers also performed there. Dressed in various disguises, Shah Abbas visited the construction site on several occasions to make sure that his orders were being followed.

The bridge also bears the name of Allah Verdi Khan, the Shah's commander-in-chief who was in charge of the construction; it is 360 m (1,170 feet) long and 13.75 m (45 feet) wide. It inspired lyrical praise from travelers. Curzon declared that it alone was worth the entire trip, and others have described it as "fanciful".

The bridge's pillars are of stone, its superstructure brick. On each side it is edged by a roofed double arcade, interrupted by several pavilions which sheltered the installations ordered by the king. Two other promenades, one above and one below this level, were created so that the bridge could be crossed on three different levels.

Julian Huxley says that Shah Abbas insisted that men's ears should be charmed by the sound of running water; so the architect made a special channel to collect every trickle of dry-season water into a sufficient stream. Only when Abbas was satisfied was the architect paid!

The Khaju Bridge

Some way downstream from the Bridge of the 33 Arches, the Khaju bridge challenges it. A little narrower and shorter than its classic rival, it is also more graceful, with its 6 semi-octagonal pavilions relieving the monotony of its arcades. The stone pillars and foundations, as well as the brick superstructure conform in style with the older bridge, but over and above all these attributes, the Khaju bridge served also as a weir. Through each arch passed a narrow channel, whose flow could be regulated by a sluice-gate, making it possible to irrigate gardens downstream. Today the water flows freely over its stone foundations.

It is thought that the Khaju bridge was built by Abbas II in the middle of the 17th century to replace a Seljuk construction which had become inadequate. A bridge was needed to enable the Zoroastrians who lived in this neighborhood to cross the river without having to pass via the Chahar Bagh. It is three-quarters of a mile from the Bridge of 33 Arches.

Originally the pavilions of the Khaju bridge were all decorated and bore philosophical inscriptions in verse and prose. Here is one quoted by Chardin: "The world is a bridge, cross it. Weigh and measure everything you find on your way. Everywhere evil surrounds good and surpasses it." This moral was illustrated by paintings suggestive enough to scandalize Sir William Ouseley. In 1873, during a wave of puritanism the paintings and verses were replaced with unexceptional faiences. A little way downstream from the bridge, on each side, a Safavid lion stands guard.

The Joubi Bridge and the Marnan Bridge

The Joubi bridge is between the Allahverdi (33 arches) and the Khaju bridges. Actually it is an aqueduct and owes its name to the *joub* (canal) which it supports; this provided water for palaces which today no longer exist.

As for the Marnan bridge, it is named after the nearby village of Marbanan. Situated west of the Allahverdi bridge, it serves mainly to connect Julfa with the center of the city.

Julfa

Julfa was built on the south bank of the river, a little upstream from Isfahan. In the autumn of 1603, Shah Abbas deported the Armenian population of Jolfa in Azerbaijan to this site, where he wished them to practice their trades. This was accomplished by the Shah's soldiers who moved the reluctant families forcibly. The king had excellent reasons to justify his action: these clever craftsmen, who lived so close to the sultan's frontiers, might have escaped from him at any moment. Depopulation of the city of Arax was a way of cutting off the Turkish trade routes. At the same time a new breath of life was infused into ancient Isfahan, where the courage, energy and skill of the Armenians worked marvels.

At first everything went according to plan. In an attempt to make it up to the Armenians for having treated them so harshly, Shah Abbas granted them all kinds of privileges—freedom of religion, the right to build churches and to designate a mayor for their community. Better still, he lent them money without interest so that they could go into business and set up their workshops and trade centers. Soon Julfa grew into a town of 60,000 inhabitants and some of the emigrés lived like princes, even inviting the Shah into their luxurious homes. Unfortunately this situation did not last, for the Shah's successors were quick to seek money where it existed. Taxes increased and privileges disappeared. During the Shah Suleiman's reign Sir John Chardin reported that the suburb of Julfa "had already been stripped of its former opulence and its population had shrunk drastically". Under Shah Sultan Hosein, who was as weak as he was pious, the people's animosity became apparent. This sovereign promulgated a law to the effect that an Armenian converted to Islam could inherit the property of his entire family; in other words, renegades were rewarded. Nadir Shah, always in need of money, completed the ruin of Julfa's merchants. Today only a few thousand inhabit this ill-fated place.

After crossing the Allahverdi (33 arches) bridge, take a right turn at the first traffic circle in Nazar Ave, which leads to the center of Julfa. Lined with vegetable stands, the main square has the rather sleepy look of an old-fashioned village. The women shoppers do not wear the chador, a reminder that this is Christian territory. In the days of the Safavids, the European population of Isfahan were forbidden to settle in the city proper and it was here in the more familiar atmosphere of this Armenian neighborhood that they made their home.

Church and Cathedral

To reach the Church of Bethlehem, take a left turn off Julfa's square. The church's main portal is on Abadat St., Built in the 17th century by the wealthy merchant Petros Khodja, the church's walls are covered with paintings of no great artistic worth. Near the entrance is a painting representing St. Gregory martyred by the Turks, a reminder to all citizens of Julfa of the dangers they had escaped by fleeing. The cupola over the choir is decorated in the style of the Chihil Sutun ceilings. Across the street, the Astvatzatzin Church is at the end of a courtyard surrounded by arcades.

Bachgah St. is on the right as you leave Julfa Sq. On the left rises the portal of Our Savior's Cathedral, locally known as Vank. The Armenians laid the foundations of their cathedral as early as 1606. Fifty years later, the city having grown in population and wealth, the little church which the pioneers had built was no longer adequate. The new one was erected by succeeding generations who bore no resentment and were conscious of their strength and wealth.

The cupola of the cathedral is indistinguishable from the rest of Isfahan's domes. The exterior of the church has been covered with a brick framework to prevent its disintegration. After admiring the stylistic spaciousness of Islamic mosques, one is struck by the cluttered look of the interior. There are paintings representing scenes of persecutions, undoubtedly meant as reminders to the faithful that they should tread prudently when dealing with authority. The most outstanding one is of the Last Judgement, a gift of the merchant Avadich, who had been much impressed by the paintings in Italian churches. Apparently this donation met with some reticence on the part of the community and the scandal caused a great deal of resentment in Moslem circles. However, closer in style to Persian taste is the ceiling of the cupola which is decorated with blue and gold knotwork of such delicacy that it might have come from the brush of a miniaturist.

A small museum containing relics of Safavid Julfa has been arranged in one of the cathedral's annexes. Next to Dutch paintings and wooden statues brought back by merchants, the masterpieces wrought by local artisans and artists reflect the stylistic influence of Isfahan. There are enameled faience tiles, illuminated manuscripts (one a 9th-century Gospel), painting on copper- and gold-plate. Tapestries depicting the apostles, sculptured crucifixes, embroidered sacred vestments and ornaments all attest to the artistic fusion of Islamic and Christian inspiration. Most evocative and interesting is the collection of costumes worn by Armenian men and women in the days of Shah Abbas, including a sumptuous wedding dress.

The Cemetery of Julfa

East of Julfa, a chaotic pile of crumbling walls indicates the site of the gigantic Farahabad Palace built by Shah Hosein. It was here that he fled when the Afghans occupied Isfahan.

The Armenian cemetery lies above these ruins and many Europeans who died in Isfahan through the centuries were buried here. It is strange to read European names on the slabs of such a faraway place. Here are the graves of the Estoile family, which settled in Isfahan in the 18th century. Reine de l'Estoile married Jacob Rousseau, clockmaker and great uncle of Jean-Jacques, who lived 48 years in Julfa and died here. The most famous tomb is that of Rodolphe Stadler, whose tragic fate Oléarius and Tavernier have recounted. Stadler, a young Swiss clockmaker, was responsible for winding the king's minuscule clock every morning. He became involved in an obscure murder plot and forced to choose between conversion to Islam and death, he chose martyrdom. Stadler was buried under a tombstone 4 m (13 feet) thick. The next day, Armenians insisted that they had seen angels come down to protect his grave.

A tall dovecote dating from the Safavid epoch rises above the cemetery. Thousands of pigeons were raised in this *Kaboutarkhan*, and their droppings, regularly gathered, helped enrich the most beautiful gardens. The production of guano became an industry and hundreds of elegant dovecotes arose around the city. Even these were beautifully decorated.

Excursions

The area around Isfahan is extensive and merges with the region described in our chapter, *The Desert*. If you have decided to make Isfahan your base, you should be warned that excursions from here are less interesting than those made from Natanz, Naïn, Kachan, etc. Nevertheless these excursions and expeditions will enable you to visit and familiarize yourself with a very original countryside of which the famous dovecotes are only the most obvious feature. There is still a great deal to discover in the Zagros foothills, where the celebrated Bakhtiars live.

The Swaying Minarets and the Temple of Fire

This excursion (7 km or 4 miles) takes you via Cheikj Bakaï Ave. to the swaying minarets (Manar Jonban), whose reputation is due more to their amusing peculiarity than their artistic value. It is a most unusual experience to climb to the top of one and, leaning solidly against its wall (in a flying-buttress position), begin swaying back and forth. The minaret will oscillate, and so will its twin situated on the other side of the portal. This mysterious affinity between the two has naturally intrigued visitors in the same way as the Leaning Tower of Pisa. This strange phenomenon must be akin to the action of a gigantic tuning fork. The building dates from the 14th century and marks the place where the hermit Abdullah Soqla was buried. The sanctuary built over his tomb supports the swaying minarets, which were added in Safavid times.

A little farther down the road, on the top of a hill, visit the Atach-gah, a fire altar, said to be Sassanid, but which is nothing more than a recent reconstitution, built on top of ancient Islamic ruins. A ten minute walk up the hill is interesting and allows one to enjoy a beautiful vista over the countryside and the city.

The Rahravan Minaret

The excursion to the Rahravan minaret (6 km or 4 miles via Hatef Ave.), in spite of the detour it obliges you to make, does not take you far out of your way. The 30 m (95 feet) of a cylindrical tower on a square base are all that remain of a 12th-century mosque. Divided into five parts, its decoration, essentially brick, develops all geometric ornamental motifs. There are also a few inscriptions.

Shaherestan

This little village, southeast of Isfahan (as you follow the banks of the Zayandeh Rud), offers the tourist the remains of a Safavid mosque (1632), a little imamzadeh (12th century) containing the tombs of two imams, Shahzadeh Hosein and Ibrahim, and, even more interesting, the austere and venerable remains of a Sassanid bridge. Most probably it was built by Roman engineers brought here in captivity by Shahpur. Nothing remains from this period except the massive stone masonry supports. Though its brick superstructure is attributed to the Seljuks, the whole displays a powerful refinement on the edge of this rather tumbledown neighborhood which still retains something of old Isfahan.

The Imamzadeh Shah Zaïd

This small mausoleum whose architecture is rather clumsy, goes back to early Safavid times. Later Shah Suleiman endowed it with a geometric faïence decoration. It is most interesting, however, for the frescos adorning its interior walls, fairly rare examples of figurative religious decoration. These are not the work of a great talent, but rather of a local artist, and reflect a touching naïveté. The slightly rigid attitudes of the figures and the vivid colors (despite the patina of time) are proof of this. The mausoleum is still used for ceremonies during Muharram.

Other Sights

The Ziar Minaret and Barsian Mosque are located southeast of Isfahan. This round trip of 120 km (75 miles) is more of an expedition than an excursion. We do not wish to exaggerate, but we should warn you that a stream can suddenly turn into a torrent, and wading in mud is no better than wading in dust.

Though not as fine as the Ali and Sareban minarets of Isfahan, this

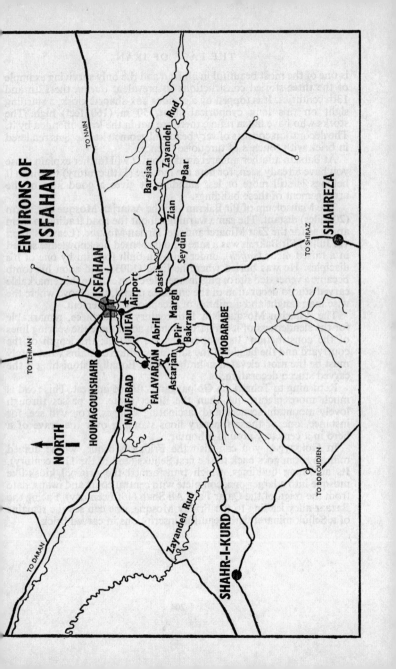

ENVIRONS OF ISFAHAN

NORTH

TO NAIN

Zayandeh Rud

Barsian

Bar

Zian

Seydún

TO SHIRAZ

SHAHREZA

ISFAHAN

Airport

Dasti

JULFA

Abril

Margh

Pir

Astarjan Bakran

TO TEHRAN

HOUMAGOUNSHAHR

NAJAFABAD

FALAVARJAN

MOBARABE

TO BOROUDIEN

TO DAAN

Zayandeh Rud

SHAHR-I-KURD

is one of the most beautiful in all Iran and the only surviving example of the three-storied constructions so prevalent during the 12th and 13th centuries. It is topped by a curious box-shaped kiosk, a startling sight on this long cylindrical shaft, 50 m (160 feet) high. The storks who have taken refuge there are not in the least offended by it. The decoration consists of very beautiful geometrical designs rendered in brick with touches of turquoise faience.

At Barsian another minaret awaits you. It will further explain those you have already seen, for here the mosque (11th century) to which it belongs is still more or less standing. It gives a good idea of the arrangement of these buildings.

The Mausoleum of Pir Bakran and the Astarjan Mosque are 30 km (20 miles) distant. The same warnings about the road leading to them apply as for the Ziar Minaret and the Barsian Mosque. (Leave Isfahan via Julfa.) Pir Bakran was a sage who dispensed his knowledge seated in a raised niche (*soffeh*), under an iwan built for him by one of his disciples. He was buried where he lived (1303), and soon his tomb became a venerated site of pilgrimage. Here you can see the remarkable carved stucco decoration of the entrance portal, the alcove where the wise man taught and a mihrab of exceptional refinement.

The Astarjan Mosque is a 14th-century masterpiece, remarkable for the slenderness of its minarets, which accentuate the soaring lines of the construction. Its proportions are perfect; the length of the courtyard and the height of the sanctuary which contains what surely must be the most elevated mihrab in Iran. Equally astonishing is the carved stucco decoration.

Returning to Tehran via Golpaygan is full of interest. This road is much more picturesque than the direct route. It passes through lovely mountain scenery and fascinating villages. You will see, for instance, one of those funerary lions standing over the grave of a hero in a cemetery around Khonsar.

In Golpaygan you can visit the Friday Mosque, whose domed mihrab room goes back to the first Seljuks (end of the 11th century). Its adjoining buildings, which transformed the original kiosk-like mosque into a larger one, complete with central court and iwans, date from the reign of the Qajar Fath Ali Shah (19th century). Facing the Bazaar alley leading to the Friday Mosque, one can see the remains of a Seljuk minaret with beautiful inscriptions in carved brick.

Practical Information for Isfahan and Surroundings

 WHEN TO GO. The spring (until mid-June) and the autumn (until Christmas) are the agreeable seasons for a visit to Isfahan. The climate however is always temperate, since the thermometer never drops below 0° C (+32° F) n winter and never rises above 36° C (97° F) in summer. One can very well enjoy a visit in summer if one avoids going to monuments during the hottest hours of the day. Museums take this into account when arranging the times at which they are open.

 HOW TO GET THERE. By air: Isfahan is linked to Tehran by daily flights; there are two flights on certain days. A traveler who is in a rush and has only 24 hours to spare can fly to Isfahan in the early morning, do a guided tour of the city and be back in Tehran in the evening. There are also daily connections with Shiraz, Kerman, Abadan and Ahwaz; two or three times a week with Yazd, Zahedan etc. The Isfahan airport is located 5 km (3 miles) to the south of the city, on the other side of the Zayandeh Rud.

By rail: The line from Tehran via Qom continues to Yazd and Kerman. **By bus:** inquire of T.B.T., Levantour, Iran Peyma or Mihan Tour for information on going to or coming from Tehran, Shiraz, Qom, Kerman, Yazd, Abadan and Ahwaz.

Coming from Tehran **by car,** you arrive via Foroughi Ave.; at the second traffic circle, take a right turn onto Chahar Bagh Ave. Coming from Shiraz or Tabriz, you approach the city via the Armenian quarter of Julfa and cross the river following Hakim Nezami Ave. as the bridge of the 33 arches to Chahar Bagh is one-way.

 WHAT TO SEE. In *one day*, this is what you should visit: the Royal Sq. (Maidan-i-Shah) and the three monuments surrounding it, the King's Mosque (Masjid-i-Shah), the Masjid-i-Shaikh-Lutfullah, the Ali Qapu Palace; the Chihil Sutun, and the Friday Mosque, ending your tour in the bazaar. As an alternative, the following is also an interesting program: the Sareban minaret and the Friday Mosque, in the early morning; the Royal Sq. (Maidan-i-Shah), visiting the King's Mosque and the Masjid-i-Shaikh-Lutfullah only, and a stroll in the alleys of the bazaar when the sun begins really blazing. In the afternoon go to the Madresseh Chahar Bagh and take a walk along the banks of the Zayandeh Rud as far as Shahrestan.

If you have *two days* combine the two programs above.

If you have *three days* or more, you can divide your visit into the different districts of the town. This is what you would visit within each zone: 1. Royal Sq. (Maidan-i-Shah) and its monuments, plus the Chihil Sutun. 2. A stroll along the Chahar Bagh, with a visit to the Madresseh Chahar Bagh, the Hasht Behesht, the Shah Abbas Hotel (Khan-e-Madar-e-Shah) and the new shopping center opposite. 3. Mosque and minaret of Ali, the mausoleum of Harun Velayat, Imamzadeh Djaffar, Imamzadeh Ismail and the Chaïa Mosque. 4. Zoleimat

THE FACE OF IRAN

Mosque, the Madresseh Sard, Madresseh Mullah Abdullah, Hakim Mosque and Sorkhi Mosque. 5. Friday Mosque, Dardacht minaret, Darb-i-Imam, Madresseh Imamieh, Mausoleum of Baba Qasem. 6. Chihil Dokhtaran minaret, Sareban minaret and the two Dar el Ziafeh minarets. 7. The bridges of the Zayandeh Rud, Julfa and the mausoleum of Baba-Rokn-ed-Din.

N.B. Visiting Isfahan is easy. Most of the city's important monuments are marked and the inhabitants can help you and guide you, which is not always the case elsewhere. There are directions pointing to the location of various monuments. Should you prefer to rely on professional guides, enquire at the Tourist Office, where you will be given several choices depending on your pocketbook.

 HOTELS. Isfahan has about 100 hotels, whose prices for every category are more comparable to those of the capital than to prices in other areas of the country. **Shah Abbas,** deluxe, Shah Abbas Ave. Fairyland atmosphere, should be visited even if you don't stay here. 500 rooms after the 1975 enlargement, good pool. Also deluxe, but cheaper, **Kourosh** just beyond and overlooking the river.

There is a sizable drop to the three-star *Ali Qapu*, Chahar Bagh; and *Irantour*, Abbas Abad Ave., both with small pools.

Pol, Chahar Bagh, we rank lower than the official category, but as the best among the two-star; *Apadana*, *Sahel*, Bisto Chahar-e Esfand; *Arya*, Shah Abbas Ave.; *Cyrus*, *Jahan*, *Keyan*, Chahar Bagh; *Naghsh-e-Jahan*, Daewazeh Doulat St.; *Nobel*, Abshar St.; *Tourist*, Abbas Abad Ave.

One-star with some private showers are the *Giti*, Shahpur St.; *Golestan*,

Pars, *Persia*, *Toos*, Chahar Bagh; *Javanan*, Bouzorg Mehr Ave.; *Karoon*, Hakim Nezami Ave.; *Persepolis*, Mohamed Reza Shah Ave.; *Rood-Kenar*, Pahlavi Ave.; *Saadi*, Abbas Abad Ave.; *Sepahan*, Sarami St. Don't hesitate to bargain about prices in this last category.

There are five small two-star *Mehmansara* (Inns) in the province, at Shah Reza about 50 km (31 miles) on the road to Shiraz; at Khonsar, in the mountains to the northwest; at Naïn and Natanz; and one in Isfahan itself.

 RESTAURANTS. Western-style meals are served in the better hotels; very indifferent except in the deluxe class. Better try the *Sahara*, Farah Pk.; *Noble*, Abshar Ave.; *Shahrzad*, Abbas Abad Ave.; *Canary*, 24th Esfand Pl. *Leon*, Khorshid St. in Julfa, is a third-class but picturesque restaurant which should also be mentioned.

Besides these, the Tchelo-Kebabi are legion. We suggest: *Soltani*, Darvazeh Dollat; *Djahan*, Chahar Bagh Ave. and *Hattam*, Fathieh Ave.

There are several snack bars, among which are the *Marmar*, Nazaar Ave. and the *Espadana*, Reghni Passage.

 NIGHT LIFE. The movie houses are located on Chahar Bagh (films in their original version are shown at the *Hafiz*). Arrange to be accompanied when you go to the theater to watch local plays: *Pârs*, Hakim Nezami St.; *Sepalan*, Chahar Bagh Ave. Nightclubs mostly in the large hotels. *Shah Abbas:*

ISFAHAN AND SURROUNDINGS

discothèque and dancing. *Ali Qapu:* discothèque and dancing; *Noble Restaurant:* cabaret-dancing; *Sahara Restaurant:* dancing.

MOSQUES AND MAUSOLEUMS. Visiting hours (be sure to check): 7.30 to 11.30; 2.30 to 6.30, in summer. 8 to 11.30; 2 to 5 in the winter. Used to crowds of tourists, the mosques of Isfahan welcome you warmly, but you are not exempt from the necessity of dressing correctly and avoiding visiting them during feast days or during prayer hours. An entrance fee is charged to visit some of them: the King's Mosque, Friday Mosque and Shaikh Lutfullah. Students pay half price. The other mosques charge no entrance fee, but it is customary to tip the guardian (at the Madresseh-e Chahar Bagh, for instance). Visits to the mausoleums and minarets are free, that is, if you succeed in getting in, which is not always easy. A boy will probably turn up and offer to get you in for 2 or 3 tomans.

PALACES. The two principal places of Isfahan are the Ali Qapu and the Chihil Sutun (entrance fee). Same visiting hours as the mosques. An entrance fee is also charged for the visit to the Vank Church and minarets in disrepair. Everywhere else visits are free of charge, but a tip is expected when visiting the oil press and the rug workshops.

SHOPPING. Isfahan's specialty is the *qalamqari*, cotton fabric, hand imprinted with bright color motifs of flowers, animals, hunting scenes and various arabesques gracefully interlaced. A piece of this fabric, 1½ by 2 yards, costs 400 to 500 Rs, maximum. Otherwise, in Isfahan you'll find all the typical tourist souvenirs sold in bazaars throughout the country, from a variety of khatam (inlaid work) to stoneware from Meshed; from brass articles of mediocre quality to the most refined silver work which unfortunately is becoming more and more difficult to find. An address where well-finished articles can still be found: *Lahiji*, on Chahar Bagh. The antique dealers are second to none when it comes to prices, which are more and more prohibitive—watch out for fakes. Another good address: *Isaac*, 308 Chahar Bagh. Here you will be shown various beautiful things: rugs, brocades, miniatures, etc.

The government shops are located on Chahar Bagh, in the Bazaar-e Boland alongside the Madresseh-e Chahar Bagh, and in the new shopping center opposite the Shah Abbas Hotel; slightly cheaper are the shops on the Maidan-i-Shah where you can find amusing hammocks for babies made out of tapestry trimmed with leather and suspended between two painted wooden bars.

There is little worthwhile to be found in the covered bazaar which is mostly given over to plastic and nylon goods; an exception are the local nougats, gaz, famous and delicious. The best contain manna, the Biblical food, which is *Alhagi maurorum* and very plentiful in Iran.

MOTORING. There are no problems about driving in Isfahan, but you must be constantly on the alert. In contrast to those in Shiraz, drivers (especially those of taxis) are quite aggressive. On the Chahar Bagh, gaps in

207

the dividing strip allows drivers to make U-turns Iranian style—in fact it is very practical and for once without danger, except of course for pedestrians. Much too narrow, the old bridges carry only one-way traffic. No parking problem on the Maidan-i-Shah and throughout most of the city; but exceedingly difficult on Chahar Bagh. There are car parks (pay one toman).

You can have car repairs, lubrication or oil change at the following garages: *Sahel*, Darvazeh Dollat; *Firdowsi*, Darvazeh Dollat. Shops handling spare parts of different models are located on Shahpur Ave. To rent a car without a chauffeur: *Khabazi*, Chahar Bagh; *Gavadi*, 24 Esfand Sq.; *Korangy*, Sheikh Bahai St.

Isfahan is the hub of an asphalted road network: to Tehran via Qom, Shiraz via Shah Reza, Yard via Naïn, Hamadan and Khorramabad. The trip Daran–Golpaygan via Khonsar is over a good graded dirt road. Gasoline (petrol) stations are spaced at about 50-km (31-mile) intervals.

HOW TO GET AROUND. As everywhere else, city *buses* ply up and down the main north-south and east-west arteries. There are two kinds of *taxis*: orange (first class) and black and white (low class). Hourly rates: about 100 Rs for an orange taxi. Besides taxis, you can also rent luxury *cars* with chauffeur, which cost about 130 Rs for the first hour and 100 Rs for each subsequent hour. Outside the city you should count on between 5 to 7 Rs per kilometer, depending on road conditions.

SPORTS. Pools: those at the Shah Abbas, Kourosh and Irantour hotels are quite expensive. Entrance is free for hotel guests. There are two pools not connected with a hotel on Datsara and Azar Aves. **Hunting.** In winter you can hunt in the vicinity, principally on the shores of the Zayandeh Rud (duck, wood pigeon, woodcock etc.); and to the west of the town for larger game. Inquire at the local office of the Hunting and Fishing Federation, Abbas Abad Ave.

CAMPING. The Shahkuh grounds, on the Shahrekord road, south of the city; kitchen, laundry room, showers etc. There is no youth hostel, but the Scout House, on Maidan-i-Shah, is ready to help you.

USEFUL ADDRESSES. Tourist Information: Shah Abbas Ave. (tel. 27667) and at the airport (28866); *Iran-Air*, 155 Chahar Bagh. Travel Agencies: *Iran Travel, Isfahan Tourist, Near East Tours* and others. Most of the bus companies are on Chahar Bagh. *Main Post Office:* Suresrafil Ave., near Sepah St.

Banks: Melli Bank, Sepah St. and Chahar Bagh. *Churches:* Roman Catholic, Sayed Ali Khan St.; Protestant, St. Luke, Abbas Abad Ave. *Hospitals:* Isfahan Clinic, Sheikh Bahai Ave. (2356); Mehragan Hospital, Sheikh Bahai Ave. (8848).

Useful Telephone Numbers. Ambulance, 7707; Police, 02; general information, 08.

SHIRAZ

Persia's Literary Capital

Was it perhaps because Shiraz was the most romantic town in the Fars that it was spared by Genghis Khan and Tamerlane—or because of its ruby wines and nightingales? Its silken rugs and fabulous gardens have lured scholars and travelers for centuries. Despite its many earthquakes there are several aged buildings, and who could not be stirred by its poets or visit their strangely beautiful tombs where lovers meet and flower beds glow? Who can resist the delicate verses of Hafiz, son of this city where the purest Persian is spoken?

Anyone coming from Isfahan by road to Shiraz enters another world. The arid mountains dotted with the black tents of the nomads, seeming blacker still under the pitiless sun, give way to high walls that hide gardens and roses, glimpsed through pine trees and high cypresses. But take your time! Here more than anywhere else, the visitor who intends to spend only a few hours at Shiraz has not yet been imbued with the spirit of the place.

A Bit of History

It would seem that the land where Shiraz stands today was already inhabited in the far-distant past. Some tablets found at Persepolis point to the presence on the construction sites of workers from the small town, no doubt a stop-over for caravans, that Shiraz appears to have been at that time. But it was in the seventh century A.D. that the future of the town was decided. In 636, the Arabs broke into the south of Iran. One of their armies regrouped and set up its quarters in the Shiraz plain before attacking and razing Istakhr, the Sassanid capital of the Fars. Shiraz consequently acquired an important political role under the Saffarids. Their successors, the Buyids (935–1055), encircled it with fortifications after having endowed it with many monuments and with a handsome library. From the 12th century on, Shiraz became the literary metropolis of Persia thanks especially to the poet Saadi (1184–1292).

Without putting up a fight, it fell under the domination of the Mongols. The eleven Khans built the Masjid-i-Now there. The following century Tamerlane appeared (1386). The conqueror was determined to spare Shiraz and even went in person to pay his respects to the famous poet Hafiz, then at the height of his glory. The city made new strides under the Safavid dynasty (1502–1722). Imam-Gholi-Khan, the governor of the Fars, was inspired to do for Shiraz what Shah Abbas had done for Isfahan. But Shiraz also passed through difficult days: in 1668, a catastrophic flood began an era of misfortunes. The Afghans had time to pillage the city in 1729 before being defeated in the neighboring plain. Nadir Shah, master of the country in turn, to punish the inhabitants for having revolted against him, took over the city after a siege lasting four-and-a-half months. During this time an epidemic of the plague accompanied the horrors of daily bombardment.

This somber period was followed by a brilliant one. Karim Khan Zand (1750–79), the new sovereign of Persia, transferred the capital to Shiraz, constructed a new mosque there, a vast bazaar, whole new quarters in the city and restored the citadel. Because of his humility as much as for political reasons, this model prince accepted no other title than that of *Vakil* (Regent). The line was short-lived: his grandson Loft-Ali Khan was the last of the Zands and was slain in 1786 by Aga Mohammed Qajar who transferred the capital to Tehran.

Despite all this, the city continued to be of some importance because of being situated on the route from Bushire, the great port of the Persian Gulf to Tehran. But the establishment by Reza Shah of the new maritime outlets of Bandar-e-Shahpur and Khorramshahr displaced the capital of the Fars from the great commercial axis. In 1957 it became a university city, and has many schools, hospitals and industries. Its importance as a regional metropolis is increasing.

Discovering Shiraz

Allah ou akbar (Allah is the greatest of all) is the name of a large valley lying deep in the mountain chain that marks the northern boundary of the Shiraz plain. This austere gorge leads to the monumental Gate of the Koran made of brick and faience. It is here that the city begins. After the aridity and so much sun, it holds out a promise of coolness and repose with its cypresses and its domes that glitter on both sides of the Knochk river.

Once one entered Shiraz through gardens, but today arrival is slightly marred by industrial installations that have recently sprung up. But this is relatively unimportant, and one goes slowly down a gentle slope to the river. Immediately at the bottom are the bazaar, the old city and streets full of activity. Karim Khan Zand Ave. is the main artery of this town of 330,000 inhabitants, living under a sky of unequaled purity, in an ever-mild climate with cool summers and temperate winters.

Surprising to see in the crowd are the strange gypsies wearing billowing gauzy skirts and garish jewelry. They are Qashqais women, belonging to the nomadic tribes that have lived in the region for centuries.

The Zand Citadel and Tomb

Regent Karim Khan had dreamt of enlarging his capital rather in the manner of Shah Abbas at Isfahan. Today, it is difficult to realize, that the monuments erected by the greatest of the Zands once edged a royal square. The modern streets have distorted the old city plan, with Zand Ave. cutting across the old quarter from east to west. In its central part, the mighty brick walls of the restored Ark-e Karim Khan still impress by their combination of strength and unexpected refinement. This citadel continues to fulfil its function, in a way, since today it houses the offices of police headquarters.

Across the avenue, at the head of an ornamental pool in a fine garden, stands a small octagonal edifice covered with delicate blue faience which once served as a reception hall, then as the Fars Museum, but which has now been deprived of most of its treasures. The façades are gay with mosaic bouquets in bloom, a popular form of decoration during the Zand period. The inside central pool is formed from one piece of marble.

The cupola is decorated with green and gold stalactites, while a

211

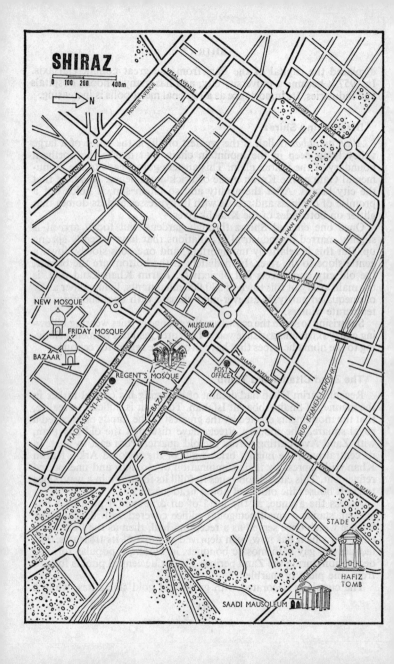

frieze of small blue and gold flowers encircles the room. There are garlands, paintings of more or less historical interest, like the portrait of Karim Khan smoking the kalian, Saadi teaching a prince, Shah Ismail in battle, but most fascinating are the dancers displaying all the attributes of the Persian ideal of beauty. A central glass case contains a collection of illuminated Korans which have elegance of line and decoration, especially one by the celebrated 14th-century calligrapher Yahya-as-Sufi. Karim Khan's saber has been placed as a relic in the same alcove where his body rested before it was taken away by Aga Mohammed Qajar.

The Mosque of the Regent

Across Pahlavi Ave. is the Masjid-i-Vakil, the 18th-century Mosque of the Regent. The 19th-century restorations have left their mark on the main portal. The demi-cupola and the faience stalactites decorating it are resplendent with bright colors. The portal is framed by two predominantly green panels of *kachis*. The mellow softness of the interior's pastel shades is striking. Below the ceramic work there is a carved stone frieze forming a plinth.

The Mosque of the Regent comprises only two iwans, one to the south, the other to the north. The latter, the "Portal of Pearls", is embellished with blooming roses and irises which were very popular in Persian designs. These colorful haft rangi faiences, in which white and yellow predominate, are characteristic of Shiraz monuments and they supply a gay note to this building.

The south iwan leads to the winter prayer hall, with arches supported by 48 spirally carved pillars whose capitals are decorated with stylized acanthus leaves. The nimbar is cut from a single block of Maragheh marble. To the left of the principal mihrab, there is a niche intended for a second ritual, which allows the audience to follow the service even though the view of the mihrab proper is blocked by a pillar.

The Mosque of the Regent is the favorite visiting place of Moslem students who come here to study the Koran. They sit cross-legged, swaying back and forth in a movement reputed to be excellent for the memory! Happily, this attractive mosque has survived numerous earthquakes, in particular those fearful ones of 1814 and 1824.

The Bazaars

Just next to the Mosque of the Regent there is the bazaar founded by this same prince, still one of the country's most colorful.

The Bazaar of the Regent (Bazar-u-Vakil) remains the commercial center of Shiraz. The solidity and beauty of its brickwork is appreciably more durable than that of the fragile and hastily put-together monuments in Isfahan. It is regrettable that Zand Avenue has cut this quarter in two.

Bazar-e-Now lies to the north, Bazar-e-Morgh, Bazar-e-Mesgarba, Bazar-e-Fil to the south; between Zand and Loft Ali Khan Avenues is Bazar-e-Nawab. Some monuments, sanctuaries and mausoleums are hidden amidst the shops. Segregation instead of repartition by trade associations which helps you find your way in bazaars elsewhere does not exist in Shiraz. Only the ironmongers and farriers group together slightly to the north of Loft Ali Khan Avenue. Nearby, the bazaar's caravanserai Saray-e-Moshir where the important transactions were negotiated, has been attractively converted into a restaurant in an authentic Persian setting, with shops offering the best of local handicrafts.

The Shiraz bazaars remain a happy hunting ground for those who are interested in Persian handicrafts. First the silver, with its repeated cherry motif. Then detailed khatam, the marquetry which was invented here. Then there is the enamel and silver jewelry. The kilims (woven rugs) and the djadims (thin blankets in gay colors) have geometric designs similar to those in the rugs made by the Qashqais nomads. And everywhere you will find the sweet but pleasant Shiraz wine, incessantly lauded by the poets.

The Mausoleum of Shah Cheragh

Dominating the south end of Loft Ali Khan Avenue—on the west side of the Ahmadi intersection—the mausoleum of Shah Cheragh is recognizable by its pear-shaped dome. Shah Cheragh (King of the Light) is none other than Amir Ahmad, brother of Imam Reza, who died in Shiraz in 835. The mausoleum erected around his tomb is a Shi'ite pilgrimage site. This is why non-Moslems are not permitted to visit it. In fact it was only in the 13th century that his remains were placed here. The earthquakes of the 1800s destroyed the dome. The bold form of the cupola was restored in the 19th century and its delicate cream and turquoise colors were renewed recently.

After passing through the splendid tiled gate into the vast courtyard, always thronged with pilgrims, you come across another sacred shrine to your left, the mausoleum of Seyed Mir Mohammed, built during the Qajar epoch and also topped by a pear-shaped dome, a design repeated over the tomb of Seyed Ala-ed-Din Hosein, another of Imam Reza's brothers, which is to the southeast of the city.

The Old Friday Mosque

From the courtyard of Imamzadeh Mir Mohammed, a small

street gives access to the Masjid-e Jame, the Old Friday Mosque, the most venerable in Shiraz, begun in 894 A.D. by Amr-Ibn-Laith of the Saffarid dynasty. In the mihrab room vestiges of the original construction are still visible: pieces of masonry and a part of the decoration. The present edifice is of a much later period. The mosaics that decorate the entrance to the Shahestan, the area for nocturnal prayers, date from the 16th century.

The most curious element of the Masjid-e-Jame is the *Khoda Khaneh* (the Lord's House), that occupies the center of the courtyard. Inspired by the Kaaba of Mecca, this square miniature temple flanked by four angled turrets was built in the 14th century. A copy of the Koran was placed inside it. It is the only one of its kind in Iran, and was restored in 1937 and 1954. The inscription, backed by dark blue enamel, is attributed to the calligrapher Yahya-as-Soufi-al-Djamali.

The New Mosque and the Khan Madresseh

Opposite the Shah Cheragh shrine, distinguished from afar by the heavily gilded cupola, a quiet alley leads to the Masjid-e-Now, the New Friday Mosque, to distinguish it from the previous one. But don't be deceived by these terms—this monument is also very old and dates from the 13th century. The story is told that *atabak* (prince) Saad-e-Zangui, who was Saadi's patron, had this mosque built to fulfil a vow. The rectangular courtyard, planted with huge old plane trees, occupies a total area of 20,000 sq m (215,000 sq feet), which makes it the largest in the country. The low, elongated mosque building features barrel vaulting and tall iwans.

On the north side of Loft Ali Khan Avenue, the great bulk of the Madresseh-e-Khan (College of the Khan), built in the 17th century to house theological students, can be seen. This building is all that remains of the numerous edifices constructed for Shiraz by Imam-Gholi-Khan, govenor of the Fars under Shah Abbas. Furthermore, only the octagonal vestibule is still of that period. The portal, restored at the end of the 19th century, bears the usual inscriptions surmounted by stalactites. In the interior, the vast courtyard is encircled by the traditional double arcade with students' rooms leading off it. The stylized decoration of the southern iwan, in which rose and blue predominate, epitomizes Safavid art. On the same avenue, further to the east is the 19th-century Nasir-ol-Molk Mosque, whose basically black and blue tiles are enlivened by a striking pink below medallions in Kufic script. The columns of the prayer hall are modeled on the Vakil Mosque.

Christian Churches

The Armenian Church, dating from the reign of Shah Abbas II (1642–67) is located in the Armenian bazaar. The nave, in pure 17th-century Shiraz style, is decorated with Persian frescoes. Formerly, matching rugs covered the ground beneath it. The English church on Nowbahr St., known as St. Simon the Zealot, was built between the two wars. Heavily influenced by Persian art, from which it has borrowed the style of its furnishings, it is the prettiest in Iran. Also, it possesses the first translation into Persian of the New Testament, published in Shiraz in 1811.

The Hafiz Mausoleum (Hafezieh)

Although the city has grown so much that it has engulfed many of the charming old gardens, to the north of the river two famous shrines have been jealously guarded in their beautifully kept surroundings: the tombs of the poets Hafiz and Saadi.

"Oh thou who pass close to my tomb, request a favor
For this will be a place of pilgrimage for all men who are free."

After having gone around the Bagh-e-Melli with its rare woods, one comes upon the mausoleum of Hafiz in a garden planted with cypresses, orange trees and fragrant flower beds. It is close to the Koran Gate. Beyond an impressive colonnade there is a delightful open pavilion, the splendid backdrop to the concerts of Eastern music at the Shiraz Festival. Here one can read his best known poems carved in relief on alabaster beneath a colorfully decorated cupola. The tomb is carved with more poems and rosettes. It is a very happy place. One poem suggests that the onlooker comes to the tomb with a pretty girl, to be gay, sip wine and not mourn. It is a traditional belief that if a young couple bring a copy of Hafiz's poems to this peaceful place and open it at random it will foretell their future. Hafiz was not a great traveler like Saadi. He loved Shiraz where he was born in 1324 and scarcely left it during his lifetime. In his own words:

"The zephyr-breeze of Musalla and the stream of Ruknabad
Do not allow me to travel or wander afield."

or again

> *"Right through Shiraz the path goes*
> *Of perfection*
> *Anyone in Shiraz knows*
> *Its direction."*

He wrote some 500 ghazals which were published 25 years after his death. As the centuries passed many collections appeared which amalgamated his work with apocryphal verses and finally they added up to a fine bible of Persian culture. From Lahore to Istanbul Hafiz has been quoted as a means to help in the complications that beset life. Even the uneducated can repeat verses which have become proverbs. The complexity of the thoughts expressed and the use of phonetics make Hafiz's masterpieces difficult to translate, their content being inseparable from their form.

The Saadi Mausoleum

Beyond the Delgosha Gardens, at the back of the "valley of joy", rises the mausoleum of Moulich-ed-Din-Shirazi, called Saadi, born in Shiraz around 1190. After a childhood spent in Bagdad, he made numerous voyages and was a captive in Syria during the Crusades, before entering the monastery which stood on the place where he was buried. He spread the fame of his native city abroad and lived to be a centenarian. As well as being referred to as Persia's greatest poet he had the gift of repartee and was a great wit. There is even a slight tinge of "sick humor" now and then:

> *"All night he wept unceasingly beside*
> *His friend, who lay inert upon the bed;*
> *At dawn they found that he who watched had died,*
> *And lo! the sick man had been cured instead."*

Saadi's tomb (the original site has just been excavated) soon became a place of pilgrimage. Though repeatedly renovated, the National Relics Society's mausoleum dates from 1952 and was designed by the Frenchman, André Godard, then director of archeological activities in Iran.

The high portico and the turquoise dome, traditional in Persian architecture, are handled with an extremely modern simplicity. There is an artificial pond, fed by a spring and full of trout, on the tiled terrace leading up to the monument. Tradition has it that this water is miraculous.

> *"From the tomb of Saadi, son of Shiraz,*
> *Issues the scent of love,*
> *Which will perfume the air you breathe*
> *A thousand years after his death."*

This epitaph, requested by Saadi himself, is inscribed on the gateway to the garden. Wisest of men, it was he who said "You can't take it with you", rather more poetical in the original but still the truest indictment against the futility of materialism.

There is yet another tale to be told. A tower in ruins, the *Gavereh Djinha* (Cradle of the Jinns), can be discerned on the mountain that dominates the mausoleum. The valley's song of love gives way to a sad chant. Up until the last century, an adulterous woman, sewn up in her veils, was led to the tower by her executioner. At the final moment, her chador was slightly opened so that she might take a last look at Shiraz. The unhappy lady was then thrown into the bottom of a well, with a strange symbol—a shepherd's crook—as a companion in misfortune.

Palaces and Gardens

Shiraz is a city of gardens which, however, can only be properly appreciated after having crossed through the furnace of the Fars. They encircle the city with a belt of greenery and flowers. A mausoleum, a small sanctuary, a pavilion serve as pretexts for the walk, and in the midst of the cool foliage one may come on a graceful little faience building designed to give pleasure.

To the north of the mausoleum of Hafiz, on the side of the mountain, the seven mystics lie at rest among the immemorial pines and cypresses. The Takieh Haft Tanan—Shiraz's only major monument not yet restored—was built during the Zand period (18th century) for the Muharram ceremonies. A large room with two adjacent smaller rooms is flanked by two monolithic columns. The walls are covered with paintings, in defiance of Koranic law, depicting Moses, Sheik Sanan, Abraham, Ishmael and two dervishes, and the ceilings with flowers and birds.

Chardin claimed that "Shiraz possesses the most beautiful trees in the world". At the end of many gardens in Shiraz, a circular enclosure bordered with poplars, plane trees and flowers constitutes a small private retreat. This is the *bonegah*, the heart of the park—its most intimate nook.

The coolest of these retreats are to be found in the Ghast-ed-Dachte, to the west of the city. But the Bagh-e-Melli (National Park) and the Park-e-Valiahd (Crown Prince's Park), which both have their special charm, should not be missed. In the months of March, April and May, Zand Blvd. and the road to the airport are lined with thousands of roses in bloom.

Still more private than these gardens are the pavilions, hidden behind high walls, which were built by the Zand princes and important Qajar personages. You will be unaware of their existence unless doors are opened for you or you are shown around by the initiated. Porticos and iwans, glittering with stucco and mirrors, are reflected in ponds edged by thickets of fragrant plants and shrubbery. Marquetry and faience alternate with panels of carved plaster. All this has the melancholy but bewitching charm of the East.

The Narenjestan and the Bagh-e-Eram

Entrusted to Pahlavi University, the Narenjestan-e-Qaram is more accessible than the many private residences. It is situated at the end of Loft Ali Khan Avenue. Orange trees (after which the palace is named) and palm trees surround the ponds in the main courtyard. A graceful colonnade with trefoiled pediments lines the southern façade. A mosaic mural with yellow, blue and rose faiences predominating, portrays the lion of the Iranian coat of arms and leopards devouring gazelles. A stone frieze reproduces the Immortals of Persepolis and there are other hunting scenes.

The handsome two-story mansion in the Bagh-e-Eram (Garden of Paradise) was constructed by the well-known architect Mohammed Hassan in the Qajar period. A central gallery, with lovely tiled alcoves and a hall of mirrors, overlooks beds of narcissi, roses and clipped hedges. Water is always an essential part of a Persian garden and here it is in abundance. In addition to a large square pond, water flows down a splendid avenue of high pines and cypresses. One of the latter is said to be the tallest in the world.

Bagh-e-Delgosha, Bagh-e-Khalili

To the left of the road to the Saadi mausoleum extends the Bagh-e-Delgosha. A wide path, bordered by orange trees, leads to the pavilion of the Zand and Qajar epoch, open to the public. The façade is decorated with molded plaster, an iwan with stone pillars, marquetried and mirrored doors, painted woodwork and kachis; the entire range of Persian pomp is found here. It is said that this old residence once sheltered a harem. A hexagonal swimming pool, now vanished, once occupied the center of the drawing room, and the royal concubines dived into it from their upstairs windows to recover the pearls that the Shah had thrown into it.

There is a delightful walk around the Bagh-e-Khalili where geraniums, wild roses, bougainvillea and water lilies form a rustic and sweet-smelling frame. To add to its glamor, nightingales have made their home in its groves.

Some Remains

The Fars is the classic seat of Iranian civilization and there are some interesting remains near Shiraz.

Qasr-Abu-Nasr, 6 km (3 miles) to the southeast of Shiraz, is noteworthy chiefly for an Achaemenid portico, doubtless borrowed from a Persepolis monument. An American mission discovered a Parthian fortress there in the thirties which had been remodeled by the Sassanids.

A little further on in the same direction is Barm-e-Dilak, where three Sassanid reliefs depict King Bahram II, with the queen and at prayer (third century). The same sovereign is found again at prayer 30 km (18 miles) to the northwest of Shiraz, at Guyum, on the road to Ardakan. The bas-relief has weathered badly. Nevertheless the excursion is enjoyable in that the return to Shiraz gives the feeling of entering an oasis and the air seems milder, sweeter and cooler than ever.

In 1973 an American archeological team discovered the buried ruins of Anshan, an ancient Elamite city dating from about the third millennium B.C. The excavations, covering some 350 acres, are located 25 miles north of Shiraz in a mountain valley, not far from Persepolis.

Practical Information for Shiraz

WHEN TO GO. From March to October the mildness of the Shirazi climate is enjoyable. The temperature does not go over 37° C (98° F) in the height of the summer. The winters are never very severe. The Shiraz–Persepolis Festival generally occurs during the first 15 days of September with Western and traditional music concerts and international ballet companies. The spectacles take place at the Hafezieh, Saray-e-Moshir, the Ariana cinema and in the impressive surroundings of the ruins of Persepolis.

HOW TO GET THERE. (See also *The Fars* chapter.) Arriving by *plane* from Tehran, Isfahan or one of the towns along the Persian Gulf, you will land at the airport situated 19 km (12 miles) to the southwest of the city. A taxi will take you into the center for 50 Rs. The *bus* station is located in Karim Khan Zand Ave. Arriving at Isfahan by *car* you enter the city after having crossed the river; turn to the right then to the left in front of the second bridge and you will find yourself on Karim Khan Zand Ave. From Bushire Nadir Ave. leads straight to the intersection of Zand Ave.

WHAT TO SEE. The atmosphere of Shiraz is inseparable from its monuments. A walk along Karim Khan Zand Ave. will disclose in turn the *Citadel* and the *Tomb of Karim Khan*, and above all, the *Mosque of the Regent* with its gay faiences and its remarkable pillared room with wreathed columns. The *Bazaar of the Regent*, with the beautifully restored *Saray-e-Moshir* annex. The *Shah Cheragh Mausoleum*, the *Old Friday Mosque*, the enormous *New Friday*

220

SHIRAZ

Mosque and the *Khan Madresseh*. The beautiful mausoleums of the national poets, Hafiz and Saadi, are of recent construction and very romantic.

A guide can be hired at the Tourist Office to take you on a tour of the city. In addition to the principal monuments, he will show you some old homes and typical Persian gardens. The travel agencies also organize guided tours with commentaries. The services of a guide for an entire day cost a minimum of ,000 Rs.

 HOTELS. Shiraz has some 30 adequate hotels, led by the deluxe 152-room **Kourosh** in the spacious Farahnaz Park in the northern suburb across the river; beauty shop, gift shop, a spectacular dining room, supper club, and coffee and cocktail lounge. Only slightly less luxurious is the 106-room **International,** Chasr-e Dasht.

The *Park*, off Zand Ave., is a good four-star. All three with large pools.

Mehmansara (Inn)***, on the road to the airport. More comfortable than the other hotels belonging to this chain, but only the new 50-room annex is air-conditioned; pool. *Grand****, Rudaki St., is small.

Among the two-stars only the *Kasra* and *Sassan*, Anvari St., have some private showers, but except the *Villa*, Zand Ave., all have restaurants.

Arya, Saadi Ave.; *Atoosa, Saadi,* Namazi Ave.; *Firdowsi, Kian, Palace,* Zand Ave.; *Tourist*, Dehnadi Ave.

No private showers among the very simple one-stars: *Baba Taher, Khayan, Shahpasand, Tehran*, Shahnaz St.; *Hafiz* (restaurant), *Shiraz Kuwait,* Daryush Ave.; *Jahan Now*, Rudaki St.; *Madayen*, Anvari St.; *Persepolis,* Saadi Ave.; *Shiraz*, Shahpur Ave.; *Takht-e Jamshid, Zand*, Zand Ave.

 RESTAURANTS. Best stick to the hotel restaurants, as few outside establishments serve Western food and alcohol as well as local dishes. Worth a try are the *Babakouhi, Haji Baba, Milk Bar* (a genuine restaurant) and *Persia,* Zand Ave.; the *103 Restaurant*, Anvari St.; *Maxim*, Mohammed Reza Shah Blvd.; *Gol-e-Sorkh*, Airport Rd. Best Persian food at the *Saray-e-Moshir*.

 ENTERTAINMENT. There are many cinemas, some of which show films in the original version: *Ariana, Persia, Pasargadae, Capri*. The Iranian restaurant *Bahar*, corner of Firdowsi and Rudaki Aves, and the *Golden Bowl*, give dinner-shows in which local dances are presented. At the *Casbah*, Zand Ave., one dines to the music of an orchestra and watches a cabaret show with variety sketches.

SIGHTS. There is no museum. Mosques and mausoleums open from 9 to 12 and from 3 to 6 except on Friday. Admission charge.

 SHOPPING. You will not want to leave Shiraz without having seen the rugs which have made the city famous. The bazaar has so many available that it is difficult to choose. The real Shiraz rugs are woven by the Qashqais nomadic tribes. One specialty is the *djadjim*, delicately woven, decorated with bright-colored geometric motifs that stand out against a velvet relief with a beige background.

The khatam, elaborate veneered inlay-work, is a specialty in Shiraz. The new work is not as attractive as the old, but the latter is rarely in good condition. Pick and choose carefully and be difficult about the finishing which have a tendency to be slapdash. A good address: *Bastani*, Zand Ave., near the Metro cinema.

MOTORING. The circulation of traffic is facilitated by wide streets. It is useless to try and park a car in the small streets of the bazaars, to the south of Zand Ave. and Lotfali Khan Ave. On the major axes, yellow signs written in Roman letters indicate the principal directions. Most of the gas (petrol) stations and car repair shops can be found on the road to the airport. The *Saadi* garage on Now Ave. and *Shahnaz* garage on Shahnaz Ave. are good and have the proper tools. A few of the major car companies have representatives in Shiraz. There are gas stations on the way out of town going toward Isfahan on Nader Ave. and in Valiahd Sq. Cars can be rented at most travel agencies.

SPORTS. Beside the hotel **swimming pools**, there is one at the Hafeziyeh Stadium, another at the Nemazi Hospital, and women only in Nader Ave. 40 km (25 miles) from Shiraz, on the road to Bushire, there is a very pleasant pool on the edge of the Darya-ye-Shiraz river and you can lunch there. **Zourkhane:** every evening at the Vakil High School on Pahlavi Ave.

HUNTING AND FISHING. Go to the Shikarbani, Rue Khayyam, local office of the hunting federation, to obtain permits.

CAMPING. The *Shiraz Tourist Camp*, on the road to the airport, provides 60 tents with camp beds. Open all year round. Campers with their own equipment can come to an arrangement with the owner. A Youth Hostel is in the process of being built.

USEFUL ADDRESSES. *Office of Tourism:* Mochir Fatem Ave., tel. 37044 and 33907. Office at the airport. *Travel agencies:* Persia Tours, Nemazi Ave. 39; Near East Tours, Municipal Center; Fars Tourist Center, Shahpur Ave. *Airlines:* Iran Air, Municipal Center, 75 Zand Ave. *Bus:* T.B.T., Iran Peyma, Levan Tour, Mihan Tour, all on Zand Ave.

Post Office: Shahpur Ave., near the police station.

Churches: Anglican, Simon the Zealot Church, located at the Christian Hospital, Nobahar St.

Cultural Centers British Council, Zand Ave.; Iran-America Society, Zand Ave.

Hospitals: Nemazi, at the western end of Zand Ave., tel. 32223; Saadi, Zand Ave., near the university, tel. 32111.

THE FARS

The Persepolis of Cyrus, Darius and Xerxes

No other place in Iran has quite the same spaciousness and a sense of contentment as the Fars. A high-level steppe, crisscrossed by fertile valleys and sheltered by the mountains from the fierce heat of the Gulf, it is the cradle of the Iranian nation to which it gave its name and its language. The chosen land of the Achaemenids it was later adopted by the vigorous Sassanid renaissance. Time passed and not until the Zands, during the 18th century, did the Fars become once again—but for less than 40 years—the heart of the Empire.

To be sure, the Persis of the Ancients was a less desolate region than it is in our day. Pasargadae was a succession of gardens and the plain of Persepolis was luxuriant with flowers and fruits. Experimental agricultural stations are attempting to turn the now barren Fars into fertile country and make it once again the granary that it was in times past.

For the time being, the charm of the Fars is austere. Under a brilliant blue sky blaze the vivid red, green and ocher of its bare mountains. In this transparent air it is easy to imagine Cyrus preparing his campaigns, Shahpur meditating his victory over the Romans. It is a gigantic archeological field that you are coming to explore here, for,

223

along with its world-famous sites, it must be rich in remains yet to be unearthed.

Discovering Persepolis

A legendary city, burnt by Alexander, Persepolis still has soaring pillars like a forest of stone. Excepting Karnak in Egypt, it is said that there was no construction in the ancient world which enclosed so vast an area. The palace site was perfect. Its situation alone sufficed for complete safety—or so it seemed to the sublimely confident Darius who, like Alexander, was oblivious to the very possibility of failure or defeat.

The Achaemenid capitals were many: Susa for winter, Ecbatana as summer residence, Pasargadae, "the camp of the Persians" for military purposes, but Persepolis was required to create a grandiose image of the empire, safe in the heart of the country, in the mountainous citadel of the Fars. It is here that petty kings and governors came to render homage to the King of Kings and bring their gifts for each New Year. More than a simple collection of taxes, it was above all the occasion for festivals and ceremonies, for which Darius (521–486) wanted a stage equal to his prestige. Artists came from the four corners of the country to build the edifices which disappeared two centuries later during the conflagration attributed to Alexander.

Archeologists have been able to reconstruct what these sumptuous ceremonies were like by examining the bas-reliefs of the palace of Persepolis and observing the ancient customs still extant in the tribes of the region. To relive imaginatively the splendid celebrations one must recall that in spring the lords and vassals put up their tents in the plain and made preparations for the solemn procession of Norouz, the New Year festival. The parade was opened by the princes of the kingdom, Persians and Medes, escorted by Susian guards and squadrons of the royal cavalry. Taking the monumental staircase, they walked in procession, each with a flower in his hand, up to the Apadana where they rendered homage to the King. Then came the "Parade of the Nations", opened by the Medes and the Susians. The Lydians traditionally offered precious vases and a war chariot. The Sogdian delegation brought furs, the Indians gold-dust, the Arabs dromedaries, etc. The King then gave a banquet and later took part in a second ceremony in which he was carried on high, seated on his throne, by the dignitaries of the 28 nations.

The Great Terrace

Cut into the hillside, with the mass of Kuh-i-Rahmat behind, this terrace, probably begun under Cyrus, was constructed on three different planes; some parts of the mountain were leveled to achieve this. An overhanging parapet is thought to have complemented the system of defense. In addition, a double row of fortifications completely encircled the site. These walls, of which some fragments have been found to the north, were mentioned by a companion of Alexander: they measured, he said, over 18 m (60 feet) high.

The Monumental Staircase and Gateway of Xerxes

The sole access to this immense plateau is a monumental staircase located on the northwest side of the terrace, close to the car park. It was made up of four individual flights of steps which opened out then came back together in pairs to make a stairway. It was probably laid out in this way to give the New Year procession an air of theatrical majesty. The steps were designed sufficiently large and flat for horses to mount.

Immediately upon reaching the summit, one sees the gateway of Xerxes or "Gateway of all Countries", located in line with the staircase. The structure consists of a square hall with two of its original four columns standing. In the floor the sockets of the door hinges are still visible. Three vast monumental doorways open to the east, west and south sides. The west doorway is guarded by two pairs of enormous bulls and the east doorway is flanked by two winged bulls with human heads. This last doorway leads to the Hall of a Hundred Columns and the south doorway opens onto the king's audience hall, the Apadana.

The Apadana

The columns of this great hall are immediately visible to the right; this is where the king held audience, receiving homage and gifts from his vassals. Begun by Darius the First, it was finished by his son and successor Xerxes the First. It is an immense hall some 75 m (245 feet) in length, its roof thrust upwards 20 m (65 feet) by 36 magnificent stone columns with decorated capitals. It is here that American archeologists discovered the texts engraved on the gold and silver plaques which you can see today at the Tehran Museum.

But the principal interest of this monument lies in the exceptional decoration of its staircases, which have been conserved almost intact under the layers of soil and ashes that accumulated after the burning of the city. What first stands out from the overall composition as major motifs are: The frieze of the Immortals, in which Medes in round caps and Susians in square ones mount the guard under the emblem of Ahura-Mazda—supreme god of the Mazdaian religion—

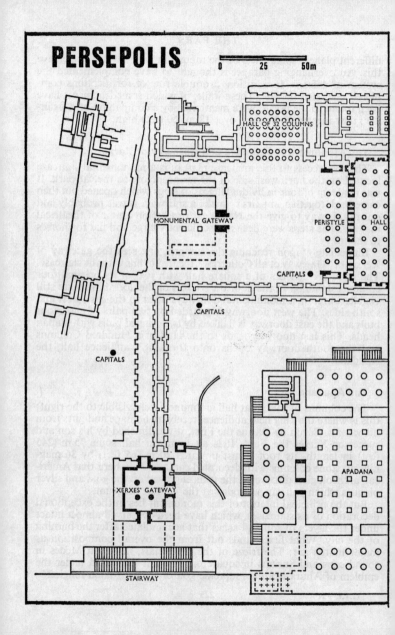

PERSEPOLIS

0   25   50m

HALL OF 32 COLUMNS

MONUMENTAL GATEWAY

PERISTYLE HALL

CAPITALS

CAPITALS

CAPITALS

APADANA

XERXES' GATEWAY

STAIRWAY

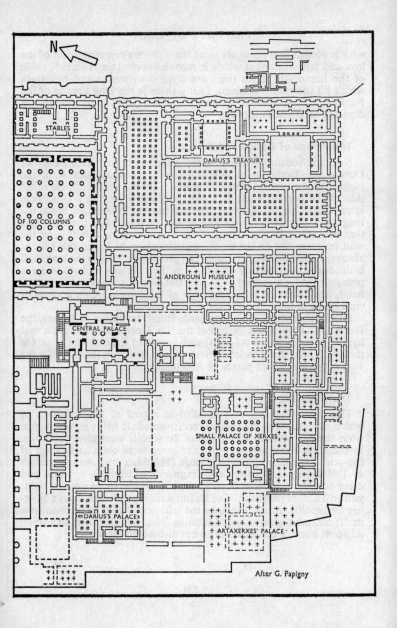

STABLES

OF 100 COLUMNS

DARIUS'S TREASURY

ANDEROUN MUSEUM

CENTRAL PALACE

SMALL PALACE OF XERXES

DARIUS'S PALACE

ARTAXERXES' PALACE

After G. Papigny

with a winged lion on either side; the vigorous representation of the lion and bull in combat which is repeated several times on either side of the Immortals. Then there are stylized cypresses and rose trees which fill the spaces between. Lastly there is the long Parade of the Nations, carved in parallel bands, in which people and animals are depicted in life-like attitudes.

The Palace of Darius and Xerxes

Near the southwest angle of the Apadana is the small palace of Darius, the Tatchara, or hall of mirrors, so-called because of the highly polished finish of its cut stones. Towards the south, on either side of the portico, there is a monolithic slab bearing a cuneiform inscription in three languages. The real interest of the place lies in the long rows of carved figures that adorn, in particular, the staircases that lead up to it. The theme of the lion devouring a bull is on the west staircase and on the south staircase again the Immortals and, as always, vassals bearing offerings. The gateway leading to the main hall is decorated with bas-reliefs in which the king sits in state under a parasol held by a servant. The east and west gateways, on the other hand, are decorated with an image of the king piercing a monster with his sword.

Still further south of the Apadana, stood the palace of Xerxes, the Hadish, on the highest terrace of the site. Once again we find a vast hypostyle hall with 36 columns, with rooms to the east and west. On the south side, the windows overlook the *anderoun* (harem). To the west is the unfinished palace of Artaxerxes III.

The Museum

This small museum was installed in a part of the anderoun of which several rooms have been reconstituted. It helps us to imagine what the chambers at the palace of Persepolis must have been like. In the main room you will discover some terra cotta sarcophagi of the 4th millennium, plaster carvings (Seljukian era), some ceramics of Tell Bakun and pottery and fragments of capitals, columns and other sculptures coming from Persepolis. In the room on the right, you will find objects from Tell Bakun and Tepe Shaura (sites adjoining Persepolis). In the room on the left, once again Islam manifests itself; ceramics, glassware and bronzes from Istakhr; then, in a small adjacent nook, a collection of pieces discovered locally.

The Hall of 100 Columns

A magnificent staircase in the center ascends to the Tripylon, the Council Chamber named after the three ornamental gates, which provides the backdrop to the performances of the Persepolis Festival. Take the stairs past the fighting lions and bulls and the jostling courtesans to the Hall, also known as the Throne Room of Xerxes. The doors giving access to it are decorated with bas-reliefs in which—under the emblem of Ahura-Mazda—King Xerxes sits in state on the shoulders of vanquished peoples. The Hall itself, which has the same horizontal dimensions as the Apadana, was only half as high. The east and west doors are decorated with the theme of the king fighting a monster or a lion. The walls of this building, made of sun-dried brick, have completely disappeared and all that remains are chiefly carved stone frames of doors, windows or niches. A large, detached bas-relief in which Darius accompanied by his son Xerxes receives the homage of an officer is passed on the way to the immense but very ruined Treasury. Divided into three parts—the first confusingly likewise called Hall of 100 Columns, the central part, Hall of 99 Columns (which served Darius as temporary Throne Room), the third the actual storeroom of the fabulous tributes—it occupied the entire southeast corner.

The Tombs

Passing the Hall of 32 Columns that extends the Hall of 100 Columns eastward and the remains of walls, rooms, shops, stables and coach houses that stretch to the south, head for the tomb of Artaxerxes II (405–361 B.C.) cut into the rock face of the Kuh-i-Rahmat. Like those their predecessors had dug at Naqsh-e Rustam, the tombs of Artaxerxes II and Artaxerxes III (361–338 B.C.) further to the south, present similar façades with doors opening into them that give access to the burial chambers. On one of the pediments the following scene is depicted. On a throne supported by the vassal nations, the king meditates before a fire-altar under the wing of the benevolent Ahura-Mazda. Very near the tomb of Artaxerxes II, you will see a well cut into the rock.

At the extreme south of the terrace, is a third tomb, this one unfinished, with the parade of the vanquished missing. The king for which it was destined, Darius III Codoman (336–330 B.C.), last of the Achaemenids, was murdered by his cousin on the flight before Alexander. You return towards the main staircase, passing by many interesting but damaged carvings scattered between the palaces: a roughed-out winged bull that was to be part of a monumental gateway still in the planning stage; a stone mastiff and a capital decorated with dragons who have rapacious looking beaks.

Just below the 33 acre platform which supports mighty Persepolis stands the lavish tented city built by the Shahansha of Iran to house distinguished guests on the occasion of the 1971 celebrations to commemorate the 2,500th anniversary of the creation of the Persian dynasty by Cyrus the Great. The Shah played host to nearly half the world's kings and heads of state.

The luxury tents, which are beige in color, were designed to blend with the sandy background and are laid out in a star shape around a magnificent fountain. The State Apartments for the Shah and Empress Farah were in fact a vast tent over 100 feet long. The walls were lined with purple velvet and specially woven purple carpets covered the floor. In the 210 foot long tented dining room guests sat on blue velvet covered chairs made in France. A French firm also made the beautiful 190 foot long hand-embroidered tablecloth. The royal tents can be visited for an entrance fee of 150 Rs (rather steep as the ticket to the ruins only costs 20 Rs).

Discovering the Fars Region

After Persepolis, the Fars has many other sites to offer and some of them are so near the royal city that you really cannot leave without going to see them. Pasargadae, which preceded Persepolis in fame and function; Naqsh-e Rustam, the tombs of the kings and the Sassanian bas-reliefs.

Pasargadae

The site of Pasargadae was chosen by Cyrus the Great (559–530 B.C.). Some people maintain that he chose it in memory of his victory there over Astyages. It is simpler to assume that Cyrus was merely continuing the movement towards the East begun by his ancestor Achaemenes, in order to put a distance between himself and troublesome Mede and Assyrian neighbors. Perhaps religious reasons also dictated Cyrus's choice. However, whatever the reason, the great days of Pasargadae were short-lived. At Cambyses's death (521 B.C.), the throne passed to Darius, descendent of a younger branch, who left Pasargadae for Persepolis. (Some historians have, in fact, maintained that the grandiose constructions at Persepolis were begun under the reign of Cyrus.)

The monuments of Pasargadae are very widely scattered, but all can be reached by car. They were contained within a vast perimeter, the layout of which can only be reconstructed with an aerial photo. Make your way first toward Cyrus's tomb. Seen from afar, it looks like a small simple house built on a pedestal. In fact, the monument is shaped like a very large sarcophagus, placed on a pyramidal foundation of enormous stone blocks, laid in six successive layers. Prior to its desecration, the burial chamber was sealed by a stone door.

Later, the Moslems built a small mihrab within the tomb itself. Close by are the ruins of a 13th-century mosque, built with materials taken from the Achaemenid edifices. Not long ago the mausoleum of Cyrus, curiously called Masjid-i-Madar-i-Suleiman (Tomb of Solomon's Mother), was a pilgrimage site frequented by housewives in the region.

About one km (half a mile) to the northeast of the tomb, the ruins of several buildings are enclosed within modern walls of terra cotta. One column remains standing in the central hall of one of these buildings. Although the shaft is of white stone, the base and capital are black (perhaps a legacy of Urartian architecture which is found in the Armenian churches). Scattered about are vestibules, porticos with columns, remains of entrances decorated with bas-reliefs but there is little of note.

Slightly to the east, another smaller ruin is noteworthy for a bas-relief representing a jinn with 4 wings, wearing a strange tiara on its head decorated with Egyptian symbols. Finally, slightly to the northwest stood Cyrus's residential palace; one of the corner pillars bears a trilingual inscription. Some 500 m (550 yards) to the north of the latter, the remains of an Achaemenid fire temple rise, resembling the one at Naqsh-e Rustam; the wall that is still standing shows how well the blocks of masonry were bonded. Still further to the north, a terrace, the Takht-i-Madar-i-Suleiman, shows a similar technique. Finally, going round the hills to the west, on the other side of a canal, one arrives at two fire altars with steps, similar to those at Naqsh-e Rustam.

Naqsh-e Rustam

At Naqsh-e Rustam, barely 5 km (3 miles) to the north of Persepolis, valuable relics of both Achaemenid and Sassanid art are found. In the high cliffs of Kuh-i-Husain, some 20 m (65 feet) above ground level, the tombs of four Achaemenid kings were hollowed out, from left to right: Darius II (425–405), Darius I (521–485), Xerxes I (485–465) and Artaxerxes I (465–424). All are practically identical in outside appearance, seeming at first sight to be but deep crosses recessed in the rock gazing over the plain to Persepolis. The bases are about 30 feet from the ground and they tower 100 feet up the cliff.

The central ledge is occupied by four pilasters crowned by bull-headed capitals supporting a molding with symbolic frieze. Each façade has a door.

Below the Achaemenid tombs, there are eight pieces of sculpture cut into the rock in memory of the Sassanid dominion (224–651), at least the first two centuries of it. The most noteworthy of them is the scene of the investiture of Ardashir I (224–241), founder of the dynasty—master of an empire that stretched from the Euphrates to Afghanistan—receiving the symbols of kingship, a tiara with long ribbons, from Ahura-Mazda. Several sculptures show the great figure of Shahpur I (241–272), particularly his victory over the Romans at Edessa in 260, while other bas-reliefs recall other less famous Sassanid sovereigns.

Two fire altars which can be seen on the left, give an idea of the religious ceremonies that occurred here and which are illustrated also by the fire temple of Kabah-i-Zardust, dating from Darius.

Istakhr

Along the road, 4 km (2 miles) to the north of Persepolis, is the site of ancient Istakhr, the religious metropolis where the Sassanid monarchs were crowned. Destroyed then rebuilt by the Arabs, it finally ceased to exist in the 10th century. There remain only several columns, some pillars and the ruins of a mosque built with pre-Islamic materials.

One kilometer and a half (about a mile) to the south of Istakhr, on the site of Kuh-i-Rahmat, there are three carved Sassanian bas-reliefs again with the scene of the investiture of Ardashir I receiving from Ahura-Mazda the beribboned tiara, symbol of kingship. There is also Shahpur on horseback, escorted by his noble guard and followed by his soldiers, once again receiving the emblems of sovereignty.

Towards Bishahpur

Persepolis and Naqsh-e Rustam might make it seem that there are relics of Persian antiquity to be found only in the north of the Fars. Though the south of the province is less well-known, and its sites less spectacular, it nevertheless has inexhaustible resources. An entire volume would be needed to list the bas-reliefs, the temples and the fire altars scattered throughout the countryside.

On the road from Shiraz to Bushire, the most interesting excursion is that of Bishahpur, if only to see the mountain landscape. Since the construction of the new road, the expedition is no longer a test of one's nerves; but you can still see here and there the dizzying hairpin bends of the dirt road crossing the famous "Old Woman" mountain pass.

The site of the Sassanid city of Bishahpur, 150 km (100 miles) from Shiraz, at the opening of a gorge, is impressively beautiful. The cliffs, the river, the valley that can be glimpsed behind, are worthy of a monarch in love with grandeur.

Opposite are peaks and hills covered with shrubs as far as the eye can see; this is Bishahpur, a vast forgotten city, founded by the Sassanid King Shahpur I in the 3rd century A.D. Continuing the work of the French archeologist R. Ghirshman, an Iranian mission is carrying on the task of excavating this ruined city celebrated during the 10th century for its orchards and olive groves. Protected by the river and a strong fortified wall, the city was once divided into four sections by two avenues.

Few buildings have been unearthed as yet, but those that have been are not uninteresting. First there is the fire temple, a square tower 14 m (46 feet) wide with foundations 7 m (23 feet) deep. A single wall is intact; at the top of it the fittings remain where stone heads of bulls held up the roof beams perhaps overhanging. The masonry work is sturdy. The sacred fire was kept perpetually burning in a dark recess protected from the sun, behind the north angle of the temple. Access to the sanctuary was by way of a vaulted staircase whose foundations can still be seen in front of the building.

To the southeast of the fire temple rises the great palace of Shahpur I. In cruciform shape it was surrounded by corridors, and had 64 recesses ornamented with stucco carvings. These were painted in the style of the period with vine branches and acanthus leaves, traces of which can still be seen. To the west of the palace, there is a courtyard, its ground covered with mosaics, fragments of which can also be seen at the Louvre museum. The mural depicts nude women surrounded by protecting jinns.

To the east of the palace and connected with it by five doors opening onto a corridor, there was a triple portal whose central arch had a span of no less than 15 m (50 feet). You can see the remains of its decorated stucco.

To the west of this site, at the end of a 500 m (550 yards)-long dirt track that skirts the age-old hillocks, rises a curious monument with two columns surmounted by Corinthian capitals. According to the inscription, this small structure was built in the year 266 by Shahpur I.

The Bas-reliefs of the River

The rock mass that dominates Bishahpur served as a fortress. One can still see the line of the ramparts with three towers and, if one looks more closely, the stone troughs in which the dead were exposed. Shahpur chose the walls of the gorge opening to the north of the city for bas-relief carvings. His successors did the same. Four of these panels are visible on the right side of the river (to the left on entering into the gorge), overrun with bushes and weeds, and some physical exercise is involved if you wish to admire them at close range. The main subject treated is once again Shahpur's victory over Emperor Valerian. There are also the traditional investiture scenes.

On the other side of the river, a track suitable for vehicles will take you first to a very damaged panel—again Shahpur's investiture and his victory over Valerian—then to a second much more interesting one. Once more the defeat of Valerian, to the left the Persian army, to the right bearers of offerings.

The Grotto of Shahpur

You must climb up goat paths towards "Mudan", the grotto that Shahpur made at the summit of the mountain dominating the Shahpur Rud, above his capital. A marvelous natural site from which the view encompasses the entire valley shimmering with heat waves in the sunlight and from the other side of which one can descend into the bowels of the mountain to a network of galleries that speleologists will find hard to resist.

At the entrance to this vast subterranean hall rises a colossal statue (8 m or 26 feet high) of Shahpur I, the only known Sassanian statue, probably carved from a stalagmite. Some smooth spaces had been chosen on the walls of the grotto for other bas-reliefs, but time and military defeats prevented them from being carved.

Firuzabad

Firuzabad, about 110 km (68 miles) to the south of Shiraz is, one of the most accessible towns in the southern Fars and the excursion is not lacking in interest, above all in the months of April or October when the Qashqais start traveling again.

Thirty km (18 miles) before arriving at Firuzabad, one follows a torrent at the bottom of an impressive gorge: the Tangab. Suddenly, overhanging the road, rises the Qala-ye-Dokhtar (Castle of the Daughter) whose fortifications protected the entire valley. This outpost is thought to have been built by Ardashir I. This is Sassanid country. A few kilometers from there, the remains of a bridge from the same period lie next to the inevitable bas-reliefs.

On the first one you will recognize Ahura-Mazda bestowing the beribboned tiara on Ardashir next to whom is the Crown Prince

Shahpur. The second is a sort of memorial of the battle of 224 B.C. that saw the victory of Ardashir over his suzerain the Arsacid King Artabanus V. At the exit of the pass, one notices the ruins of the palace of Atesh Kadeh, built by Ardashir at the beginning of his reign.

In the plain, 3 km (2 miles) to the northwest of the present little town, the ruins of the old Sassanid city of Gur are still indicated under hillocks. The outline of it is still visible by means of a slope and a moat. In the center of this perfect circle are a fire altar, the remains of a fire temple and a masonry tower. Robert Byron in his book *The Road to Oxiana* says of the latter: "The tower has no name, but is said to mark the site of a stone fallen from heaven. All round it, within the radius of half a mile, the ground shows the contours of Ardashir's capital. Many of the foundations seem to be only a foot or two below the earth and there is one platform still above it. This is built of rectangular blocks, neatly cut and fitted in the Achemenian way and very different from the higgledy-piggledy masonry of the tower, where stones of any shape are embedded in a sea of mortar. I should like to dig here; it must be the richest site in Persia still untouched." These words were written in 1937.

Towards Fasa and Darab

The roads to the Sassanid sites southeast may be paved throughout by 1977. The first stop will be Savestan 98 km (60 miles), where the tomb of Sheikh Youssouf (13th century), alas in bad repair, is the principal attraction. The ruins of the old city are 10 km (6 miles) to the south of the modern town and are worth visiting from the rather well-preserved 5th-century palace.

Fasa is only 3 km (2 miles) from its original site, the Tell-i-Zohak. The moat that encircled this rectangular city is still visible. Finally, before arriving at Darab, 110 km (68 miles) further on, stop at the fortified village of Djuzdjan. From here you will have a view towards the northeast of the circular outline of ancient Darabgird with its moats and ramparts. A mountain footpath on the right leads to a bas-relief located above a small pond. The triumph of Shahpur over Emperor Valerian is carved into a hollow in the rock. This scene was once used by the nomads for target practice. If you have the courage to follow the path for 5 km (3 miles) more, you will discover, cut into the mountain, an old church transformed into a mosque—the Masjid-i-Sang.

Neyriz

At Neyriz, a small city of 16,000 inhabitants slightly to the north, go to see the Friday Mosque, one of the oldest in the country. The south iwan is the most interesting part of it. It is the original core of the mosque, dating from the 10th century, a simple iwan with a pointed arch, ornamented with a handsome mihrab of carved plaster flanked by 5 niches on either side. Buttresses and additional buildings were added later. The mosque of Neyriz is a typical example of desert architecture, prompted by the lack of timber. Along with Firuzabad, Neyriz is the main center of the still partly nomadic Qashqais tribes.

The Qashqais

These tribesmen are a law unto themselves. They move according to the season wherever their flocks can find good grazing. These migrations may take weeks and it is a captivating sight to see the Qashqais on the move. In summer they put up their black tents close to the terraces of Persepolis. In autumn they again take to the road to the south, towards the "garmair", the warm lands on the edge of the Persian Gulf. At the end of March they go north again, stopping at Sarhad Shahar Dongan, their seasonal capital. With their proud bearing, these people seem to be the true masters of the country. For a long time they ruled the Fars, terrorizing the towns.

One wonders how this tribe with a Turkish tongue chose to wander through lands so far away from their original habitat. It seems that it was the Safavids who transplanted them, so as to entrust to these rough primitive fighters the defense of southern Iran against the Portuguese. Alas for the Qashqais, today there are other ways of driving out the hated foreigner. Determined to put an end to this war-like nomadism, Reza Shah, whose methods were direct, threw the principal leaders into dungeons. When the Great King was exiled, those who survived imprisonment were freed. Since then, the Iranian government has been trying to domesticate these incorrigible wanderers by building them villages and distributing land, as well as exercising a tight control over their territory by a network of police station outposts. Along with this goes education and a hundred or so schools now move with the nomads, white tents among the black. At Shiraz there is a junior and a high school, thanks to which it is hoped that finally the Qashqais will be integrated into national life.

Sedentary or no, the Qashqais keep their specific character. Their women are tall, well-built with strong features. They often wear spangled bright dresses and long, full skirts. Their jewelry is fascinating and includes necklaces of gold and silver coins, which often represent the wealth of their own particular family. Seated before their tents they continue to weave and knot the rugs that have made Shiraz famous.

236

THE FARS

Practical Information for the Fars

WHEN TO GO. The same time of year as for Shiraz. From March to May the traveler sometimes is fortunate in seeing the nomadic tribes of the Qashqais on the move. Their principal headquarters are at Sarhad Shahar Dongan in spring, between Pasargadae and Persepolis in summer and near the Persian Gulf in winter. The Shiraz-Persepolis Festival takes place early in September.

HOW TO GET THERE. By air: one visits the Fars starting out from Shiraz, capital of the province. An Iran Air flight from Tehran—stopping at Isfahan—lands there each morning. There is a return flight in the evening. There are several flights during the week to and from Abadan, Kuwait and the ports along the Persian Gulf. **By bus:** the buses of the T.B.T., Iran Peyma, Levantour and Mihantour companies stop at Shiraz coming from Isfahan, Abadan, Ahwaz or Kerman (via Yazd). They have daily service to the principal towns of the province, Neyriz, Firuzabad, etc.

WHAT TO SEE. The Fars is an extremely rich region from the archeological point of view. Its principal attraction is the site of *Persepolis*, summer capital of the Achaemenids. In the same area are Naqsh-e Rustam, the grandiose necropolis of its kings, and the Sassanid bas-reliefs that are connected with them, and *Pasargadae*, the city of Cyrus, in which his tomb is located. The Sassanid bas-reliefs of Naqsh-e Rajab are of minor importance.

To the south of the province, the Sassanid city of *Bishahpur* will interest you because of its collection of Sassanid bas-reliefs in an impressive location and its grotto with the monumental statue of King Shahpur I, rather than for its immense excavation site.

The travel agencies in Shiraz organize day trips such as a guided tour by minibus to Persepolis and Naqsh-e Rustam as well as including the Eram garden and the tombs of Hafiz and Saadi. These agencies can also arrange special tours on request.

HOTELS. You can now stay near the ancient site of Persepolis at two excellent hotels: the deluxe 187-room *Daryush* with open-air dining room, shopping arcade, games room and swimming pool; the 100-room *Mehmansara* ***, air-conditioned, pool, is also very comfortable. The small *Apadana* ** is 5 miles away at Marvdasht.

You will find small, two-star *mehmansara* (inns) at the towns of **Abadeh**, north of Shiraz on the Isfahan road; **Darab, Estahbanat, Jahrom** and **Neyriz**, east; **Bushire, Fasa**, south; and at **Nourabad**, west. Otherwise, there are very simple, small hotels in these places.

THE FACE OF IRAN

CAMPING. At Shiraz: Tourist Camp on the road to the airport. At the police station at Persepolis they will tell you where you can put up a tent.

SHOPPING. The Fars region is famous for its *gelims*, tapestries woven from goat's hair or sheep's wool, which make wonderful rugs and covers. Sold inexpensively at the bazaars.

MOTORING. From Isfahan to Shiraz 478 km (300 miles), of paved road makes for easy driving. There is a 2,100 m (6,900 feet) high pass before Dehbid. From Shiraz to Bushire 309 km (192 miles) over the paved road passes of the "Old Woman and her Daughter". From Shiraz to Dogonbadan (towards Abadan and Ahwaz) there is 160 km (100 miles) of paved road, then a bad track with better sections in the vicinity of some model villages. This itinerary can be difficult in winter. From Shiraz to Neyriz (220 km, 140 miles), the dirt road is in bad repair. From Shiraz to Firuzabad (116 km, 68 miles), 56 km (35 miles) are paved and the rest is a dirt road in good repair. From Shiraz to Lar (334 km, 205 miles), the road is paved as far as Jahrom (172 km, 105 miles); after that there is a very difficult mountainous route. A four-wheel-drive vehicle is recommended.

Excursion to the Achaemenid sites of the Fars. Leave Shiraz via the Isfahan road. 59 km (36 miles) further on, you will come to the monumental terrace of Persepolis (entrance fee). Then, go again in the direction of Isfahan, glancing briefly at the Sassanid bas-reliefs of Naqsh-e-Rajab, to the right of the road. Several kilometers further on there is a turn-off to the left (sign-post) for Naqsh-e Rustam. A good road for 3 km (2 miles) laid out across the remains of the city of Istakhr.

Approximately 100 km (62 miles) to the northeast of Shiraz there is a turn-off to the left (arrow) for Pasargadae (paved road).

Excursion to Bishahpur. Leave Shiraz via the Ahwaz road. After about 100 km (62 miles) there is a road-fork: turn to the left in the direction of Bushire. After 9 km (6 miles) you will reach the village of Bishahpur, marked by signs of the Iranian archeological mission. There is no gas (petrol) station between here and Kazarun 22 km (14 miles) further on. The Sassanid bas-reliefs are in the valley on both sides of the river, to the left of the road on arriving.

In order to visit the grotto of Shahpur, go beyond the bridge and take the upstream path on the left side of the river (sign: Shahpur Cabe). You pass through a village and see two others on the other side of the river. On a level with the second village (5.5 km, 3 miles) take a path to the left which crosses the river by a ford. Beware of flooding. You go through the village following the path which climbs the slope of the mountain 2 km (1 mile) from the fork. Leave the car. It takes an hour by foot to reach the grotto which opens at the summit of the mountain—and forty minutes to come down again. This excursion can be a difficult one and it may be easier to hire mules at Bishahpur or in one of the villages.

LURISTAN AND KHUZISTAN

Ziggurat and Oil Country

Luristan and Khuzistan are the two western provinces of Iran that form the natural prolongation of Azerbaijan and Kurdistan towards the south. The Lurs and the Kurds, and even the Bakhtiaris, were moreover lumped together for a long time by the Arab geographers who saw these mountain tribes as more or less wild "peasant-nomads" belonging to one and the same people. For the traveler, Luristan is above all a region of high and very beautiful mountains that conceal in the hollows of their valleys villages having a fortified air about them and inhabited by the people of the tribes. The capital of the province is Khurramabad, where you will find only a few historical remains. As a matter of fact, Luristan is of interest primarily to ethnologists.

Khuzistan is known as "the green country" an expression true only in the middle of winter, for all greenery is burnt to a crisp by mid-April. The mountain slopes down gently to the edge of the immense plain, the Susiana. This is the melting-pot of the ancient world from which the early beginnings of our civilizations sprang.

However, here the past fades away rapidly before the present. This is the rich province from which the country derives its wealth, the realm of black gold. Pipelines, flaming gas chimneys and the oil refineries themselves form today's landscape, while in the distance there is the sea, bordered with the great ports, Iran's main front on the world of trade.

Discovering the Region

Coming from Iraq or Azerbaijan, the main north–south road enters Luristan via Shahabad. The shortest route from Teheran is via Saveh and Arak to Borujerd (55,000 pop.), after which begins Luristan with some small forts made of dried mud, then some villages where occasionally the glass lanterns of the hammams glow. Now the road begins to twist through the mountain, the hamlets become increasingly austere and the scenery more grandiose. You cross a pass at an altitude of 2,000 m (6,500 feet) and Khurramabad is only 40 km (24 miles) away.

Khurramabad and the Lurs

The city appears at the junction of two rivers, in a rather majestic mountain setting. The massive silhouette of the citadel, built at the summit of a rocky peak, adds to this impression. The city was originally named after it, Diz-i-Siyah, the Black Fortress. A retreat of the Lurs chiefs, the Atabets, it was a permanent threat to the region. As early as 1386, Tamerlane tried to put an end to the ravages of these highwaymen. At the beginning of the 17th century, Shah Abbas attacked the fortress, executed Atabeg and made one of his deputies governor of the province. From then on the Lurs kept quiet, but they have remained the fiercest of all the tribes. Their 300,000 members though subject to the Shah, still bow to the authority of their own local chief. You will meet the Lurs in the narrow streets of the bazaar at Khurramabad, the men dressed sometimes in their long brightly-colored covercoats with a black collar; the women in ankle length dark dresses, their long hair floating around their faces, their heads bound in a turban made of two intertwined scarves. One passes them also along the main road on the outskirts of their villages, where they take care of the orchards. When they lead their herds to pasture on the steep slopes of the mountains, they erect curious encampments made of woven mats, stitched together with strands of black wool.

Khuzistan

From Khurramabad, Khuzistan is approached via a paved road that goes down the mountains towards the plain of Susiana. It crosses through beautiful landscapes, at times austere, at others charming, revealing in passing the coolness of a cascade. The road at one moment goes along the river, which offers the picturesque spectacle of its twists and turns, its gorges and its sandy banks. Malavi, with its few palm trees, has something tropical about it. At Pol-i-Dokhtar, the Bridge of the Daughter, the road passes under an arch, the remains of a bridge dating from Shahpur I (3rd century). Across the Karkha river is the partly excavated fortress town of Ivan-i Karkha built by Shahpur II to replace Susa which lies beyond Andimeshk; the branch left leads to Dizful, Shushtar and Masjid Suleiman.

Dizful and Shushtar

The city of Dizful (25,000 pop.) is perched on a cliff that dominates the Ab-i-Diz, its clay houses built right down to the banks of the river. In summer it is so hot that the inhabitants dig underground retreats at the edge of the water in order to keep cool. Wander around in the narrow streets of the old town, which the modern avenues have opened up, in order to admire the subtleties of the geometrical ornamentation of the door lintels. Do not leave without having looked at the remains of the combination dam and bridge built during the reign of Shahpur I by the Roman soldiers captured during the battle of Edessa in the year 260 A.D.

Some 35 km (21 miles) to the northeast of Dizful, the Mohammed Reza Shah Pahlavi dam across the river Diz rises to a height of almost 200 m (650 feet). Besides irrigating approximately 150,000 hectares (600 square miles), it generates enormous quantities of electrical energy.

The ruins of Jundi Shahpur are visible about 15 km (9 miles) from Dizful on the road to Shushtar. Founded by the Sassanid sovereigns, this city was famous at that time for its medical school.

Shushtar, 60 km (37 miles) southeast of Dizful, is worth a visit. Here again are the underground cool rooms and a Sassanid combination bridge and dam over the Karun. You can cross the town towards Masjid Suleiman to see the water wheels, still operating on a diversion canal of the Karun and also the nearby ruins of the castle of Salasil.

Masjid Suleiman

The road going towards Masjid Suleiman (40,000 pop.) twists through a beautiful landscape with a broken relief that will arouse the enthusiasm of geologists. The city itself stretches over many kilometers, connecting the residential areas to the oil-field installations, and the old city. The surrounding areas are not lacking in historical interest. The road to the airport will take you to a Parthian site: an immense terrace reached via a staircase 25 m (82 feet) wide. At Meidan-i-Naft, another oil field, remains of an Achaemenid temple are close by. At Pardeneshandeh (25 km, 15 miles, to the northwest), there is a site similar to Masjid Suleiman. Archeology and oil get on well together, indeed it is probable that the ancients fed their fire altars with the naphtha oozing from the ground.

The Bakhtiaris

The Bakhtiaris' camping grounds are in the mountains that separate Masjid Suleiman from Isfahan, where they are hollowed out by the upper valley of the Karun and its tributaries. In winter, the Bakhtiaris come down into the *sardsir*, the plains with a milder climate surrounding Dizful, Shushtar and Susa. The only people to be acquainted with the trails for moving flocks, they make their way in small groups—the herds on one side, the families on the other—to the Aradal region in spring and in summer to the pasture lands stretching out between Isfahan and Borujerd.

The Bakhtiaris make up a confederation of tribes still highly organized and powerful today. For a long time the Bakhtiaris considered the Shah's authority to be purely nominal. They were, however, obliged to furnish him with an army of several hundred men of which half were retained in Tehran as a pledge of fidelity.

Like the Kurds and the Lurs, the Bakhtiaris were chased towards the mountains by the Arab invasions. According to the ethnologists, these peoples, who had become sedentary, were forced to return to nomadic life in spite of themselves. One proof of this is that they use the cow as a beast of burden unlike the real nomad who uses the camel.

Like all mountain tribes, the Bakhtiaris have traditions of honor, hospitality and vendetta. Their women are known for their skill in treating wounds and especially in extracting bullets, happily an art they rarely have occasion to practice today. You will recognize the men of these tribes by their wide black trousers, their striped dark blue and white tunics and their felt skull caps. Their cemeteries are characterized by the lions and weapons carved on the tombstones.

Susa

This is in the eastern borderland of the Fertile Crescent that spreads from the delta of the Nile to the mouth of the Euphrates. At the borders of the Mesopotamian and Iranian plateaux Susa, as early as the IVth millennium, was affected by the impact of the Sumerian and Semite civilizations. Dynasties followed each other, crushed each other. With ant-like tenacity, the architects rebuilt what conquering armies had razed. From the cuneiform letters of the clay slab inscriptions we learn about this patient labor and of the wealthy agricultural society with its commercial organization that prospered in the region.

Towards 640 B.C., the Assyrians wanted to get rid of Elamite power once and for all. Susa was razed by Assurbanipal. The inscriptions also boast of the methods and actions of this bloody sovereign. One hundred years later, the Achaemenid dynasty appeared on the scene. Susa became the capital of Great Susiana. Ahura-Mazda, the single god, took the place of the ineffectual idols of the Indo-Iranian pantheon; man would no longer offer up his own son on the sacrificial altar.

Then came the conquest of Alexander which resulted in new disasters. The Sassanids rebuilt Susa, making it more sumptuous than ever, till Shahpur II flattened the town, which had become a Nestorian Christian stronghold, with an army of elephants. In the 7th century A.D. the Arabs arrived and built a great mosque on the site of the fire temple. From the 13th century on, Susa was a dead city located on a once fertile steppe. Since 1884, excavations (still continuing) have brought to light fifteen different strata of occupation. The most spectacular find is the enameled turquoise-blue frieze of the Apadana of Darius, depicting lions, bulls and the Immortals, which is now in the Louvre Museum.

The main ruins belong to the Achaemenid period, the Shushan of the Bible, in which the great Hall of Audience, the Apadana of Darius, is so vividly described. 72 column bases stand in orderly rows, and, as at Persepolis the capitals have bulls' head motifs. The inscription proclaims: "For this palace that I built at Susa, the materials were brought from afar. The earth has been dug out down to the rock under the ground." In this truly royal residence lived the beautiful Esther as wife of King Xerxes.

To the right is the mound of the Acropolis. The fortified castle with battlements, a curious whim of scholars, was built at the beginning of this century to keep looters at a distance. To the east of these two sites lies the "Mound of the Royal city", residence of dignitaries. Further still to the east was the "artisans' city". Outside the city walls, across the Shahpur river, a late Achaemenid palace with a frescoed columned hall, has recently been dug up.

From the terrace of the fortress, the entire site can be taken in at a glance, and, from the other side, the modern village of Shush. At the foot of the fortress, in a garden, is a museum.

In the village, on the bank of the river, rises the white sugar-loaf dome of a mausoleum that houses the remains of a prophet named Daniel (not necessarily *the* Daniel, though he, like another Old Testament prophet, Nehemiah, served at the Achaemenid court). In spite of its extremely modern aspect, the bee-hive type of decoration dates from the 13th century.

Haft Tepe and Choga Zanbil

Going to Choga Zanbil, 45 km (27 miles) to the southeast of Susa, you will notice to the right of the road the dug-up mounds of Haft Tepe. Since 1965, an Iranian archeological mission has been excavating at this Elamite site and has uncovered a temple, an inscription and 21 skeletons embalmed in red clay.

Choga Zanbil is Sumerian for "ascending to heaven", a fitting name for the religious center of the Elamite capital Dur-Untash, founded in about 1250 B.C. by King Untash-Gal and destroyed in 640 B.C. by Assurbanipal. The city was surrounded by an enclosure inside which a second wall marked the boundaries of the sacred quarter. In the middle of this rose the ziggurat, the most beautiful sacred tower in the Middle East.

Built entirely of sun-dried brick covered with baked brick, this unique example of Elamite architecture with its 5 floors once soared 53 m (170 feet), but today only 3 floors remain, making a total of 25 m (80 feet). The base of each level rests on the ground itself, probably for symbolic reasons; it would seem that the tower was built from the inside outwards, in accordance with a certain ritual ceremony.

At Choga Zanbil excavations revealed a large number of tablets covered with cuneiform letters and enormous "votive nails" of terra cotta, sometimes enameled, suggesting giant mushrooms often bearing a crown of "eyes". They indicate that this tower was dedicated to the god Inshushinak. There are also the remains of twelve temples on this site, in addition to those discovered in the ziggurat, as well as vestiges of three palaces.

Ahwaz, Khorramshahr and Abadan

Towards the south, remote antiquity and the 20th century come together; industrial expansion has brought Susiana back to life.

Ahwaz (270,000 pop.), the city of Ahura-Mazda of the Sassanids, is given over to fire worship as in the past, but today the fire is that of the flaming gas chimneys. These stand rigid and neat like troops on a parade ground and those, 10 km (6 miles) to the north of the city, have become a meeting place. On winter evenings the people come to picnic, sing and talk together in the light of these immense torches. Ahwaz is the region's capital city and chief market town.

Without lingering in this large city, located on both sides of the Karun and in whose residential quarters palm trees already appear, let us move on towards Khorramshahr. At the junction of the Karun and the Arvend Rud, lies a port with the same type of installations created by the British from Arabia to Bengal. Located at the terminus of the Trans-Iranian railroad, it is the nation's main commercial port. Along with this prosperity goes the casualness of the tropics, and you will enjoy watching the Karun ferrymen in their pretty boats decorated with spiral-shaped prows.

A few kilometers of super-highway lead to Abadan (300,000 pop.), the largest and oldest refinery in the Middle East. Along with shipping, oil, the local deity, is all powerful. The museum, surmounted by an open-work cone which tries to resemble the sugar-loaf of Susa, contains an excellent choice of objects that are representative of Iranian art of all periods. Here you will find inlay work, glass, bronzes, rugs, and jewelry. There is enough to make the stopover interesting.

Practical Information for Luristan and Khuzistan

WHEN TO GO. Since Luristan is the natural extension of Kurdistan, it enjoys a similar climate and thus should not be visited during the winter months. However, at Khurramabad, the cold is less severe; the first palm trees appear at Malavi and the mountain disappears and is superseded by the immense plain of Susiana, the green country of Khuzistan. The winter months are preferable but punctuated with torrential rains. From April to August, the thermometer climbs slightly higher each day and reaches a maximum of 47° C (116° F).

HOW TO GET THERE. By plane: you land at Abadan or Ahwaz. Daily service to Tehran, Shiraz, Isfahan. The Dizful-Andimeshk airport is used mainly by the oil companies. **By train:** daily service to Tehran. Though Luristan is by-passed by the railway which stops at Arak and Aligurdarz, Khuzistan is well-served and, after a night spent on the train, you can get off at Andimeshk or at Haft Tepe to visit the archeological sites of Susiana, or continue to Ahwaz, Khorramshahr or Bandar-Shahpur. **By bus:** two large principal itineraries connect Khuzistan with the rest of the country: Tehran, Kazvin, Hamadan,

THE FACE OF IRAN

Khurramabad, Ahwaz, Abadan and Abadan, Ahwas, Behbahan, Shiraz. Daily service to Kermanshah and all the towns of the province, leaving from Ahwaz.

 WHAT TO SEE. In Luristan beautiful landscapes and people in picturesque costumes. Khurramabad is not lacking in charm with its citadel and its mountain scenery. In Khuzistan, you can go to *Susa* with its open-air museum, *Haft Tepe* and *Choga Zanbil* where the most beautiful ziggurat (sacred tower) in all the Middle East is to be found. As for the oil cities, Ahwaz, Abadan and Masjid Suleiman have only their flaming gas chimneys, their pipelines and the other accessories of the oil industry to offer.

HOTELS

Abadan. Deluxe 132-room *Abadan International*, Braim (near airport), nightclub, bar, travel agency, pool; the four-star 100-room *Karvansaray*, Khorramshahr Rd., is just as luxurious and expensive. Nearby, the three-star 23-room *Abadan* is above average.

Azar, *Shekoufeh*, Zand Ave.; *Carlton*, Shadari Ave.; *Keyvan*, Shahpur Ave.; *Tehran*, Ahmad Abad Ave., are two-star.

Some private showers in the one-star *Firdowsi*, *Miami*, *Taj*, Shahpur Ave.; *Jam*, Amiri St.; *Kakh*, Amir Kabir Ave.; *Palace*, *Park*, *Pars*, *Plaza*, Zand Ave.

Ahwaz. On the road to Masjid Suleiman *Ahwaz*****; *Khorram****, *Royal***, Pahlavi Ave.; on the same street but no private showers the one-star *Naderi*, *Park* and *Park Now*; *Jahan*, Reza Shah Ave.

Andimeshk. *Eghbal**, Shahnaz Ave.; *Azerbaijan*, Firdowsi Ave.

Behbahan. *Mehmansara* (inn)**; no star for the *Shariati*, Hafiz Ave.

Borujerd. *Moghadam*, Shahpur Ave.

Dizful. *Iran Dez**, Mossalas Sq.

Khorramshahr. *Anahita****, Pahlavi Ave.; *Bakhtar***, Ibn Sina Ave.; no private showers in the *Iran*, Kamal-el-Molk Sq.; *Karun*, Pahlavi Ave.; *Park*, Milanian Ave.

Khurramabad. *Mehmansara***, on the road to Dizful, as is *Karun*. *Azita**, in town after bridge to the right.

Shush. *Mehmansara***, at entrance to the city.

Shushtar. *Mehmansara***.

 MOTORING. A paved road from north to south crosses Luristan and Khuzistan as follows: Hamadan, Khurramabad, Andimeshk, Ahwaz, Abadan. The Kermanshah-Malavi road is also paved. For the different itineraries from Kermanshah to Khurramabad, see the chapter *Kurdistan*, following.

 HOW TO GET AROUND. If you do not have a private *car*, there are *taxis* either at Andimeshk, Dizful or at Ahwaz to use for a visit to Susa or Choga Zanbil. The price is by arrangement but Andimeshk–Susa should not cost over 120 Rs and Ahwaz–Susa not more than 250 Rs.

LURISTAN AND KHUZISTAN

Excursion to Susa: about 46 km (28 miles) after Andimeshk on the Ahwaz road, turn off to the right for Susa. The modern village is 5 km (3 miles) away; the site is at the entrance to the village.

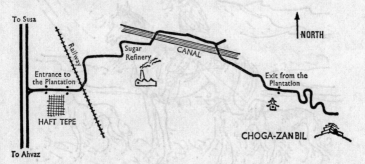

Excursion to Haft Tepe and Choga-Zanbil: From Susa return to the Ahwaz road and follow it for 14 km (8 miles), a large arrow indicates a fork in the road to the left. You enter a sugar plantation through a gateway and Haft Tepe is on the right. To reach Choga Zanbil you carry on across a railway towards a factory which you pass on your right. You cross a canal, go along it for some distance and then recross it and come to the exit from the plantation. At this point you will have covered 23 km (14 miles) since leaving the Ahwaz road and you have a further 6 km (3 miles) to do. The ziggurat at Choga Zanbil comes into view only at the last minute.

USEFUL ADDRESSES. *Abadan:* You will find travel agencies and airlines (Alitalia, BA, TWA, KLM) as well as shipping companies after leaving the airport, in the Braim Sud quarter. Swissair is, however, in town. Iran Air: Sunshine Block no. 15, and at the airport.

Churches: Anglican: Saint Christopher Church, Braim Sud, Khorramshahr Rd.; Catholic: Sacred Heart Church, Bahmanshir, near the Central Post Office.

247

IRAN'S FAR WEST

Hamadan, Kermanshah and Kurdistan

Travelers coming from Iraq will approach Iran through this region. Life in this part of the country is dominated by the mountains which rise to over 4,000 m (13,000 feet) in several places. The harsh winters last from December to March and summers are always cool, especially in Kurdistan, which is still partly covered with forests.

While the region has been little affected by foreign influence, the neighboring cities of Khosravi, Kermanshah and Hamadan are situated along the ancient caravan link between the Mediterranean and Central Asia. This explains the rather cosmopolitan character of these towns and, going further back into history, the important position held by the Medes, whose homeland this was. It is therefore not at all surprising that this highway, made centuries ago, should be marked by mementos of their presence for, during each epoch, successive rulers naturally endowed the most prominent sites with monuments to their own glory.

Mountains rise on both sides of the narrow roadway. Along it sun-tanned peasants drive slow migrations of livestock upward toward summer pastures or meander downward in the autumn. Small villages are hidden in the vales.

Exploring: Khosravi Border Point to Kermanshah

Leaving behind Mesopotamia, Bagdad, the Euphrates and the Tigris you enter the Persian empire. In fact you were and still are in Kurd country which has been, by the vagaries of modern politics, divided into three separate states. After driving 20 km (12 miles) or so, you reach Qasr-e-Shirin and its ruined fortress. Sassanids, Arabs and Turks succeeded each other as masters of the city but the Sassanid remains will detain you here for a few minutes. The *Shahar Qapu* (4 doors) and the *Emaret-e-Khosroés*, a palace dating from the reign of Khosroés II (6th century) are the most important. There are a few wall sections, some very thick and sufficient to give you an idea of the overall plan.

Thirty km (18 miles) further on the little Kurdish village of Pol-e-Zohab, undistinguished at first glance, has bas-reliefs dating from the third millennium. These sculptures extol the grandeur of the Akkadian kings, ancient rulers of Mesopotamia.

As always the theme is warlike. King Annubanini is shown offering his prisoners to the goddess Ishtar. Similar in subject but prehistoric are the carvings found at Darband-e-Sheikh-Khan, northwest of Pol-e-Zohab.

About 3 km (2 miles) farther is David's Booth (Doukan Daoud) which is reached via a track on the right. This is a Mede tomb dating from the 7th century B.C. After returning to the main road you stay on it until you reach Kermanshah. There is nothing to distract you except the admirable scenery.

Kermanshah

Kermanshah (170,000 inhabitants) will not detain you for long, but it is an excellent stopover for travelers coming from Iraq and a good place from which to make the excursions to Bisutun and Taq-i-Bostan.

It would be wrong, however, to neglect the city of the kings of Kerman which was founded in the fourth century by the ancient governor of Kerman, Bahram IV, the brother and successor of Shahpur III. Kermanshah in fact claims to go back even further in history.

In any case, being strategically located, it was the site of numerous battles. Pillaged and ruined each time, the city changed masters often. Occupied for the last time by the Turks during World War I, Kermanshah has since been free of foreign rulers. Though the city lacks famous monuments, its bazaar is one of the most colorful and original in the country. It is slightly dilapidated; the roof is caving in and corrugated iron has replaced the brick cupolas. Nevertheless its alleyways teem with a life and commerce not entirely dedicated to the distraction and entertainment of tourists. Here one should look for the beautiful Kurdish rugs made in the region. The Kurds in their local costumes who come here to do their shopping add a great deal to this picturesque scene.

Taq-i-Bostan

The one must at Kermanshah is the short drive to Taq-i-Bostan (The Garden Arch). Though the site is not as large as Bishahpur (see chapter on Fars) the quality of its sculptures surpasses it.

At the end of the road in the lee of a mountain there is a charming water garden fed from a nearby spring. Here, with a suitable setting of rocks, pools, trees and flowers, you see two artificial grottos and a panel carved in bas-relief, representing the investiture of Ardashir II (379–383). The king, standing between two gods, Hormuz on his right and Mithras on his left, is trampling a prisoner underfoot, while Hormuz hands the sovereign the beribboned ring, symbol of royalty.

The sculptures of the larger grotto (610–626) show garlands, cornucopiae and pilasters decorated with flowers and trees and are said to have no Sassanid equal.

At the back of the same grotto there is a carved figure of Khosroés II (590–628), menacing in his armor, mounted on his favorite charger Shabdiz. The detailed precision of this imposing equestrian group is characteristic of Sassanid sculpture.

Admirable hunting scenes decorate the side walls of the grotto. The elegance and ease of execution make both the stag and wild boar hunts unique masterpieces. On the left, slightly out of place here, is a 19th-century sculpture of Ali Mirza, son of Fath Ali Shah.

In the second grotto which has an oblong opening with a barrel-shaped roof there are carvings of Shahpur II and Shahpur III showing the investiture of the latter (383–388).

Bisutun

The bas-reliefs of Bisutun (40 km, 25 miles east of Kermanshah) are just as famous as those of Taq-i-Bostan. When you reach the immense sugar refinery recently built, look no farther, for you have reached your destination.

The two bas-reliefs carved in the rock at eye level date from the Parthian epoch. The most ancient of the two represents Mithridates II (124–91 B.C.) receiving tribute from four dignitaries. The other commemorates the victory of Gotarzes II over his rival Meherdates which took place here in the year 50. Unfortunately, both panels have suffered considerably from the ravages of time.

The Achaemenid sovereign, Darius I (521–485 B.C.), ordered the bas-relief commemorating his triumph over Gaumata to be carved in the cliff at a height of 60 m (200 feet). The latter wished to succeed to Cambyses (529–522 B.C.), son of Cyrus, and Darius was forced to fight no less than 19 battles to conquer his throne. The nine figures standing behind the King of Kings represent rebel princes taken prisoner. Thanks to the patience and erudition of Colonel Rawlinson, a British officer attached to the Qajar staff, the trilingual (ancient Persian, Akkadian and Elamite) inscription was deciphered.

Sanandaj and Kurdistan

In the Kermanshah bazaar there are men of proud mien, wearing fringed turbans, baggy trousers and shirts with flat pockets. These are the Kurds, unsubjugated warriors. They live in the mountains north of Kermanshah, west of Hamadan as far south as Lake Rezaiyeh, and their domain extends in Turkey to Lake Van and over the entire northeastern corner of Iraq. The Kurds, with their ancient traditions, are essentially semi-nomadic people who lead a pastoral life.

You can see them in Sanandaj, their capital. To get there, rather than taking the asphalt road from Kermanshah, you could follow the Qorveh dirt road which starts at the northeast end of Hamadan. Here the Zagros is revealed in all its majesty, and the mountain pass through which Sanandaj is reached opens out on a vast panorama.

The little town, built in the funnel-like depression formed by the river, has an interesting bazaar. Here the Kurdish families come to sell their rugs and make their purchases: not only spices but also fabrics and silver coins with which the women decorate their hair and bodies. Decked out in complicated turbans as though they were off to a feast, the women wear quilted coats with flaps turned up over long full dresses and baggy trousers.

The Kurds are generous, simple, hospitable and reticent. If you are invited to visit them you will wish to learn something about their life. Their homes are protected against drafts by rugs, and the underground stables which shelter their herds are a measure of their wealth.

Hamadan

In spite of its 180,000 inhabitants. Hamadan resembles a large provincial village, strung out along the six branches of its main arteries which radiate out from Pahlavi Sq. The big colorful bazaar, where one finds shepherds' goatskin coats as well as iridescent ceramics made especially for tourists, gives the city the character of a huge rural market, in spite of the neon lights which pierce the darkness around the square.

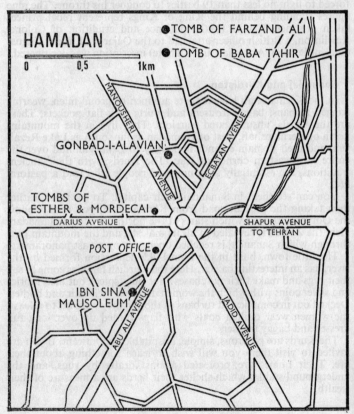

This is antiquity's famous Ecbatana, capital of the Medes, conquered by Alexander in 331 B.C. It was the favorite summer residence of the Achaemenid, Parthian and Sassanid rulers, pleasantly cool below mighty Mount Alvan (9,000 feet). The ancient stone lion to the southeast of the city, in a sadly mutilated condition, is a reminder of Parthian times. Then came the Arabs followed by the Seljuks, the Mongols and Safavids. Next Turkey invaded the territory and two years later Ahmed Pasha of Bagdad captured Hamadan after two months' stubborn resistance. In 1732 a peace treaty handed the town back to Iran and Hamadan, with remarkable recuperative powers, flourished again.

The Mausoleum of Esther and Mordecai

It is said that the most important Jewish colony of Iran was established in Hamadan. Their presence here as well as throughout the country is explained in two ways. The first and quite plausible explanation is that the Hebrews settled in Iran at the time of Xerxes (485–465 B.C.). Esther, presumed to be his wife, sought and obtained the king's protection for her people and sent for her uncle Mordecai, so that he might organize the settling of Jewish colonies in Iran. The other and more prosaic explanation stems from more recent times. According to this hypothesis, the wife of the Sassanid king Yazdegerd I (399–421), herself a Jewess, established a Jewish colony in the town. Most probably it is the body of this queen which lies in the mausoleum said to be that of Esther and Mordecai. The dome of the mausoleum looms in a narrow street, to the right of Dariouch Ave., not far from the Pahlavi Maidan. When visiting this monument, don't fail to notice the guardian's gestures as he opens the doors. This portal is a large stone slab with a hole pierced through it, into which the guardian passes his arm in order to remove the heavy wooden bolt. Inside are two carved wooden sarcophagi covered with draperies. The remains, however, are in the basement. You will also be shown an ancient Bible, written in Hebrew characters on gazelle skin. As when you enter a mosque it is customary to remove your shoes before going inside the mausoleum.

The Mausoleum of Avicenna

Ibn Sina, alias Abu Ali, is none other than the Occidentals' famous Avicenna (980–1037) whose wisdom and knowledge was known very early in Europe. Ibn Sina was probably born in Balkh. He worked first in Bukhara and later in Hamadan, where he died. A physician and philosopher, he left important scientific, metaphysical and mathematical works as well as poetry which greatly influenced the West during the 13th and 14th centuries. His writings were still studied in universities during the 19th century. Dating from 1952, the mausoleum is one of the most modern monuments in Iran. Its style is inspired by Mongol and Seljuk funerary towers, and its silhouette is reminiscent of the Gonbad-i-Qabus (see chapter on Caspian Sea). There are two very simple tombstones, placed one above the other in the Mongol fashion, one on the terrace and the other on the ground floor. The little museum next door contains several original manuscripts and reproductions of the scholar's work. Gifts from different parts of the country are also on display, among which is a copy of the *Shah Nama* (Book of Kings) illustrated with miniatures.

Speaking of modern monuments, the mausoleum of Baba Tahir, a contemporary of Avicenna and a predecessor of Omar Khayyam, is to the north of Hamadan. It is 20th-century baroque and lacks the elegance of Avicenna's mausoleum. One translation of a quatrain written by this mystical poet is as follows.

> *"If heart is sweetheart, what's my sweetheart's name?*
> *And whence heart's name, if sweetheart be the same?*
> *Heart and sweetheart blend all in one, I see,*
> *Nor know I which—sweetheart or heart—to claim."*

The Stone Lion

To reach this monument follow the Khiaban Djadid, also called Khiaban Sirous, to the last traffic circle. Then take a small street slightly to the right which leads to an open space. The "Sang-e-Chir"—the Stone Lion—stands here, hidden by a rise in the ground. At one time it is said to have crowned one of the city's gates. There is a superstition that, if it is kissed on the nose by a pretty girl and a little stone is deposited in one of the many depressions, she will find a lover.

On the way back towards the center of Hamadan you can visit the town's main rug factory.

The Gonbad-i-Alaviyan

The Gonbad-i-Alaviyan, though less famous than the lion, is more beautiful. You can reach it without difficulty by going down Manoutchéri Ave. (or Baba Tahir) until you get to a square easily recognizable because of a chapel with a green dome. Then take the large avenue on the right; soon the Gonbad-i-Alaviyan will loom on the right above the surrounding rooftops. Built in the 12th century, it is one of the innumerable Seljuk funerary towers which one sees all

254

over Iran. This is one of the best preserved. Its façades are decorated with large panels of carved stucco. Though its cupola has disappeared, most of the interior decor is original and it has a stucco mihrab densely decorated with floral and calligraphic motifs.

Ganj Nama

A lovely 12 km (7 miles) drive takes you to Ganj Nama (Treasure Book) with its Achaemenid trilingual inscriptions cut in rock. The site was probably much frequented long ago because it is cooled by the bubbling waters of the nearby cascade and framed by the mountains. Ganj Nama commemorates the titles and the genealogy of Darius (521–485 B.C.) and his son Xerxes (485–465 B.C.). The two sovereigns are offering prayers to Ahura Mazda, the supreme godhead, in ancient Persian, in neo-Elamite and in neo-Babylonian.

Malayer

Many of this town's 40,000 inhabitants are employed in the government rug factory (Cherkat-e-Fareh), a good place to purchase carpets at comparatively low prices.

At Nushijan Hill, 20 km (13 miles) away, the British Institute for Persian Studies finished in 1974 the excavation of a 3,000-year-old Median fire temple, large hall and protecting fortress. To preserve the building, the temple had been filled with big stones when the inhabitants left for as yet unexplained reasons. A steel frame and canopy now protect the site. The valuable jewelry and clay pottery found are on view at the Iran Bastan Museum in Tehran.

Practical Information for the Far West

WHEN TO GO. Winter is long in this, the highest region of the Zagros. Late spring and summer are pleasant at this altitude. The rain comes early in the autumn and snowfalls occur sometimes as early as November. The ideal time is September to mid-October for nature then dons her mantle of bright warm colors.

HOW TO GET THERE. By air: the cities of Hamadan and Kermanshah are linked to Tehran two or three times a week by Iran-Air flights. **By bus:** there are buses every day from Tehran to Kermanshah and Hamadan, to most of the towns and villages in the region and notably to Sanandaj which has daily direct bus service to Tehran and bi-weekly service to Azerbaijan. T.B.T. Levan-

THE FACE OF IRAN

tour and Iran Tourist will answer inquiries. The Saadat Now and Sedaqat companies have buses to Hamadan, Marivan and Saqqez from Sanandaj.

 WHAT TO SEE. In Hamadan: the *Tomb of Avicenna* (Ibn Sina or Abu Ali) the *Esther and Mordecai Mausoleum* and the *Gonbad-i-Alaviyan*, a 12th-century Seljuk monument. There is a pleasant mountain excursion to the Achaemenid site of Ganj Nama. Kermanshah has nothing special to offer except its picturesque and authentic bazaar. Go to Bisutun (Sassanid bas-reliefs) and Taq-i-Bostan (Sassanid bas-reliefs) both nearby. If you are coming from Iraq you can stop at Qasr-e-Shirin (Sassanid remains) Pol-e-Zohab (Akkadian bas-reliefs) and Doukan Daoud (Mede tomb). In Sanandaj you can stroll through the bazaar, which has nothing special about it except for the Kurds in their gaily colored costumes.

HOTELS

Arak. *Laklak*, *Mehmansara* (inn)**; *Arya*, *Miami**.

Hamadan. *Abou Ali*** and its annex*, Abou Ali Ave.; some private showers in the *Kakh***, none in the *Roshan**, Pahlavi Sq.; *Tavakoli*, Shahpur Ave.

Ilam. *Mehmansara* (inn)**, 10 rooms.

Kermanshah. *Motel Glayol***, air-conditioned, pool, off the Hamadan road, follow the signs; *Dariush***, Kourosh Ave.; *Asia*, *Bisutun***, Shahpur Ave.; *Persepolis***, Firdowsi Ave.; *Motel Madaen**, on the Hamadan road; some private showers in the *Bozorg*, Hasht-e-Mordad Sq., *Jahan*

and *Pars*, Shahpur Ave.; none in the *Aftab*, *Asre*, *Jadid*, *Eslamieh*, *Karoon*, *Maleki*, *Takht-e Jamshid*.

Malayer. *Mehmansara* (inn)**.

Nahavand. *Kakh*, Valiahd Sq.

Qasr-e-Shirin. *Mehmansara***; no private showers in the *Farhad*, *Khayyam*, *Parastoo*.

Sanandaj. *Abidar*, *Raoof**; even simpler *Naderi* and *Shahriar*.

Saqqez. *Bakhtar*.

Shahabad Gharb. *Mehmansara***.

Tuyserkan. *Alvand**.

 SHOPPING. Hamadan is famous for its ceramics and painted dinnerware which are sold at prices much too high for their quality. The bazaar has everything you have already seen in Azerbaijan. The huge goatskin coats—the local people's principal protection against the cold—are made with the fur on the inside. Usually the skins are dyed yellow and embellished with elaborate orange embroideries, In the Kermanshah bazaar your eye will be attracted by the Kurdish knotted rugs made in the nearby villages; though coarse, their colors are attractive.

 MOTORING. From the Iraq frontier one can drive to Tehran via Kermanshah and Hamadan on a good asphalt road. Equally good roads north from Kermanshah to Azerbaijan via Sanandaj, Saqqez, Miyandoab to Lake Rezaiyeh and Tabriz; south via Shahabad and Malavi into Luristan and Khuzistan. For the direct route via Nourabad, one needs a Land-Rover (beautiful scenery). The road is paved all the way southeast from Hamadan to Isfahan via Malayer and Borujerd; from the latter there exists a good about equidistant alternative to Tehran via Arak and Saveh. Halfway between Borujerd and Dorud on the Isfahan road the newly widened highway branches west to Khurramabad. The Hamadan–Sanandaj road is a good dirt road; over the last 15 km (9 miles) one passes through picturesque mountain scenery. (Not feasible in winter because of snow.)

Gasoline (petrol) is available on all these routes. The first Iranian petrol station is located right after the frontier post of Khosravi. For car repairs and maintenance there are garages in Kermanshah, north of the city on the Hamadan road, and service stations on Pahlavi Ave. (Bisutun Station), on Shahpur Ave. (Mahmoudi Station) and on Shahnaz Ave. (Nasr Station).

Excursions. From Kermanshah you can make the excursions to *Taq-i-Bostan* and to *Bisutun*. Leave the city heading north on the Tehran road and drive to the traffic circle (about 5 km, 3 miles). The left road leads to Sanandaj (135 km, 83 miles), the right to Tehran passing by the Bisutun bas-relief (40 km, 25 miles) and the road straight ahead leads to Taq-i-Bostan (9 km, 6 miles). The *Paru Cave*, one of the world's largest, is located in the mountain of the same name about 12 km from town. *Ganj Nama:* leave Hamadan on Dariouch Ave. and stay on it until you reach the last traffic circle. Take the asphalt road slightly off to the right and continue for about 12 km (7 miles).

 **USEFUL ADDRESSES.** *Khosravi:* Tourist Bureau at the frontier post. *Kermanshah:* Iraqi Consulate, Pahlavi Ave. Iran Air, at the airport. Melli Bank, Shahpur Ave. Reza Pahlavi Hospital, Pahlavi Ave. T.B.T. and T.C.C. bus companies, Sepah Place.

Useful Telephone Numbers. Police, 02; highway police, 2166; ambulance, 2444.

THE DESERTS

Great Salt and Great Sand

The center of the Iranian plateau consists of vast hostile lands where life cannot flourish without a heroic struggle against the forces of nature. There is a continual search for coolness and water and the oasis villages with their earthen cupolas and thick walls are designed to combat the climate. Some of the larger dwellings have a high iwan opening out onto a court and leading to two small vaulted rooms. The room in the back, which is slightly lower, is always cool. *Badgirs*, (wind traps) resembling large hatchways which open out on the roofs, catch the cool breezes and create a constant draft in the *zirzamins*, the subterranean rooms, and frame the cupolas of the underground cisterns. Thus the water which is drawn at the bottom of a staircase leading below ground, is always fresh and cold. In the desert there are kanats, subterranean canals carrying mountain water, and, alongside at intervals, roofed wells.

The problems of life in the desert have not been solved entirely by modern techniques. In this extremely conservative area live the last of the Zoroastrians, rebels against Islam for the past thirteen centuries. Here also the Shi'ite rites are most strictly observed. There is not a village which does not boast its *Hoseiniyeh* where the Muharram festivities are celebrated and where *Taziya* is played. The *Cher*, the enormous wooden catafalque which represents the idol of Hosein, occupies the place of honor in the processions during the month of mourning. You will see it in every bazaar, and village.

Finally, to the joy of connoisseurs, the desert has preserved some of the most interesting examples of Seljuk and Mongol architecture. The first truly Persian mosques are still standing, their stucco decoration having withstood the ravages of time.

Discovering the Region

From Ray on, 10 km (6 miles) beyond the capital, one is already traveling on the edge of the desert. Qom, Kashan, Natanz, Naïn, Yazd: this ancient route offers the inconveniences as well as the charms of forgotten roads. To one side is the mountain; to the other, the desert, with its vast pans of shimmering salt, which engulfs these five cities scattered over a 500 km (310 miles) stretch. You will see a few dry and thorny tufts of vegetation. In spite of the rather desolate picture which the map suggests, the landscape of the east–west transverse road to Tabas is no more arid.

Qom

Qom (Qum, Ghom, Khum) is the first stop along the desert road, about 160 km (100 miles) from Tehran. From afar the golden cupola sparkles beside the beautifully tiled dome framed by six minarets.

Qom (150,000 pop.) is the second most important holy city in Iran after Meshed. As always in Moslem countries, great discretion should be practiced when photographing, especially in the vicinity of the sanctuary which harbors the remains of Fatima, sister of Imam Reza, himself venerated in Meshed. You can enter the Safavid monument's vast courtyard, always thronged with pilgrims apparently camped there for days on end, their crumpled clothes and soiled bundles forming a strange contrast with the almost clinical cleanliness of the splendidly restored tiles and marble. Access to the shrine itself is strictly forbidden to non-Moslems but you can stroll at leisure through the souvenir bazaar, a typical appendage of all pilgrimage sites, no matter what the religion.

There are other monuments to visit, particularly the imamzadeh (14th century) with its curious conical roof and the Friday Mosque, a kiosk-like building whose construction betrays surviving elements of a Sassanid fire temple. You will also find in the bazaar (entrance: first traffic circle after the bridge), uncharacteristic of the Orient, a remarkable triple-domed hall piled high with rugs.

Kashan

From Qom to Kashan, the road runs over 100 km (62 miles) between the already distant chain of tinted mountains and the flat desert, cracked and salt white. Villages, some abandoned, others with the iwans of their façades facing north, dot the landscape. The kanats, resembling the underground passageways of giant moles, are the life lines of these foothills.

Kashan appears (70,000 inhabitants), bristling with bulbs, domes and minarets, bathed in the golden light. Although this is the home of the kachi, you will see few of the beautiful enameled faience tiles named after the city, nor will you see any of the marvelous tiles with metallic reflections. The relics of those sumptuous years are in the Tehran museum.

Monuments: the Masjid-i-Maidan-i-Fays, situated in the middle of the bazaar, is Timurid; one of the minarets of the Masjid-i-Jami is Seljuk, as is the Manai-i-Zein-ed-Din, whose solitary dilapidated silhouette rises above a large modern boulevard. Shah Abbas I's predilection for Kashan is evident; his body lies near the Mausoleum of Habib ibn Moussi. Of the Great Safavid's splendid estate, described by travelers of the time, in Bagh-i-Shah (Garden of the King) west of the city, nothing is left but 300-year-old cypresses and the tiled canals where the waters of the Fin spring flow. The present palace is the work of Fath Ali Shah (19th century).

A site of very different interest awaits you not far from Bagh-i-Fin. A French archeological expedition excavated the necropolis of Tepe Sialk between 1933 and 1938. Even though most of the objects which were found are today in various museums, Tehran and the Louvre among others, it is a must to visit this site where, 6,000 years ago, generations of craftsmen lived and created their artistic treasures for posterity.

Natanz

Beyond Kashan the desert remains on one side of you for a while and then vanishes, as the road starts to wind up into the foothills of the Kuh-i-Kargas (4,000 m or 13,000 feet), whose dark and jagged mass is outlined against the horizon. In this impressive site, 80 km (49 miles) from Kashan, Natanz lies with the cupolas of its mosques prominently displayed. The Masjid-i-Jami is the only interesting one. Easily recognizable by its minaret and conical cupola, it faces a pretty little square shaded by ancient trees. It consists of several buildings, all 14th century: a khanegah (convent) whose portal is very cleverly restored, the mosque itself, the mausoleum of Sheikh Abdel Samad Isfahani and a minaret. Before leaving Natanz, you can also visit the Koutche Mir Mosque and admire its Seljuk mihrab in carved plaster.

Ardestan and Zawareh

Between Natanz and Ardestan, the road meanders for 66 km (41 miles) through rather uninteresting mountain scenery. Before reaching Ardestan, a trail on the left leads to Zawareh (18 km or 11 miles), an isolated village seemingly at the end of the world. At the rear of the village a large blue dome shelters a handsome arcaded hall. Here take a right turn towards the Friday Mosque (12th century). This is probably the oldest mosque with 4 iwans in Iran and was planned this way from the beginning. Don't miss the Pamenar Mosque with its beautiful carved plaster decoration in the Mongol style. Notice especially the surfaces underneath the arcades. A climb to the top of the minaret (18 m, 60 feet) will afford an interesting overall view of the local architecture.

In Ardestan, Zawareh's former rival, visit the Friday Mosque (12th century), whose iwans were added to the original building. It boasts three beautiful mihrabs and the remains of very original decorative motifs on the surface of the vault of the principal iwan.

Naïn

Naïn (13,000 inhabitants), 95 difficult km (59 miles) from Natanz, is the last important settlement before Yazd. Yet another Friday Mosque, also 12th century, awaits you. Practically nothing remains of its Abbasid origins, but the decoration of the mihrab room and of the mihrab itself is probably the most delicate of any to be seen in the country. Notice the carved wood mimbar (14th century). Be sure to look at the outside, especially the south portal and the minaret, by which you recognize the monument on the left as you enter the village (beautiful decorative theme under the flange). You probably should make the effort to see the ruins of the Baba Abdullah Mosque (14th century). If you are going to drive onto Yazd it is best to allow plenty of time, for the road is full of stopping places. Aqda, about 70 km (43 miles), is the first oasis you will reach. Ardakan, about 40 km (24 miles) farther on, hides its charm in narrow dirt streets. On the left a sign indicates the direction to Maybod, a large village of potters huddled at the foot of an imposing cliff. Now you are 60 km (37 miles) from Yazd.

Yazd

Yazd is practically encircled by desert and stands at an altitude of 4,075 feet on a plain edged on the north and south by mountains. It has 70,000 inhabitants and bristles with activity. Trucks loaded with merchandise prepare to make their way towards Zahedan and Khorasan. Bicycles move in every direction, laden down with silks or woolens, for Yazd is a textile center. In the bazaar you can watch the local sweet merchants at work. Their giant cauldrons are filled with simmering syrup, sugar is molded in the shape of missile shells, and sugar loaves are decorated with colored paper. Here whit, wood chests are lined with velvet; there leather is braided; farther one copper is beaten.

Throughout its long history, Yazd, its domes and cupolas hidden in the heart of its ancient quarters, has always been a prosperous and respected city. During the 14th century the Muzaffarids endowed the city with its monuments: the Masjid-i-Jami and the Masjid-i-Vaqt-o-Saat (Time and Hour). The latter doubtless got its name from the observatory in this maze of important buildings which had a most elaborate device for recording the time. Of the madresseh, library, college and observatory nothing remains but the mosque (1326) and its magnificent interior decoration of faience and stucco. The same style is echoed in the mausoleum of Shams-ed-Din, located in the suburbs of the city. The mausoleum of the twelve iwans dates from the 11th century.

Mir Chaqmaq, an officer of the Timurid ruler Shahrukh, is responsible for the mosque which bears his name. Its high, imposing minarets are an outstanding feature of the town and are similar in style to the minarets standing at the bazaar entrance. The latter are of much later vintage.

The Gabars and Zoroastrians

The faithful of the ancient Persian religion live mostly around Yazd and Kerman. The Zoroastrian villages are situated in arid valleys which no one else wanted. They are recognizable by a large tree towering over the rooftops, for this is the indispensable decorative element of the courtyard of the temples. There are several communities between Yazd and Taft.

The religious practices of the Zoroastrians differ little from those of the Indian Parsees, their co-religionists who went into voluntary exile at the time of the Moslem conquest. Their religion is based on the belief in one supreme being, Ahura-Mazda, the "Wise Lord", who is honored by leading a righteous life rather than through complicated rites. Zoroaster's reforms (probably 6th century B.C.) dealt mostly with this point and with the repression of blood sacrifices. For a Zoroastrian the sacred fire is the image of the god to whom he prays. The fire is kept in a huge bronze urn situated in the middle of the sanctuary and accessible only to priests. A much larger rectangular hall, open to the public, is used for the celebration of the rites. The celebrants, their faces masked so as not to sully the sacred fire with their breath, recite from memory the 72 most important chapters of the Avesta in a language unintelligible to the faithful. When the ceremony is over, those present are invited to partake of the food offered as sacrifice.

Everything which contributes to the earthly happiness of the community is considered beneficial and worldly pleasures are not spurned. Women are not veiled, but wear brightly-colored cowls and full trousers.

The most important event in the life of a Zoroastrian is *naojote*, the initiation ceremony which must take place before the age of 15. The child is undressed, then clothed in a white garment with a cord around his waist symbolizing his responsibilities. It is impossible not to mention the funeral rites, for they are most peculiar. The bodies are placed on tiers inside the large windowless towers called Towers of Silence. Within an hour at the most, the corpse has been devoured by vultures. The bones are then thrown into the central pit of the tower. This custom ensures that neither fire, water nor earth will be contaminated with impure matter. No one, except for those in charge of this ceremony, has ever seen the inside of such a tower.

The Desert Crossing

The vast desert expanses in the center of Iran are surrounded by mountain ranges which catch the rain. There is the Kevir, the Great Northern Desert, and the Lut, the Southern Desert. The Kevir, at an average altitude of 700 m (2,300 feet), is colder but less hostile. Numerous rivers lose themselves in its spaces transforming crusty salt surfaces into muddy swamps. The Lut, altitude 300 m (1,000 feet), though torrid and invaded by sand, is easier to cross because of its large palm tree oases.

There are no nomads wandering over the Iranian desert. They settle around water holes wherever the climate is conducive to the ripening of dates. The ancient caravan trail crossed the great Iranian desert from oasis to oasis. Today trucks have replaced dromedaries and it is possible to travel across this sterile expanse following their tracks.

From Naïn or Ardestan, one first reaches Anarak, a small sleepy mining town at an altitude of 150 m (500 feet). At Choupanan (1,000 inhabitants), situated in the midst of a palm grove, leave the trail on the left leading to Djandaq and Khor, and take the road for Robat-e-Posht-e-Badam. Here you join up with the shorter and more traveled route which starts on the highway 27 km (16 miles) from Yazd. The road first goes through dunes; then you come to Khowrnaq with its cisterns and its soil riddled by wadis. For a considerable distance the road is bordered by large scintillating salt crusts, which finally give way to reddish soil covered with thorny bushes. Robat-e-Posht-e-Badam (600 inhabitants) is a crossroads of desert routes. From there you can reach the beautiful oasis of Khor (3,000 inhabitants) with its palm grove sheltered behind high walls and its narrow streets.

Robat-e-Posht-e-Badam, Robat-e-Khan, Robat-e-Kour are police posts where there is little to relieve the boredom. The driving is treacherous as the sand surface moves beneath the wheels. Then comes the plain, where camels graze and green palm trees indicate villages. Farms increase in number and finally you reach Tabas.

Tabas

Tabas (12,000 pop.) prides itself on its thousands of palm trees, its orchards and its agriculture. All along the two modern avenues you can watch cotton fiber being separated from the seeds with small primitive gins. At the end of the principal avenue a spring feeds the canals of a beautiful garden. Don't overlook the Masjid-i-Jami and its impressive supporting buttresses. You will walk through amazingly narrow streets resembling deep trenches, pierced by angular door-frames and stairways leading down to the cisterns.

All Tabas's wealth is revealed to those who climb to the top of the ruins of the Ark tower. This citadel, which was the hideout of "Assassins" during the 11th century, was dismantled by Sultan Sanjar. The clumsy minarets of one of the city's madares date from this epoch.

The End of the Road

Tabas was only a stopping place. The parched landscape looms again. Beyond Abbas Abad, a solitary mountain range must be crossed. Deyhouk with its dappled roofs marks the return to the plain. Next is Firdows, a little town of 12,000 inhabitants, which was completely ravaged by earthquakes in 1968. Ruins and refugee tents intermingle with brand-new construction. Then comes Gonabad, famed for the vividly colored enamel tableware made in the hamlet of Mend. The town boasts a 16th-century Masjid-i-Jami. Here you

THE DESERTS

join the road of the Allies, which connects Zahedan with Meshed. To the north you cross Khorasan. Towards the south, another adventure awaits you in Seistan.

Practical Information for the Deserts

 WHEN TO GO. During the summer one can make the trip from Qom to Yazd without suffering too much, although the sun makes itself felt rather violently from Naïn on. The spring or autumn are more agreeable. Although there is a risk of snow storms in winter, this is the best season to traverse the Naïn–Gonabad or Yazd–Gonabad routes. Rain can be worrying too. These are some of the most difficult roads in Iran and cross regions where the temperatures can vary from +40° C (104° F) to −5° C (23° F) in one day.

 WHAT TO SEE. In *Qom:* whatever you are allowed to see of the sanctuary where Fatima, sister of Imam Reza, is buried. In *Kashan:* an interesting bazaar and a few Seljuk remains; this is a secretive city with great character. In *Natanz, Ardestan, Naïn* and *Zawareh* one can visit the most ancient mosques of the Seljuk, Mongol and Abbasid epochs. In *Yazd:* The Friday Mosque (14th century) and the Vaqt-o-Saat Mosque (same epoch); the Zoroastrian quarters with their pebble-paved streets (to the west and south); a brief glance at the Towers of Silence, near the Saffayeh Motel.

 HOW TO GET THERE. By air: there are daily flights between Tehran and Yazd. There are also several flights a week between Yazd and Kerman, Zahedan, Shiraz and Isfahan. **By train:** Tehran–Yazd–Kerman–Zahedan line is completed as far as Kerman. **By bus:** Mihan Tour has daily buses from Tehran to Zahedan via Qom, Kashan, Natanz, Naïn, Yazd and Kerman. Buses of the export company service the area around Qom and Kashan. Consult the section *Bus Service* in the chapters on Isfahan and Shiraz. To cross the desert, the Golchan Ser Company has buses three times a week between Yazd and Tabas, from which point there is a daily bus service to Meshed via Gonabad (Golchan Ser and City Navard companies).

HOTELS

Firdows. *Charbani*, small hotel near the municipality.

Kashan. *Mehmansara***; *Sayiah*.

Naïn. *Mehmansara***.

Natanz. *Mehmansara***.

Qom. *Apadana**, Mohammed Reza Shah Ave.; *Bahar**, best but no private showers; *Chahar Fasl, Nikoo* and *Boolvard*, all on Moojeh Ave.; *Arya*, Astaneh St.

Tabas. *Mehmansara***, Shah Sq., on the left coming from Yazd. Rest lounge in the *Café Saadi*, Shah Sq. and in the Gity Navard *Terminal*.

Yazd. *Motel Saffayeh****, pool, Kerman Rd.; *Cirous**** (expensive for what is offered), Pahlavi Ave.; *Arya* and *Pars*, Valiahd Ave.

THE FACE OF IRAN

 CAMPING. In Yazd, you can camp in Karkhaneh Agha 4 km (2 miles) before the town as you arrive from the north. Comfortable. On the desert road and in Tabas, ask the police, who will indicate where you may set up your camp.

 MOTORING. From Tehran via Qom and Kashan good asphalt road beyond Natanz; but it would be foolhardy to continue over the "corrugated" sections as far as Naïn which can be reached painlessly from Isfahan on the paved road to Yazd; the long section southeast to Kerman is scheduled for completion by 1977. As for the road across the desert (Yazd–Gonabad), even though most of it is perfectly passable, a Land-Rover is needed to get across a few sandy stretches. In case of rain, the road can pose problems for vehicles of all kinds. Furthermore, a supply of petrol is needed until Tabas—take 30 percent more than your normal consumption. The same holds true for the trip between Tabas and Firdows. In case of breakdown or accident, practically no repair facilities exist in Tabas. You'll have to go to Yazd or Meshed to have repairs done and get the necessary spare parts.

 SHOPPING. Wherever you stop, you'll have a chance to spend your money. There are a few antique dealers in Qom (a good address: *Abbas Sabahi*, Hasrati Ave.) and in Kashan. They are less expensive than those in Tehran and Isfahan, but this will not last much longer. Qom specializes in sweets, as does Yazd. The latter is also famous for its silks. In Tabas you'll find brightly colored woven cotton rugs and *givehs*, felt-soled sandals for walking in the desert. The finest modern rugs, mostly of silk, are made in Qom and Naïn.

MESHED AND KHORASAN

The Eastern Marches of Nomads and Farmers

At the time when the Roman empire was crumbling under the attacks of the barbarians, the "Eastern March" under the Sassanids withstood the assaults of nomads from Central Asia. During the seventh century, danger from the west shattered the tottering Sassanid kingdom and, for a brief period, Khorasan became the refuge of Iranian civilization. In 820, Khorasan became the domain of the Taharids but for less than half a century.

From then on the province was to have many ups and downs, passing from one ruler to another until the invasion of the Seljuks, led by Togrul Beg (1038) and culminating at the end of the 12th century with Genghis Khan's Mongol tidal-wave. What men did not succeed in destroying through the ages, nature did. In 1968 violent earthquakes again destroyed several towns.

This vast territory has about two million inhabitants, nomads in the south, farmers in the north. Water from the melting snows is brought underground through a system of kanats to even the smallest parcels of land. Each cultivator takes his turn for a supply of the precious liquid and it is considered a crime to open one's sluices when it is a neighbor's turn to irrigate his land. No one here lets others take advantage of him. "I have never seen more ferocious peasants than in Khorasan," one of Gobineau's characters says. "They live in fortified villages; when a poor soldier approaches, they close their doors, climb on the walls and, should you be so rash as not to leave immediately, you will find yourself the target of a volley of shots, which rarely miss" (1875).

There is no reason for you to fear the Khorasanis' rifles today. During the last century they had cause to resent visits from plundering Turkomans as well as from the regular army which was supposed to bring them under control. Since then Uzbeks and Turkomans have been brought to their senses by the Russians and formed their own republics and they now have better things to do than go slave-hunting in Khorasan. The peasants have had time to cultivate their gardens and the fruits they produce are among the finest in the country.

Discovering Meshed

Meshed (Mashad) has pride in its traffic circles and large avenues laid out by Reza Shah. The city is just as proud of its parks, its modern monuments such as the station, and its sugar refineries, which cause roads to be jammed with convoys of beet-laden trucks in the autumn. The population has doubled in 20 years and is now over 300,000, to which must be added pilgrims who come by the thousands every day during the period of religious feasts. For Meshed is a city with one of the greatest concentrations of religious buildings in the world.

A Bit of History

Since the beginning of the ninth century, chroniclers have mentioned the small village of Sanabad near Tus, once an important city but now reduced to a hamlet. History and legend become very confused when Harun al-Rashid, Caliph of orthodox Moslems, is put face to face with Imam Reza, venerated by the Shi'ites. In 809, the Caliph of Bagdad died and was buried in Sanabad. Ali Reza then asked to be buried next to his archenemy as a sign of eternal reproach. Upon his death (817), poisoned by Ma'mum—his son and successor— his wishes were carried out, and the site of his tomb was called Meshed (the place of the Martyr). Ghaznevids, Mongols and Timurids took turns destroying both the tomb and the town and rebuilding it whenever they wished to consolidate their empires. The 16th century saw the beginning of raids by the Turkomans and the Uzbeks, the picturesque as well as devastating henchmen of Sunnite fanaticism.

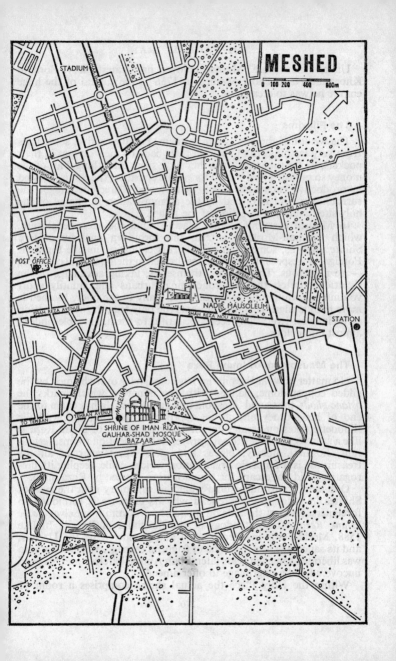

MESHED

0 100 200 400 600m

STADIUM

GRAMAR AVENUE

KANAL AVENUE

NADIR SHAH AVENUE

DANESHGAH AVENUE

KHWAJ RABI AVENUE

POST OFFICE

PAHLAVI AVENUE

BALUKABAN AVENUE

KHWAJA NASIR TUSI AVENUE

NADIR MAUSOLEUM

SHAH REZA AVENUE

SHAH REZA NOU AVENUE

STATION

NADERI AVENUE

ENGHELAB-YOU AVENUE

TO TEHRAN

TEHRAN AVENUE

MUSEUM

TABARSI AVENUE

SHRINE OF IMAN RIZA
GAUHAR-SHAD MOSQUE
BAZAAR

SAFAVI AVENUE

Under Nadir Shah, Meshed enjoyed its greatest glory. Born in Khorasan, Nadir chose Meshed in 1736 as the capital of the huge empire he was to create.

The Pilgrims

The wealth of the city is due to them. Families arrive, sometimes from very far off, a rug to sell on their back or their savings in their pockets. By the time they leave they have spent everything. Part of the money so piously given is used for public charities; the rest is invested in productive enterprises, such as factories. Three-quarters of the surrounding land is owned by the administration in charge of the holy sites under the direction of the Imam.

In Meshed everything takes place around the sacred enclosure, which for non-Moslems is also the forbidden enclosure. Here Shi'ite pilgrims, some from neighboring countries, mingle together. Foreigners—especially the Afghans dressed in their national costumes —are numerous. The Iranians themselves, taking advantage of the situation, stretch the law concerning turbans and jauntily sport voluminous white tulle head-gear. For many of the poor, Meshed is more than a pilgrimage; it represents the only trip, the only vacation of their lives. Everything seems beautiful to them, enviable, indeed almost miraculous.

The Mausoleum of Imam Reza

No matter how far the pilgrim has come, he is overwhelmed by the gilded copper dome, flanked with two minarets, which marks the *astane-ghods*, the sacred threshold of Imam Reza. He has come to the end of his journey and as he approaches the city, the symbolic silhouette takes on greater depth. The mausoleum of Imam Reza is like a sacred city complete with prayer halls, reception rooms, restaurant, hospital, library, offices and—most spectacular of all—its treasury. It is a fantastic organization which, while keeping its prerogatives, did not escape the secularization decreed by Reza Shah.

One must try to understand what this sanctuary is in the eyes of Shi'ites in order to comprehend why its entrance is forbidden to foreigners. Did not the Safavid monarchs proclaim themselves *Kalbe astane Reza*, "the watchdogs of the threshold of Reza"? In late 1588, Meshed was invaded, sacked and plundered by the Uzbeks, and its sanctuary was the scene of frightful carnage. When Khorasan was liberated some ten years later, Shah Abbas, barefoot and his head uncovered, led a pilgrimage to offer amends.

Within the Holy Place the actual shrine comprises a room 11

m (36 feet) square, covered by a cupola 34 m (112 feet) high. Until very recently pilgrims coming to pray did not hesitate to kick Caliph Harun's tomb as they went by! The new reliquary was installed in 1957. To show you how impressive this is here are some figures: 1,693 kilos (3,750 pounds) of silver, 35 kilos (77 pounds) of 18-carat gold, a ton of bronze, two tons of iron, and two tons of walnut. The whole thing is decorated with inscriptions enumerating the hundred attributes of Allah. The initials of the first 44 give the date of its inauguration and the jeweler's name. A huge chandelier has just been installed, which is the largest one ever made by a Bohemian crystal works. It is 5 m (16 feet) high, 5 m (16 feet) in diameter and weighs 2 tons. This chandelier is accompanied by 35 more each weighing 200 kilos (440 lbs).

Once a year the "dusting" ceremony takes place in the presence of all the dignitaries. The grill is opened, all the donations of the pilgrims are gathered up and deposited in the treasury. The walls of the room bear the marks of the various tastes of the succeeding dynasties of benefactors. A few faiences date from the Seljuk period. Shah Tahmasp has left a fine specimen of calligraphy. The shape of the tiles varies between octagons, crosses and stars. A large Safavid inscription, 80 cm (31 inches) high, runs around under the cupola, and between the frieze and the kachis the inevitable mark of the Qajars—mirrored mosaics.

Most of the different rooms and courtyards surrounding the mausoleum were repaired by Nadir Shah and the Qajars. Inside the ancient enclosure, the north room, that of Shah Abbas, is remarkable for the embossed design of its kachis, the south room for its silver door and the east room for its balcony from which the kettledrums are played at sunrise and sundown.

The mosque of Gowhar Shad, wife of Shahrukh (15th century), unfortunately is also inside the forbidden enclosure. It is regrettable that one cannot see the magnificent Timurid faiences which decorate it, the inscriptions of the queen's own son, Shah Abbas's kachis, and the carved wood pulpit.

The Museum

In the midst of all these forbidden fruits there is one visit which is allowed: the museum. It illustrates the Shi'ites' contributions to Islamic art. There is a collection of Korans as beautiful as they are ancient, for the oldest date from the 1st century of the Hegira; one having been copied by Ali in person and the other by his son Hassan. The Baisonqur Koran is a masterpiece of great size: its pages are 1·80 m (70 inches) long. The scribe was none other than Tamerlane's grandson, who first practiced by copying a Koran in miniature. His grandfather reproached him for having diminished the sacred book, and so Baisonqur decided to design a Koran whose size would be in accordance with the majesty of the text. Only about fifteen badly damaged pages are left of this precious work. Also very curious is the Koran of Babur, son of Baisonqur, for it is written in characters invented by this artist prince.

The other objects on display have to do with the history of the sanctuary, such as the Imam's first tombstone (12th century), a fountain (13th century), ceramics, tableware and tiles, brocade fabrics, Safavid arms and carved wooden doors. The ancient reliquary displayed here is the object of further veneration by pilgrims.

The accessories used during the celebrations of Muharram are grouped in one room: the *alamats*, metal ensigns, and the nuptial chamber of Kassem, decorated as for a wedding.

Around the Sanctuary

Since all gifts and legacies are donated to the sanctuary, it is not surprising that the other monuments cannot compare with it. Such is the case with the Shah's Mosque, which dates from the Seljuk epoch, but whose mihrab is incorrectly placed according to the Shi'ites.

Yet there is no lack of mosques and madares, suddenly looming before you at the bend of a narrow street in the bazaar. The most arresting of these is the little mausoleum of Pir-i-Palandus, located in Chour St., which runs into Safavid Ave. The Mongol Oljaitu built this lovely colored dome for the great mystic.

The old city of Meshed is remembered more for its bazaar than for its faiences. It is a mixture of strange bric-a-brac, things brought and given by the pilgrims. First of all there are rugs, the currency used by most peasants. Through some strange mix-up these products of Khorasan are commonly thought to be Baluchi. There are some extremely original examples, brightly colored and with designs which often include a tree of life.

Among the souvenirs which the Meshedi—official title given to one who has made the pilgrimage—must bring back with him are prayer beads with 33 or 100 grey (*pazar*) or black (*yost*) stone beads and little tiles made of Meshed clay, on which he can lean his forehead when he prostrates himself in prayer. In fact hotel keepers leave some in the rooms at the disposition of guests, just as Americans provide bibles. The traveler can also acquire a weighty gift, tableware of pazar stone, much appreciated in the region, or if he prefers he is free to choose turquoise jewelry.

The Mausoleum of Nadir Shah

The mausoleum of Nadir Shah is a modern edifice with bronze horsemen in Naderi Ave. The proud Afshar dreamed of a monument in the style of the Taj Mahal and had stones brought from Maragheh to this end. However the Qajars had no place for him in their hearts. It was only in recent years that a building worthy of the great conqueror was erected. Very sober, sturdy and vigorous in style, it is perfectly suited to the personality of this hero. The little museum which is devoted to him contains arms and 18th-century objects.

The Environs of Meshed

There are many excursions to be made around Meshed. The closest is the Kuh-Sangi, at the end of a beautiful avenue lined with eight rows of trees. This "Paradise Avenue" leads to a graceful building which stands in the middle of a park equipped with sports facilities. 550 m (1,800 feet) from the pool, to the left, is an iwan built by Shah Safi as a shelter for the tombs of Imam Reza's descendants.

Six km (3 miles) northwest of Meshed, the mausoleum of Khadje Rabi still attracts pilgrims. The man venerated here was one of the Prophet's companions, and he is included among Islam's eight ascetics. This monument was built by Shah Abbas in 1622. Octagonal in shape it is topped by an 18-m (60-foot) dome, and faced with faiences. The inscriptions are the work of the famous calligraphist Ali Reza Abbassi. Recently restored, this mausoleum is said to have been the source of inspiration for the architects of the Taj Mahal. In the autumn, when the sweetly perfumed ice plant flowers turn yellow and a soft mist hangs like a veil in the distance, a calm spreads over this place of meditation.

Capital of Khorasan from time immemorial until shortly after the advent of Islam, Tus is the birthplace of Firdowsi, the celebrated author of the Shah Nama (Book of Kings—10th century), an account in Persian verse of the Sassanid epic. Another famous person born in Tus was Nizam-al-Mulk (1017–92), reformer and administrator, minister to the Seljuk sultans Alp Arslan and Malik Shah and ardent champion of the Iranian cause against foreign occupiers.

Turks, Mongols and Timurids swooped down on the town. The pyramids of severed heads made by Miran Shah, son of Tamerlane, forever discouraged the survivors of Tus from rebuilding their city which in any case had been supplanted by Meshed.

Of the large town practically nothing is left except for vague traces of fortifications. "The peasants cultivate the land in the middle of the city, growing wheat and barley," M. Freyser wrote in 1821. In the middle of this desolate scene stands the mausoleum of Firdowsi. The story is told that when the mullah refused to bury the poet in the Moslem cemetery because he was a Shi'ite, his friends buried him in his garden. Here he rests to this day. In 1934, his tomb was covered with a kiosk which has since been replaced by a sumptuous mausoleum surrounded by pools.

Not far from the garden of Firdowsi is an ancient building which bears a certain resemblance to a fire temple. It is called the Boqeye Harunieh, even though it has nothing to do with the Caliph buried in Meshed. This square structure is built of brick and surmounted by a dome. It is thought to be a monument started by the Seljuks but never finished because of the Mongol invasion. The villagers point with pride to the remains of a bridge attributed to Firdowsi's own daughter and built thanks to a posthumous gift from the sultan Mahmud of Ghazni, to whom the poet had dedicated his work.

On the way back to Meshed, you can see the market town of Qahqaheh, a solid earthwork fortress pierced by four large gates.

Radkan is situated in the mountains northwest of Tus, accessible only by a dangerous track. It is interesting not so much for its fortress, which was restored by Nadir's son, as for the *mil*, the tower of Radkan, located 3 km (2 miles) from the village. It has yet to be established whether this tower marks the tomb of a Mongol governor (13th century) or whether it was built two centuries earlier by the Buyids. The dimensions of the tower are height 25 m (82 feet), exterior diameter 40 m (132 feet), and the interior diameter 28 m (92 feet). The interior is octagonal. The fluting (36 large grooves) of the exterior surface abuts on a faience and carved brick frieze decorated with Kufic inscriptions.

Discovering Khorasan

Khorasan is immense: 314,286 sq km (120,000 square miles). Months could be spent wandering over it in every direction, discovering ancient monuments which await restoration. Unfortunately Khorasan's chaotic past has left it richer in history than in surviving works of art.

Kalat-i-Naderi

This excursion offers adventure. One hundred and twenty-five km (77 miles) of difficult dirt road to the north of Meshed will bring you to the heart of the steep and rugged mountains whose strange

274

geological formations have witnessed historical events equally curious.

Kalat's strategic position in the path of northern invasions was first recognized in the days when history and legend were still intermingled. Firdowsi mentions it in the Shah-Nama, but it was Nadir Shah who gave the town its luster and fame. Since his death, Kalat is but a slumbering ghost town.

Kakh-i-Korshid (the Sun Palace) was obviously at one time the home of a great prince. Its plan gives us an excellent insight into the warlike style of life of his court and the constant dangers which threatened the conqueror. The palace is encircled by five gardens, surrounded by a brick and stone wall. The building itself looks like a cylindrical monolith. Its exterior is faced with large tiles. The interior was brilliantly decorated with gilt paneling and ornamental designs. In the central court only the portraits of the Afshar princes, on horseback preceded by their servants, have survived.

At the end of his reign Nadir decided to abdicate and retire to Kalat. This is why in less than six years he not only built this palace but also restored Arghavan Shah's Derbent fortress, built the Kabud-Gonbad Mosque, laid out 7 km (4 miles) of canals, dug 365 cisterns, erected a bridge, etc. . . .

The Kabud-Gonbad (Blue Dome), located near the little village which bears its name, is falling in ruins. Arghavan Shah's Derbent fortress, which dates from the Mongol epoch, is a crude brick construction in the form of a truncated cone situated 35 m (115 feet) above the Jarf Rud. Beyond the fortress, on the right, there is an inscription, carved 15 m (50 feet) up in the cliff, celebrating the glory of Nadir Shah in 24 Persian and Turkish verses (1747).

Four km (2 miles) to the east of the Blue Dome rises a dam, 70 m (230 feet) high, which is probably the work of the Seljuks. Three of its arches still stand. At the cost of a few repairs it could probably still be used for irrigation. On the top of the highest mountain of Kalat, 7 km (4 miles) north of the Blue Dome, is Abadie Khechte, where Nadir stored his treasure. The place was guarded by a detachment of elite soldiers whose descendants populate the region. The 365 cisterns built to assure the garrison's water supply are unusable today.

From Meshed towards the Caspian

Quchan (Ghoochan), northwest of Meshed, was built on the site of ancient Estaka, the first capital of Parthia. During the 12th century the region was inhabited by a Mongol tribe, the Guerailis, to which were soon added immigrants brought by Khan Hulagu. Later, the turbulent Uzbeks threatened Shah Abbas's authority, so he brought Kurdish tribes to Quchan to reestablish order. This is why today Turkish, Persian and Kurdish are all spoken in this district. Nadir Shah was assassinated in Quchan. His cruelty had incited one of the Kurdish chieftains to revolt in the region. The city was about to be attacked by Nadir's troops but on the eve of the assault the monarch was slain by conspirators.

There is little to see in Quchan, which was badly damaged in the 1929 earthquakes. You may want to take a look at the tomb of Sultan Ibrahim, son of Imam Reza, built shortly before the Mongol invasion and rebuilt during the last century. It is here that the famous pages of the Baisonqur Koran, which may be seen in Meshed, were found. Bojnurd is 120 km (74 miles) beyond Quchan. Above the city rises the imposing fortress of Narine. South of Bojnurd, the mausoleum of Sultan Seyed Abbas occupies the summit of a hill. Not far from it are the remains of the ancient city of Kjamarghan, sacked by the Mongols. This field of ruins has given rise to a local group of treasure hunters who work for profit and indiscriminately sell objects of great value for prices that are sometimes ridiculously low. Between Shirvan and Bojnurd, the town of Djalian, huddled in the bottom of a valley, is an impregnable natural hideout. The mausoleum of Baba Tavaqqol is decorated with a beautiful black stone dated 1524.

Towards Afghanistan

The road southeast is clearly marked and well-paved. Descending from the mountains into the plain, stop at Turbat-e Jam. Sheikh Ahmad Jam was one of the famous 11th-century ascetics despite being afflicted with the nickname Jemdeh Pil (Enormous Elephant). Near his mausoleum (14th century) stands a mosque with a very beautiful carved plaster mihrab and a madresseh. Finally, in Taybad (Tayebat), the tomb of Zein-e-Din erected by Shah Rukh is a good example of the Timurid style.

Nishapur

About 130 km (80 miles) west of Meshed, Nishapur (Neyshabur) is a peaceful town of 33,000 inhabitants, hidden among orchards which are spread out like an amphitheater against the foothills of the Kuh-e-Binalud. Its name quite betrays its Sassanid origin. Later, during the 7th century, the city was the residence of the Arab governors of Khorasan, who were followed in the 9th century by the Tahiric princes. Then began the curious interlude of the Safavid dynasty, known as "The House of the Tinker", which says a great deal concerning the modest beginnings of its founder. But in 903 the Samanid Emirs—authentic princes this time—took over Nishapur. Soon it was the Seljuks' turn (11th century). There are two great figures of this period whom we later find at the court of Sultan Malik Shah (1072–92): Omar Khayyam, poet and sage, and his friend the Grand Vizier Nizam al-Mulk who was a great philosopher.

Omar Khayyam is buried 4 km (2½ miles) southeast of the city. Designed in 1934, the girders of the mausoleum seem to be striving to retain the delicate soul of the great man. Next to it is the tomb of the mystic poet Farid ud-din Attar. "Attar has roamed through the seven cities of love while we have barely turned down the first street." He was among the innumerable victims of Genghis Khan's invasion.

Not far from this exalted place, amidst shady trees and gardens, stands the tomb of one of the prophets of Islam, Mohammed Mahruk, who was burned alive.

Nishapur is also the city of turquoise. The mountains to the north contain many deposits which are actively exploited, such as the mine of Ma'dan. You can visit the mines but you will be much more interested in going to one of the workshops, where stones are polished and matched. All turquoises are not blue. Some are dark green, occasionally veined in grey, in which case they are used for costume jewelry. The most beautiful stones are clear blue without impurities.

Sabzevar

About 130 km (80 miles) west of Nishapur, on the southern road running along the desert towards Tehran, Sabzevar (27,000 inhabitants) is a very active center. It is the cradle of the Shi'ite sect and the religious zeal of its inhabitants is proverbial. The local clan of Sarbedars even tried during the 14th century to establish authority over all Iran through proselytism. The restoration of the Friday Mosque dates from this period. A minaret which stands on the plain marks the site of the ancient city of Khosroeguerd, razed by the Mongols. This monument built around 1112 is one of the most beautiful in Iran.

Practical Information for Meshed and Khorasan

WHEN TO GO. From June to September because of the severity of the continental climate. More than elsewhere in Iran, the month of Ramadan should be avoided because of the religious fervor displayed by the inhabitants of this region: all restaurants are closed at noon and even good hotels refuse to serve breakfast. In Meshed the feasts of Shi'ite calendar are celebrated. Avoid

THE FACE OF IRAN

these dates, for there is no room in the hotels. The whirlwind of popular exaltation can be annoying, especially in the month of Muharram.

HOW TO GET THERE. By air: there are 2 or 3 flights a day from Tehran; two flights a week from Zahedan; several flights a week from Karachi (Pakistan). **By rail:** Tehran–Meshed, 926 km (585 miles), 49 stops, among which are Sabzevar and Nishapur. Schedules vary according to the season, but throughout the year two or three trains a day run between Tehran and Meshed. The station is in the northeastern part of the city. **By road:** there are two routes from Tehran (see section on motoring). Buses use the first one, via Amol and Quchan. T.B.T., Mihan Tour and Levantour have bus services between Meshed and the capital. The Meshed bus station is on the Tehran road.

To reach the sacred enclosure, cross the city on an east-west axis, driving down the Vakilabad Blvd. and those following it until you get to Roudaki Circle. At the end of Tehran Blvd., on the left, you will find the sanctuary. Coming from Afghanistan and Nishapur, you enter the city at the southwest, ending up also on Roudaki Circle, where you turn right to reach the sanctuary.

WHAT TO SEE. In Meshed you cannot visit the mausoleum of Imam Reza. On the other hand, nothing prevents you from watching the pilgrims. Within the walls you may visit the museum and the library. There is also the modern mausoleum of Nadir Shah. In Tus nearby try to see the Tomb of Firdowsi and especially the Mausoleum of Khadje Rabi with its superb faiences. One day is enough to visit Meshed and its surroundings. In Nishapur see Omar Khayyam's tomb and the turquoise mines. Kalat Naderi offers grandiose natural decor and 18th century historical relics. There are Timurid mausoleums in Turbat-e-Jam and Taybad.

HOTELS

Meshed. *Mashad Hyatt*, deluxe, Farah Ave., 150 rooms with balcony, pool, tennis, all amenities; *Apadana* and *Iran****, Kosravi Now Ave.; *Tehran**** and *Darbandi***, Tehran Ave.; *Amin***, Tabarsi Sq.; *Amir***, Shah Reza Ave.; *Bakhtar* and *Pars***, Pahlavi Ave.; *Kourosh* and *Sepid***, Daghighi Sq.; *Sina*** Shomali Sq.; these have some private showers, but not the exceedingly simple one-star *Alizadeh, Arya, Birjandi, Firdowsi, Golkar, Johari, Kakh, Kasra, Majid, Malaekeh,* *Marmar, Rasooli, Shahsavar, Toos, Zohreh*, which do not even always provide running water in rooms.

Birjand. Mehmansara, *Arya**, Sepah Ave.

Bojnurd. *Mogadam**.

Gonabad. *Mehmansara***.

Nishapur. *Mehmansara***, *Laleh*.

Sabzevar. *Shardari** and *Arya*. Tourist Camp.

Shahrud. *Mehmansara***.

Turbat-e Jam. *Haghighat*.

RESTAURANTS. Meshed: those in the principal hotels. *Khayyam*, Daneshgah Ave., and *Arya-Mehr Park* serve international food and alcoholic beverages. The *Pars* and the *Hatam*, both on Farah Ave., are excellent Persian restaurants.

MOTORING. The northern route from Tehran east via Gorgan, Bojnurd, Quchan to Meshed is paved throughout and much preferable to the southern route via Semnan, Shahrud and Sabzevar (asphalt from Sabzevar). South of Meshed the roads are paved to Firdows and Kakh via Gonabad as well as to Taybad (Afghan frontier) via Turbat-e Jam. Dirt road south of Gonabad to Zahedan.

CAMPING (in Meshed). There is no official camping ground but tents may be pitched in Arya-Mehr Park and along the airport road.

ENTERTAINMENT. *Khou-Sangui Club*, Arya-Mehr Park. There are many movie theaters on Pahlavi Ave. Performances start very early. *Hammans:* the Pars, Maidan-i Sarab; Villa, Ahmadabad Ave. *Zourkhane:* Maqbereh, Bagh-e-Naderi; Eydgah in Eydgah; Bahman, Tehran Ave.

MUSEUM. The *Meshed Museum*, within the shrine, has very interesting collections of Islamic art and a beautiful library of manuscripts and miniatures. It is open every morning except Friday. Ladies must wear scarves over their heads. The *Museum-Mausoleum of Nadir Shah* is open in the morning and in the evening after 4, except Saturday.

SPORTS. Tennis: Pahlavi Club, on the Kuh-Sangi road. **Golf:** Pahlavi Club. **Pools:** Pahlavi Club, the Said Abad Sports Center, Said Abad Ave. **Fishing** in the Kashaf Rud and *mountain climbing* with the local chapter of the Mountain Climbing Federation.

SHOPPING. In the larger bazaars around the sacred enclosure turquoise from Nishapur and Quchan are to be found (merchant cutter: Djavedani et Fils Sarai Nassereh Bazaar, # 212); poustines, coats and vests made of embroidered skins; platters, vases and figures carved in soap-stone; silverware; rugs brought in by the peasants; several antique dealers who have charming bric-a-brac; religious souvenirs for the pilgrims, such as Meshed clay tablets and prayer beads.

USEFUL ADDRESSES. Tourist Bureau, 44 Jahanbani Ave., tel. 25878; the office at the airport is permanently open. *Consulates:* Afghanistan, between Pahlavi Ave. and Shah Reza Ave., near the Pars hotel. Pakistan, Asadi Ave. *Post, telegraph and telephone:* Pahlavi Ave. *Banks:* Melli Iran, Pahlavi Ave. There are 7 other banks in Meshed. *Hospital:* Shah Reza, Jahanbani Ave.

279

Travel Agencies: Iran Air, Pahlavi Ave.; T.B.T. Mihan Tour and Levantour: Falakeh Jonoubi. *Bus terminal:* Tehran road.

Churches: Roman Catholic, Shah Reza Ave.; Armenian Church, Sevom Esfand Sq.; Synagogue, Bagh-e-Mostoufi Ave.; there is a Protestant church on Shah Reza Ave., in the Armenian Hospital.

Useful Telephone Numbers: Police, 02; highway police, 2111, 4700.

THE SOUTHEAST

Kerman, Zahedan and Minab

The two ostans (provinces) of Kerman and Baluchistan-Seistan
with their barren lands and tropical climate, in sharp contrast to
Azerbaijan, make up the southeastern part of Iran. They are the
extensions of the great deserts, some of whose characteristics you will
recognize here. First of all there is the southern end of the Kevir-i-Lut,
whose sand stretches in long dunes on which the wind traces decorative patterns. There is more sand and salt as you cross the Seistan
before reaching the cool air around the lakes, which are surrounded by
greenery. There are date palm oases at Iranshahr, at Bam and Minab
besides those existing in the many villages along the road. All the
signs that characterize lands hostile to men are here: badgirs, underground cisterns, kanats, nomads' tents and the inevitable "corrugated
iron" road surface.

Coming from Yazd, you will first discover the province of Kerman,
ancient Caramania, whose capital was Sirjan. In spite of its mountainous topography, with some peaks over 4,500 m (14,700 feet)
it has traditionally been a passageway. Under the Safavids, the caravan traffic between India and the Persian Gulf helped maintain the

prosperity which the Safavids had bestowed on the province. During the succeeding centuries, Baluchis, Afghans and Qajars brought the misery and desolation from which the province has not completely emerged.

Farther east, Zahedan is situated at the intersection of roads leading to Seistan and Baluchistan. The first is a vast dry plain, but endowed with the emerald waters of Lake Hamun, which gave rise to the local industry of *assirs* (reed window-blinds). As for Baluchistan, it is marked by the Mokran, whose bristling peaks range parallel to the coastline. Between these mountains there are narrow and sometimes fertile valleys where fruit trees compete for space with cereals, sugar cane and tobacco. Beyond the oases is the land of the squat black tents of bearded and hospitable nomads.

Discovering the Southeast

This southeastern region is a vast sandy desert. Distances are great, the roads often difficult and devoid of hotels between the main stopping places. When accommodation is available, do not expect the comforts of the tourist centers of Isfahan and Shiraz. However it is worth it, for you will travel through splendid landscapes of exceptional interest, some of them unique: the Persian Gulf at Bandar-e-Abbas and its curiously masked women; the Seyyed people who live on the shores of Lake Hamun and use reed boats; the Baluchi, driving their herds along the rocky slopes of the Mokran which is covered in the spring with the purple corollas of the little desert flowers (*goul-e-Lala*).

Furthermore, there are plenty of old monuments and faience mosques to satisfy the amateur.

Kerman

History and legend blend when recounting the origins of this city of 55,000 inhabitants whose founding is attributed to the Sassanid sovereign Ardashir I. In the period between the Arab conquest (7th century) and the rise of the Safavids, some 900 years later, Turks and Mongols took turns occupying the city. Under the Safavids, Kerman enjoyed a certain prosperity, which was unfortunately destroyed by Nadir Shah's campaigns and above all by the savagery of the Qajar Agha Mohammed (1794).

Fortunately, the most beautiful of Kerman's monuments, the Friday Mosque, built in 1348 and restored in the 16th century by the Safavids, was spared. It is a very beautiful example of faience decoration with different shades of blue enlivening its surfaces. Rectangular in plan, it has the four classic iwans and an entrance which is surmounted by a cupola set upon squinches.

Within the labyrinth of narrow streets between Shah Ave. and the Regent's Bazaar (Vakil Bazaar) rises the King's Mosque (Masjid-i-Malik) dating from the Seljuk period and restored several times. The portal of the Timurid Pamenar Mosque is a lovely sample of 14th-century mosaic work. If you plan to stay in Kerman for several days, the city is full of mosques to visit, as well as the Gonbad-e-Jebeliyeh, a 12th-century Seljuk mausoleum situated outside the town, the Bagh-e-Sirif, a large shaded garden and the Qala-yé-Ardashir, a ruined citadel attributed to the Sassanid monarch whose name it bears.

Mahan and Bam

Forty km (25 miles) southeast of Kerman over a good asphalt road is the charming village of Mahan (8,000 inhabitants), surrounded with greenery against the backdrop of the snow-capped mountain range of the Kuh-e-Djoupar. As soon as one enters the town, the blue dome is visible with its graceful white faience knot work of the tomb of Nur-ed-Din-Nimat Allah (15th century), the founding poet of a brotherhood of Dervishes. The mausoleum which shelters his remains and those of several of his disciples was built thanks to the generosity of an Indian Moslem king. Shah Abbas endowed it with its elegant blue and white cupola before the Qajars came along and added their traditional flowery decorations.

After driving about 150 km (93 miles) on dirt roads from Mahan, you reach Bam, the loveliest oasis in Iran, famous for its oranges and dates. Though recently founded (19th century), it is nonetheless most attractive with its decorated brick portals.

Bam (18,000 inhabitants) derives all its character from the Ark, a fortified town, today abandoned. Protected by a double wall, the fortress of Bam was for many years a key position and was often besieged. In 1794, Loft Ali Khan, last of the Zands, sought refuge here, vainly hoping to escape Agha Mohammed Qajar's persecution. Unfortunately the citadel was taken and the inhabitants executed.

You go through the monumental gateway in the wall and past the guard room to find yourself in the streets of a deserted city. In the half caved-in cupolas, walls of sunbaked bricks and badgirs you will recognize the typical desert architecture. The mosque, situated to the right of the principal alley, still attracts a few faithful. Through a very discreetly placed door in the second wall, you enter the citadel proper. A ramp which goes around a cliff to the left, leads to the court-yard of what used to be the castle. Each embrasure commands a magnificent view of the oasis with its checker board of irrigated fields, earthen roofs and the swaying fringe of palms.

Towards Pakistan: Zahedan

From Bam to Zahedan located at an altitude of 1,400 m (4,600 feet), the sandy and sometimes difficult road crosses the southern part of the Lut. One hundred km (62 miles) from Bam, one passes a marker, the Mil-e-Naderi (11th century), built years ago to guide caravans across a plain devoid of natural landmarks.

Do not expect too much of Zahedan. Only a few years ago it was nothing but a few houses huddled around the one and only kanat. Today this little town (12,000 inhabitants) has an international airport, a tourist office and a provincial governor. Not only is it the end of the line for Pakistani trains into Iran, but also the obligatory transit point for those heading towards Pakistan on a good road via Mirjaveh, 80 km (49 miles) away.

In the bazaar, well stocked with Pakistani bric-a-brac, you will find a few Baluchi embroideries, red and green on black and admire the stature, the expression, the magnificent black beards and the muslin turbans of the region's inhabitants.

The Baluchi

To visit the Baluchi, the tall nomads who live in black wool tents, one must go into the Mokran, the mountainous and arid region which occupies the extreme southeastern corner of Iran.

Be prudent with a camera despite the graceful, embroidered dresses of the women who also wear unusual jewelry—large open-work bracelets and heavy gold earrings studded with turquoise.

In the summer the Baluchi seek the coolness of the mountains but return to their oases when the date harvest begins. The crop is theirs by right and the sedentary peasants were their vassals. Such was Baluchistan's traditional background until recently. Agrarian reforms have completely toppled the old medieval order and the proud masters have been reduced to seeking work in Zahedan. Soon, their black tents will disappear.

Today, they are still the most interesting feature on the road to Khash, a small town situated in a superb setting of volcanic formations, where rises the Kuh-e-Taftan (4,000 m, 13,000 feet), a volcano with twin cones. Whenever the mountain stops smoking, a sign of catastrophe according to tradition, the inhabitants start talking about leaving the area. Iranshahr is frankly tropical with its palm groves and white houses.

Zabol and Beyond

The region of the Hamun Lakes—Seistan, whose capital is Zabol— is one of the most original in Iran. The area was not always surrounded as it is today by deserts: the Greeks, Parthians and Sassanids considered it a rich farming area and the ruins of their cities, lost in the sand, are tempting quarries for archeologists, especially the Italians. The ruin of Seistan was wrought for the most part by the Mongols. In 1383, Tamerlane systematically destroyed the kanats, the patient work of generations.

Lake Hamun which gives life to the entire region, is fed by the Helmand, a major river whose course runs entirely in Afghanistan, except for its delta. The capricious flow of this river determines the water level of the lake. North of Zabol lies Lake Seistan, whose sources are the Afghan Hari and Farah rivers. The precious waters are a bone of contention between the two countries. Since the Afghans drain off water from the Helmand for irrigation, the water level of the lakes remains very low.

Leaving Zahedan, you first cross a region of brilliantly colored and jagged mountains. Shortly after leaving the small palm grove of Harmak, you descend into the plain, a desert where a few lonely dromedaries graze. Then turn off the Meshed road towards Zabol, driving through an increasingly desolate landscape. Beyond Shileh, on the left, is the track which leads to the recently excavated ruins of Shahr-e-Soukhteh, "the burning city". In Zabol proper (13,000 inhabitants) there is nothing to see. The only points of interest are along the lake shores. Coming from Zahedan, turn left at the first traffic circle and follow the road until you reach the village of Adimi (10 km, 6 miles). About 2 km (1 mile) farther on, you reach the outskirts of Posht-e-Adimi, a small village made up of a mixture of mud houses and straw huts. Here you will get your first look at *toutens*, small boats made of tied reeds, floating on the shallow waters. If you venture out in one you will discover how stable and water-tight they are.

In order to make the excursion to the Kuh-e-Khaje, you must return to Zahedan and cross the Helmand bridge. A good dirt road on the right leads to Kuh-e-Khaje, a flat-topped mountain which soon looms against the horizon. During the 1st century A.D. the Parthians built a city there which was protected by the lake, the mountain and a line of ramparts along its summit.

The Meshed road is known as the "road of the Allies", because this was built during the Second World War to transport military material to the Soviet Union from India. A few of the road markers with V for victory on them still remain. Until you reach Birjand the towns indicated on the map often consist only of a police station, and not a soul lives between Harmak and Sefidabeh. Those who are observant will notice windmills in the Hosein Abad region. Beyond Birjand, Qaen is recognizable by its mosque which was fortified at one time.

From Kerman to Bandar-e-Abbas

The road takes you over a pass more than 2,000 m (6,500 feet) high and winds through spectacular mountain scenery down to the sweltering coastal plains along the Persian Gulf. The only stopping place in the area is Sirjan, named after the ancient city which lies in ruins only 9 km (5 miles) farther to the east. A dismantled old castle rising in the plain can be seen from the road. Here the last troops faithful to the Muzaffarids took refuge until 1393, when Tamerlane decided to destroy it along with its stubborn garrison. The siege lasted three years. Finally the citadel and town were razed and the inhabitants deported. This eagle's nest can be reached by the Baft road; its debris may yield a few mementos of a past described in a 14th-century text by a Muzaffarid prince. Crags, vast horizons and solitude reign. The road traverses the small parallel ranges which separate Kerman from the Gulf. The first oasis is Hadji Abad, with palm trees, tamarisk thickets and blossoms bursting forth in the dust. From here one heads south.

Bandar-e-Abbas (12,000 inhabitants) is rather disappointing. First you go through suburbs of forlorn straw huts, then down a large avenue until you reach the seafront which is planted with brand-new lawns. There is nothing very picturesque about the vista, except for the pot-bellied boats which ply between the mainland and the islands seen in the distance.

Across from Bandar-e-Abbas is the island of Qeshm in the Straits of Hormuz. 140 km long and 36 km wide, it's the largest island in the Gulf and a good place to go for a get-away-from-it-all day trip. A boat takes you across in 45 minutes (or check whether the planned causeway is operable); there are sandy beaches, a good restaurant, the ubiquitous bazaar, and some historical exploring to do: Portuguese ruins and, on the mountainside, an ancient sun-worshipping site. Although the waters of the Straits are actively fished the little port itself is a sleepy affair.

Minab

The charm of the coastal plain lies in its oases, of which the most famous is Minab, about 100 km (62 miles) from Bandar-e-Abbas. An incredible number of palm trees trees crowd the banks of a dry river bed. A background of bald mountains stands against the horizon. This town of straw huts and mud shanties comes to life on Thursdays. The craftsmen and stock breeders of the vicinity converge on the town, bringing pottery and gaudily-colored basketwork to sell as well as their goats and lambs, their donkeys and camels. The pebbled river bed then becomes a fairground. Most of the women, in their brightly-colored flowing robes and embroidered pantaloons, hide their faces behind cotton or taffeta masks which are decorated with embroidery. These are peculiar to the region.

In Minab as in Bandar-e-Abbas, you will notice the extreme diversity of races. There are Indians and Arabs, as well as blacks. Climate, customs, and dwellings all combine to make this coast a colorful world apart, a place of mystery.

Practical Information for the Southeast

WHEN TO GO. Even though Kerman is in the south, its altitude of 1,800 m (5,900 feet) assures it of cool summers and mild winters. In spring and autumn frequent sandstorms may obscure the usually clear skies. The beginning of winter (December–January) is preferable to any other season for a visit to Bandar-e-Abbas, its neighboring oasis of Minab and for the drive between Bam and Zahedan. Rains make travel hazardous during the end of March. Summer is torrid in these regions; Iranshahr is the hottest city in the country. Seistan (Zabol) is agreeable in winter unless one hits on the rare days when the north wind brings temperatures down to −20° C (−4° F). In summer the 120-day wind is destructive and adds the discomfort of dust to the heat.

HOW TO GET THERE. By air: Kerman is linked to Tehran and Yazd by thrice-weekly flights, twice a week to Zahedan and once a week to Isfahan. There are 4 flights a week between Zahedan and Tehran via Meshed or via Kerman and Isfahan. **By bus:** Kerman is linked to the capital, Yazd, Zahedan, Bam and Bandar-e-Abbas by daily bus service provided by the companies: Etminan, M.A.M., Mihan Tour and City Navard. Zahedan is connected to the capital (via Kerman and Yazd) and Iranshahr by daily buses of Etminan M.A.M. and Mihan Tour. M.A.M. and City Navard buses leave everyday for Meshed. Daily buses going towards the Pakistan frontier (Mirjaveh) take on passengers on Pahlavi Ave. Connections the next day for Quetta (Pakistan). **By train:** Tehran–Isfahan–Yazd–Kerman; the Kerman–Zahedan section is under construction. Zahedan is linked to the Pakistan railroad system. Regular service is interrupted in case of cholera epidemics in Pakistan. Enquire in Zahedan about eventual resumption of services. The station is located 3 km (2 miles) east of the city.

THE FACE OF IRAN

WHAT TO SEE. In *Kerman:* the Masjid-i-Jami and its Safavid faiences. In *Mahan:* the Nur-ed-Din-Nimat Allah a 15th-century mausoleum. In *Bam*, a superb palm tree oasis and the abandoned citadel. In *Zabol:* the lakeside population of Seistan and the reed boats. In *Baluchistan:* volcanic landscapes and nomads. In *Minab:* an oasis of several thousand palm trees and masked women.

HOTELS

Bam. *Mehmansara***, as you leave town, on the Zahedan road. *Shafahi*, Reza Shah Ave. *Kesra*, very simple, Pahlavi Ave.

Bandar-e-Abbas. *Gameroon*****, private beach, pool, tennis; half of 104 rooms overlook the sea; *Motel Welcome***, Eskeleh Ave.; *Kourosh***, *Iran*** and the one-star *Kasra, Naz*, the latter being the most pleasant with private baths and air-conditioning and *Roya*, all on Reza Shah Ave.

Bandar-e-Lengeh. *Kourosh**.

Chahbahar. *Mehmansara***.

Kerman. Some private showers in the *Sahra***, Zaboli Ave.; none in the one-star *Akhayan, Kazra*, Kazem Ave.; *Arya, Naz*, Pahlavi Ave.

Minab. Very primitive hotel across from the power station.

Mirjaveh (Pakistan frontier). *Mehmansara***.

Nosrat Abad. *Mehmansara***.

Rafsanjan. *Mehmansara***.

Sirjan. *Mehmansara***.

Zabol. *Kourosh**; small very simple hotels are *Tavakol, Fars* and *Nasiri*.

Zahedan. *Arya**, Sepah Ave.; *Keramati** (restaurant), Pahlavi Ave.; *Laleh, Guilan, Roya*, all on Shahpur Ave.

CAMPING. In Zahedan: *Tourist Camp*, well-equipped. On the airport road.

RESTAURANTS. A good address in Kerman: Tchelo-kebabi *Fard*, Pahlavi Ave.

MOTORING. The road from Tehran via Isfahan is paved as far as Yazd and is scheduled for completion by 1977 all the way to Kerman. Then another (40 km, 24 miles) of asphalt to Mahan. Beyond it is dirt, with a "corrugated iron" surface and puddles of water, which after rain can pose serious problems. From Bam to Zahedan there is the added inconvenience of sand, which makes certain sections of the road particularly treacherous. The Zahedan–Meshed route is also over a corrugated dirt road till Gonabad. The branch to Zabol is as adventurous as the road south from Zahedan to Iranshahr via Khash; considerably better to the Pakistan border at Mirjaveh. From Kerman via Sirjan to Bandar-e-Abbas, asphalt road in good condition; likewise thence to Minab and Manujan.

From Bandar-e-Abbas one can reach the towns of the southern Fars and Shiraz. Between Bandar-e-Abbas and Lar (250 km, 155 miles), the track is difficult and crosses desert regions. There are several impassable fords during heavy rains. Kahgom to Darab (180 km, 111 miles), a well maintained dirt road. Sirjan to Neyriz (160 km, 99 miles) very rough. The dirt road, more or less hugging the coast southwest from Bandar-e-Abbas, is adequate as far as Bandar-e-Lengeh, but deteriorates on the longer stretch northwest to Bushire.

Driving through this area, one can cover over 200 km (124 miles) without finding a gas station. So take precautions. Comprehensive repairs and spare parts available only in Zahedan and Kerman.

Excursions: Zabol: about 200 km (124 miles) from Zahedan. In order to make the excursion to Zabol and Seistan, permission must be obtained. This can be done through the Tourist Office in Zahedan. You will be asked to show your permit in Zabol; numerous police checks along the way. To go to Kuh-e-Khaje (30 km, 18 miles, from Zabol), leave Zabol on the Zahedan road, cross the bridge, and a few hundred meters farther on, turn to the right onto a good dirt road. To get to the lake at Posht-e-Adimi (12 km, 7 miles, from Zabol), go to the first traffic circle as you enter the city, turn left and go straight ahead.

For Khash and Iranshahr a permit is also needed (through the Tourist Office). Remember that there are no hotels in the region. In towns you can resort to the governor's guest house. To leave Zahedan toward the south take the avenue which lies to the west of the Khiaban Shahpur, and which runs parallel to it.

USEFUL ADDRESSES. In Kerman: *Iran Air*, Pahlavi Ave. *Mihan Tour:* Meidan-e-Ark. *Hospital:* Chir-o-Khorchid, Pahlavi Ave., tel. 2842. *Melli Bank:* Pahlavi Ave. *P.T.T.:* Kasemi Ave. *Garages:* at the end of Pahlavi Ave.

In Zahedan: *Tourist Office*, Shahpur Ave., tel. 2502; *Iran Air:* Shahpur Ave.; *Autobus:* M.A.M., Auto Taj, Etminan, Pahlavi Ave.; *Mihan Tour*, Alam Ave.; *Chir-o-Khorchid Hospital*, Shahpur Ave. *Pakistani Consulate*, Sisdametri Ave. *Indian Consulate*, Mehran Ave. *Melli Bank*, Shahpur Ave. *P.T.T.*, Alam Ave. *Garage:* Ghazi Zadeh Auto-Service, Pahlavi Ave.

Useful Telephone Numbers: Kerman: Police, 02 and 2221; Highway Police, 2277; Ambulance, 3829. Airport Information, 2920. *Zahedan:* Police, 2092; Highway Police, 2500; Ambulance, 2800; Airport Information, 2228.

SUPPLEMENTS

ENGLISH-IRANIAN TOURIST VOCABULARY

The pronunciation of Persian is subject to broad dialectal differences, and different versions of the same name or place are often found in maps, books and signposts. The situation is further aggravated by the fact that Persian is written in the Arabic script, which omits the short vowels. The following are some useful words and phrases: (a as in hat, ā as in car, o as in hot, e as in get, oo as in noon, kh as in Scottish "loch", or German "Buch", i as in machine; the stress is usually on the last syllable).

General

Morning—noon—evening	Sob(h)—zo(h)r—shab
Good morning, good evening	Sob(h) bekheir—shab bekheir
May peace be with you (used at any hour)	Salām aleikom
Goodbye	Khodā hāfez
How are you?	Hāl-e-shomā che tor ast?
Do you speak English (French, German)?	Shomā englisi (faransavi, almāni) baladid?
Thank you	Teshekor (sometimes the French word "merci")
Very well	Kheili khub
Pardon me—excuse me	Bebakhshid
Please	Lotfan
I don't understand	Namifahmam
Today—yesterday—tomorrow	Emrooz—dirooz—fardā
Yes—no	Baleh—nakheir (or na)
British (American) Consulate	Konsoolgari-ye-englisi (amerikā'i)
A day—a week	Yek rooz—yek hafteh

At the Station and Airport

Station—airport	Istgāh—foroodgāh
Is there an express train for . . .?	Aya yek ghatar (tren) sari barāyeh . . .?
Are there any sleeping compartments?	Couchettes dārid?
I would like a ticket for . . .	Yek belit barāyeh . . . mikhāham
First class, second class	Darajeh yek, darajeh do
What time does the train leave for . . .?	Tren-e . . . kei harakat mikhonad?
Going—returning (return trip)	Rafteh—bargashteh
Porter	Hammāl

293

ENGLISH-IRANIAN TOURIST VOCABULARY

In the City

Street—avenue	Kocheh—khiyābān
Square—crossroads	Meidān—chekār
Bridge—city gate	Pol—darvāzeh
Hotel—restaurant	Mehmānkhāneh—restorān
Government-owned inn (or hostel)	Mehmānsarā
Mosque—palace	Masjed—kākh
Pharmacy	Davākhāneh
Doctor	Doktor (tabib)
Bank	Bank
Post office	Postkhāneh
Police station	Police (also kalāntari)
Hospital	Bimāristān

Shopping

Rug store	Maghazeh-ye-fārsh
Rug (carpet)	Fārsh (ghāli)
I would like to see . . .	Mikhāham . . . bebinam
Souvenirs	Soghati
It's too expensive	Kheili gerān ast
I don't like that one	Khosham nemiāyad
I'll take it	Barmidāram
Stamps	Tambr (Fr. timbres)
Postcard	Kart, or Kart-postal (Fr.)
Roll of film	Film
Black and white	Siyāh-o-sefid
In colour	Rangi

At the Hotel

Do you have a room available?	Yek otāgh khāli dārid?
One bed, two beds	Yek takht—do takht
With bathroom, shower	Bā van, bā doosh
Breakfast	Sobhāneh (also nāshtā'i)
The key	Kelid
The washrooms	Mostarāh
Hot water	Āb-e-garm
Blanket—towel	Patoo—hooleh
The bill please	Lotfan hesāb-ra bedehid

At the Restaurant

Wine—white—red	Sharāb—sefid—ghermez
Mineral water	Āb madani
Beer	Ābjoo
Fruit juice	Āb miveh
Bread—butter—jam	Nān—kareh—morabbā

ENGLISH-IRANIAN TOURIST VOCABULARY

Salt—pepper—sugar	Namak—felfel—ghand
Vinegar—oil	Serkeh—roughan
Omelette	Omelet
Fish	Māhi
Vegetables—rice	Sabzi—berenj
Chicken	Joojeh
Beef	Goosht-e-gāv
Lamb (mutton)	Goosht-e-gosfand
Roast lamb	Goosht-e-bareh
Tea—coffee (with milk)	Chai—kahve (bā shir)

On the Road

Road	Rāh (also jāddeh)
Which is the way to . . . ?	Rāheh . . . kojāst?
How many kilometers?	Chand kilometr?
To the right—to the left	Be-rāst—be-chap
Gas (petrol) pump	Pomp-e-benzin
Water	Āb
Village	Deh (yakdeh)
Ambulance	Ambulance
Highway police	Gendarmerie (Fr.)
Accident	Hādeseh (also tasadof)

At the Garage

(Many technical words in Persian are taken from French)

I have broken down	Machine kharāb shod	Electric wire	Sim-e-bārgh
Can you tow us?	Mitavānid mārā bekeshid?	Clutch	Klach
		Tires	Lāstik
A jack	Jak (Eng.)	Headlights	Cherāgh
Spark plug	Sham	Rear axle	Defrensiel (différentiel) Fr.
Points	Plātine	Radiator	Radiateur (Fr.)
Carbureter	Carburateur (Fr.)	Gears	Dandeh
Carbureter jet	Gicleur (Fr.)	Gasoline	Benzin (Fr.)
Throttle	Kond	Oil	Roughan
Muffler (silencer)	Exoss	Fill it up!	Por konid!
		Change of oil	Taviz roughan
Dynamo	Dinām	Lubrication	Roghankāri
Starter	Estārtes	Recharge the battery!	Bateri shārzh konid!
Brakes	Tormoz		

Days of the Week

Sunday	Yekshambeh	Thursday	Pānjshambeh
Monday	Doshambeh	Friday	Jomeh
Tuesday	Seshambeh	Saturday	Shambeh
Wednesday	Chārshambeh		

Colors

White	Sefīd	Blue	Ābi
Black	Siyāh	Green	Sabz
Red	Ghermez (also sorkh)	Yellow	Zard
		Dark—light	Tireh—roushan

Numbers

It is useful to learn the following numbers. It means you can tell the prices in shop windows, your hotel room number, bus number and so on.

1	yek	40	chehel
2	do	50	panjāh
3	seh	60	shast
4	chahār	70	haftād
5	panj	80	hashtād
6	shish	90	navād
7	haft	100	sad
8	hasht	150	sado panjāh
9	noh	199	sado navādo noh
10	dah	200	divist
11	yazdah	300	sisad
12	davāzdah	400	chār sad
13	sizdah	500	pun sad
14	chahārdah	600	shish sad
15	punzdah	700	haf sad
16	shunzdah	800	hash sad
17	hevdah	900	noh sad
18	hijdah	1000	hezār
19	nuzdah	2000	do hezār
20	bist	10,000	dah hezār
21	bisto yek	100,000	sad hezār
22	bisto do	1,000,000	yek milion
30	si		

296

INDEX

Abbreviations used in this Index are as follows: E for Entertainment; H for Hotels; R for Restaurants; S for Sports; Sh for Shopping.

297

MAP OF IRAN

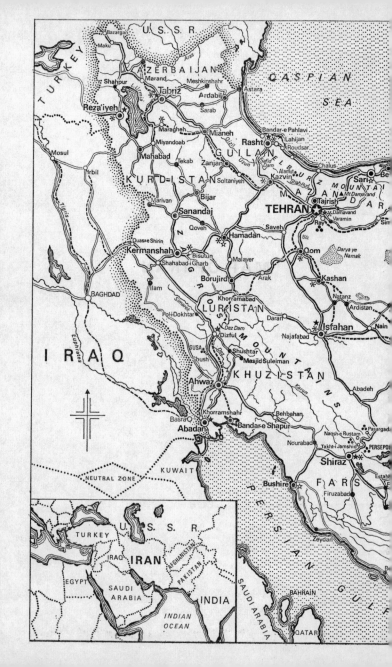

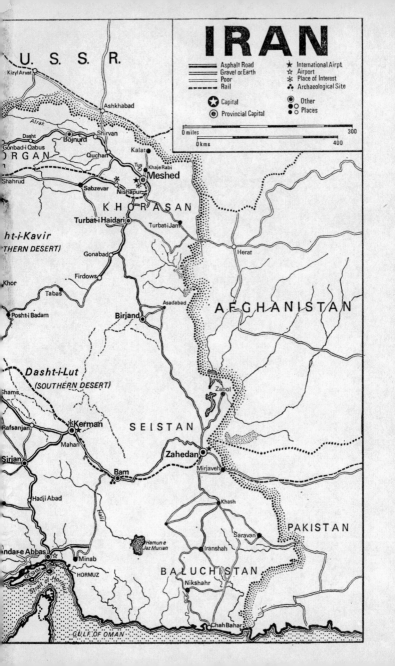